MULTICULTURAL GENDER ROLES

MULTICULTURAL GENDER ROLES

Applications for Mental Health and Education

Edited By

Marie L. Miville

WILEY

Cover Image: © iStockphoto/petekarici
Cover Design: David Riedy

This book is printed on acid-free paper.

Copyright © 2013 by John Wiley & Sons, Inc. All rights reserved

Published by John Wiley & Sons, Inc., Hoboken, New Jersey
Published simultaneously in Canada

No part of this publication may be reproduced, stored in a retrieval system, or transmitted in any form or by any means, electronic, mechanical, photocopying, recording, scanning, or otherwise, except as permitted under Section 107 or 108 of the 1976 United States Copyright Act, without either the prior written permission of the Publisher, or authorization through payment of the appropriate per-copy fee to the Copyright Clearance Center, 222 Rosewood Drive, Danvers, MA 01923, (978) 750-8400, fax (978) 646-8600, or on the web at www.copyright.com. Requests to the Publisher for permission should be addressed to the Permissions Department, John Wiley & Sons, Inc., 111 River Street, Hoboken, NJ 07030, (201) 748-6011, fax (201) 748-6008, or online at www.wiley.com/go/permissions.

Limit of Liability/Disclaimer of Warranty: While the publisher and author have used their best efforts in preparing this book, they make no representations or warranties with the respect to the accuracy or completeness of the contents of this book and specifically disclaim any implied warranties of merchantability or fitness for a particular purpose. No warranty may be created or extended by sales representatives or written sales materials. The advice and strategies contained herein may not be suitable for your situation. You should consult with a professional where appropriate. Neither the publisher nor the author shall be liable for damages arising herefrom.

For general information about our other products and services, please contact our Customer Care Department within the United States at (800) 762-2974, outside the United States at (317) 572-3993 or fax (317) 572-4002.

Wiley publishes in a variety of print and electronic formats and by print-on-demand. Some material included with standard print versions of this book may not be included in e-books or in print-on-demand. If this book refers to media such as a CD or DVD that is not included in the version you purchased, you may download this material at http://booksupport.wiley.com. For more information about Wiley products, visit www.wiley.com.

Library of Congress Cataloging-in-Publication Data:

Multicultural gender roles [electronic resource]: applications for mental health and education / Marie L. Miville.
  1 online resource.
    Includes bibliographical references and index.
    Description based on print version record and CIP data provided by publisher; resource not viewed.
    ISBN 978-1-118-14522-7 (print)
    ISBN 978-1-118-22577-6 (ebook)
    ISBN 978-1-118-23911-7 (ebook)
    ISBN 978-1-118-26375-4 (ebook)
       1. Sex role—United States. 2. Sex differences (Psychology)—United States.
  3. Sex role—Cross-cultural studies. I. Miville, Marie L.
    HQ1075.5.U6
    305.30973—dc23
                                                                    2012046323

Printed in the United States of America
10 9 8 7 6 5 4 3 2 1

For my parents, Roland and Beatriz Miville,
and
for Jill

Contents

Preface	xi

Chapter One Gender Role Construction among Men and Women of Color   **1**
Marie L. Miville, Lucinda Bratini, Melissa J. Corpus, and Manuel A. Diaz

Gender and Gender Roles	2
Racial-Ethnic Contexts of Gender and Gender Roles	6
Constructivist Grounded Theory Method	14
Concluding Remarks	17
References	18

Chapter Two Gender Roles among African American Men   **23**
Marie L. Miville and Joel Sahadath

Negotiating Gender Roles	25
Negotiating Gender Roles Revisited	54
Applications for Mental Health Professionals and Educators	56
References	63

Chapter Three Gender Roles among African American Women   **65**
Jorja A. K. Redway and Marie L. Miville

Conflict and Evolution of Gender Roles	67
Applications for Mental Health Professionals and Educators	88
References	94

Chapter Four Latino Male Gender Roles 97
Manuel A. Diaz, Marie L. Miville, and Natalia Gil

Defining Male Gender Roles within a
Latino Cultural/Family Context 100

Applications for Mental Health
Professionals and Educators 125

References 130

Chapter Five Latina Gender Roles 133
Lucinda Bratini, Marilyn C. Ampuero, and Marie L. Miville

Latinas in Process of Transformation
and Negotiation 135

Applications for Mental Health Professionals
and Educators 162

References 167

Chapter Six Gender Roles among Asian / Asian American Men 169
Michael Y. Lau, Yu-Kang Chen, Jill Huang, and Marie L. Miville

Culture, Socializing Influences, and Agency in
Gender Role Constructions 171

Applications for Mental Health Professionals
and Educators 198

References 204

Chapter Seven Asian American Female Gender Roles 207
Melissa J. Corpus and Marie L. Miville

Model Minority, Model Woman 209

Applications for Mental Health Professionals
and Educators 224

References 229

**Chapter Eight Negotiating Multicultural
Gender Roles: A Proposed Model** 231
*Marie L. Miville, Lucinda Bratini, Melissa J. Corpus,
Michael Y. Lau, and Jorja A. K. Redway*
Summary of Our Analyses 232
Multicultural Gender Role Model 235
Future Directions for Research and Practice 244
Concluding Remarks 245
References 245

Appendix Supporting Research Materials 247
Gender Role Interview Guide 247

Acknowledgments 263

About the Editor 265

Contributors 267

Author Index 269

Subject Index 273

Preface
Marie L. Miville

> *There was a book that I was reading in fifth grade that was about this young Black girl who wanted to fight in the Civil War and in order to be able to do it she had to dress like a boy. And I think it was in the dialogue, she's talking about being a slave and being, being a child, so being under every adult; being a slave and so being under every White person; being a girl, and so being under every male. And that she was the very, very, very bottom of the ladder. . . . And I remember sitting there thinking that that was me, that I was, as a child, I had no power; as a woman I had no power, and as a Black person, I had no power.*

This compelling story, from a young African American woman we interviewed, illustrates how the multiple experiences of race, ethnicity, and gender often intermingle in how we define ourselves as gendered beings. These experiences are embedded within sociopolitical contexts involving interlocking oppressions communicated by powerful messages that, like our interviewee, we first perceive as children (Hurtado, 2010). These messages come from a variety of people, including those we love and respect; institutions that we fear or hold dear; settings that open up our capacities for understanding and success or shut them down; and events that can embolden or inhibit the ways we see ourselves and each other. These messages teach us how we *should* as well as how we *can* think, feel, and act, including the ways we walk or talk, the clothes we wear, the values we cherish, and even the dreams to which we aspire.

Today the roles that women and men play in their families, communities, and the larger society are diverse, constantly evolving, and at times in conflict with each other. The preceding narrative illustrates the painful realities linked with the multiple oppressive challenges people of color face in constructing these roles. Moreover, cultural beliefs, values, and norms profoundly influence the meanings that may be imbued within these roles. Unfortunately, although psychological theories and interventions exist focusing on how people develop their sense of selves as men and women, few studies have explored the impact of race and ethnicity on *gender roles*, that is, "behaviors that men and women enact congruent with the socially constructed ideals of masculinity and femininity" (Mahalik, Cournoyer, DeFranc, Cherry, & Napolitano, 1998, p. 247). Moreover, some of these theories and interventions still reflect race- and sex-based stereotypes rather than being informed by the actual lived experiences of the individuals whom they purport to explain and help (Shields & Dicicco, 2011). Thus little information is available to guide mental health professionals, educators, and students entering these fields about how people of color might construct their gender roles in today's world.

OUR GOAL

In this book, we explore the multiple sources and ways that men and women of diverse racial-ethnic backgrounds learn about and negotiate gender roles. In Chapter 1, we provide a brief review of the current literature in this area, highlighting sociohistorical contexts in which these processes are best understood. We also explain our qualitative research methodology, constructivist grounded theory, which guided our data analyses. By incorporating this research method, our participants' voices helped us frame the multicultural gender role model we describe in Chapter 8.

In Chapters 2 through 7, we present extensive qualitative data based on semistructured interviews with more than 60 individuals from African American, Latina/o, and Asian/Asian American racial-ethnic backgrounds who described what gender and gender roles meant to them. These chapters present many personal and poignant stories that highlight the various challenges men and women of color overcome in constructing gender roles.

In Chapter 8, we put forward a multicultural gender role model based on our interpretations of participants' experiences.

The core narrative of our model is *negotiating gender roles*, which crystallizes processes men and women of color engage as they continuously create their gender roles. These processes include: (a) resolving conflicts; (b) navigating privilege and oppression; (c) understanding one's impact on others; (d) transforming self-perceptions; (e) intersecting identities; (f) navigating emotions; (g) constructing their own gender styles/expressions; and (h) constructing their roles in family, community, and society.

FROM THE "BOTTOM OF THE LADDER" TO THE "TOP OF THE MOUNTAIN"

In addition to sharing the many themes and stories our participants revealed to us, in each chapter we also provide applications of our findings for mental health professionals and educators who work with diverse populations. In particular, our findings will be of use to mental health and school counselors, professional psychologists, and social workers who work with a racially and ethnically diverse clientele, including Black or African Americans, Latinas and Latinos, and Asians and Asian Americans. Our participants' poignant stories as well as our theoretical model help identify the multiple influences that affect how young people come to see themselves as gendered beings as well as the roles they can and should play in their families and communities. These stories also point out the variety of conflicts that can arise and the many ways, healthy and otherwise, that these conflicts might be resolved individually, in therapy, or through outreach programming. For example, clients might read portions of the book chapters in order to help them articulate the emotions they are struggling with as a result of the double jeopardy of being both a woman and a person of color. Moreover, this book will be of interest to educators, particularly those in secondary and postsecondary institutions. For example, given its reader-friendly narrative style, our book might be used as part of a set of required readings in undergraduate and graduate university courses that focus on gender or racial-ethnic studies. The book also may serve as a resource for high school teachers in their efforts to help students and their parents to learn about some of the challenges students of color face in negotiating gender roles as they transition from adolescence to adulthood (e.g., equating academic success with being viewed as a sellout). Some of our suggestions focus on promoting leadership development, improving academic success, and establishing healthier relationships.

It is our sincerest wish that the stories we have shared, the theoretical model we created, and the suggestions we provide may help others strive for and reach the mountaintops of their dreams.

REFERENCES

Hurtado, A. (2010). Multiple lenses: Multicultural feminist theory. In H. Landrine & N. F. Russo (Eds.), *Handbook of diversity in feminist psychology* (pp. 29–54). New York, NY: Springer.

Mahalik, J. R., Cournoyer, R. L., DeFranc, W., Cherry, M., & Napolitano, J. M. (1998). Men's gender role conflict and use of psychological defenses. *Journal of Counseling Psychology, 45*, 247–255.

Shields, S. A., & Dicicco, E. C. (2011). The social psychology of sex and gender: From gender differences to doing gender. *Psychology of Women Quarterly, 35*, 491–499.

Chapter One

GENDER ROLE CONSTRUCTION AMONG MEN AND WOMEN OF COLOR

Marie L. Miville, Lucinda Bratini, Melissa J. Corpus, and Manuel A. Diaz

> *I feel like there's this image that we just have dealt with so much, and that's a part of who we are, but we're supposed to keep going. Like unbreakable. . . . I think there's this real shame of us having to seek mental health services or us feeling like we're not that strong independent Black woman, even though there's some acknowledgment that our life is hard and it's expected to be hard.*

> *My father taught me to be masculine. And he taught me to be a fighter, don't give up. When somebody comes at you, push you, don't take it. Hit 'em back. He taught me to don't care who it is, where he's coming from, how big it is. You hit. And you hit. And you hit.*

> *In the Filipino culture, I think women are strong people in the family. They kind of are the leaders . . . they take care of the household and they make decisions.*

These quotes from an African American woman, a Latino man, and a Filipina woman highlight some of the unique challenges that men and women of color face in our society as they begin to develop or construct their sense of themselves and others as gendered beings. This book introduces you to the experiences of more than 60 people of diverse racial-ethnic backgrounds, including African Americans, Latinas/os, and Asians/Asian Americans. These individuals were interviewed about their views of what it means to be a man or woman and the roles their racial-ethnic heritage plays in constructing these meanings. We present stories of poignancy and complexity, as these young people struggled with a number of questions: What does it mean to be a man or a woman today? What messages continue to be taught by families, schools, and the larger society, especially through the media, about the roles we can or should play as men and women? How do we make sense of the often-conflicting images, stories, and lessons that are a part of the current narratives on gender? We live in times of changing expectations regarding how men and women *should* act as well as how they actually *do* act. The themes presented here depict the continuing challenge of how to hold on to traditional cultural beliefs while at the same time seeking more equality, acceptance, and access.

In this chapter, we present some of the current thinking mental health professionals have used to study gender and gender roles. Our review of the literature is not meant to be comprehensive or exhaustive but instead to highlight important theoretical constructs and findings that formed the empirical basis of our interview project. We also describe the research methodology we used in conducting our interviews, constructive grounded theory (CGT), which helped us analyze our data for common themes among our interview participants.

GENDER AND GENDER ROLES

According to Unger (as cited in Suzuki & Ahluwalia, 2003), *gender* refers to the "socially constructed attributions and expectations assigned to individuals on the basis of their biological sex" (p. 120). In other words, when talking about roles men and women may play in their private lives and in the larger society, "It is now widely accepted that gender is a social construction, that sex and gender are distinct, and that gender is something all of us '*do*'" (Lucal, 1999, p. 782). Thus, rather than identifying individuals as male or female and their related behaviors as biologically (or sex) based, scholars today argue that social and cultural conditions, not biology, have much to do with the beliefs, behaviors, and norms that men and women display (Stets & Burke, 2000).

One of the ways we "do" gender is through the enactment of *gender roles*, "behaviors that men and women enact congruent with the socially constructed ideals of masculinity and femininity" (Mahalik, Cournoyer, DeFranc, Cherry, & Napolitano, 1998, p. 247). Gender roles express our respective place or position in the larger society relative to traditional beliefs of masculinity and femininity and reflect essentialized qualities of appearance, mannerisms, personality traits, and beliefs regarding domestic and work roles. Examples of traits associated with masculinity include action, competition, and instrumentality, whereas femininity incorporates passivity, cooperativeness, and expressiveness (Stets & Burke, 2000). In many cultures, women traditionally have been associated with feminine gender roles (e.g., domestic settings) and men with masculine gender roles (e.g., work settings). However, since the early 20th century, researchers, particularly anthropologists such as Margaret Mead, have found numerous societies and cultures that do not adhere to these kinds of roles. Mead found, for example,

> Among the Arapesh, both males and females displayed what we would consider a "feminine" temperament (passive, cooperative and expressive). Among the Mundugamor, both males and females displayed what we would consider a "masculine" temperament (active, competitive and instrumental). Finally, among the Tchambuli, men and women displayed temperaments that were different from each other, but opposite to our own pattern. In that society, men were emotional, and expressive, while women were active and instrumental. (Stets & Burke, 2000, p. 3)

Moreover, scholars have pointed out that in many, but not all, societies, gender roles often are imbued with social status and differential access to power and resources, generally resulting in men in the dominant or superior position and women in the submissive or inferior role. The role or process of power, "the ability to do, to act, or to effect" (Collier, 1982, in Jones, 2003, p. 31) and relevant constructs have long been ignored in the field of psychology. Sociologically, power can be understood systemically as "the ability of persons or groups to command compliance from other persons or groups, even in the face of opposition. Power requires resources superior to those controlled by the compliers" (Chavetz, in Jones, 2003, p. 32). A simple example of the continuing power of gender-based social positions today involves the gender wage gap, wherein women in the United States earn $.77 for every dollar men earn, all other variables being held constant (Institute for Women's Policy Research, 2011).

The past four decades have yielded a great deal of research exploring gender, *gender identity*—"the degree to which persons see themselves as masculine or feminine given what it means to be a man or woman in society" (Stets & Burke, 2000, p. 1)—and gender roles. Rigidly held shared beliefs about gender and gender roles (i.e., *gender stereotypes*) have had a negative impact on both men and women, including psychological theory and research conducted in this area.

For example, adolescence has been identified as a key phase of development in which boys and girls construct their initial meanings of what it means to be men and women, respectively. Writing more than a half century ago, Simone de Beauvoir (1949/1989, in Tryon & Winograd, 2003) observed that during this period, and in contrast to their childhood, girls become passive, "waiting for them to have their identity defined for them by the men they marry. Boys, however, make their way actively toward adulthood. Whereas boys are permitted to question and challenge the status quo, girls are expected to define themselves according to it" (p. 185).

Unfortunately, this can result in girls becoming secretive, aspiring "to a dreamy and romantic future" (Tryon & Winograd, 2003, p. 186) à la the fairy princess tales of Disney films; a girl dreams because, as de Beauvoir notes, "she is too much divided against herself to join battle with the world" (p. 186). The end result is that "she neither accepts the role that biology and society have prescribed for her nor does she relinquish it completely" (p. 186).

More recent theories about gender role and gender identity development of girls and women emphasize the importance of social context and the role that power and conflicting expectations play in promoting mental and physical health or distress (Enns, 2004; Jones, 2003). Emphasis in these recent theories is placed on redefining power-based constructions of gender, from a focus on the center or presumably normative views (i.e., male), to marginalized but still influential groups in society, such as those of women and people of color. Feminist psychotherapy, for example, emphasizes the "unequal power between men and women, abuse, and empowerment of women in their individual lives" (Miville & Ferguson, 2006, p. 91). Awareness of the negative impact of *patriarchy*, a system that casts men and women "as opposites in an oppressive gender hierarchy dominated by male control and female coercion and submission" (p. 91), and *sexism*, negative beliefs about women, have become a primary focus of negotiating healthier gender identities and helping girls and women to lead more empowered lives. The impact of gender-based disparities still can be seen in such varied contexts as the inequitable distribution of domestic labor in the home and career barriers in the workplace (e.g., discriminatory hiring practices, "the glass ceiling," Heppner, Davidson, & Scott, 2003).

For boys and men, pressures to conform to the masculine gender role can lead to *gender role conflict (GRC)*, "a psychological state in which socialized gender roles have negative consequences for the person or others" (O'Neil, 2008, p. 362). GRC occurs when "rigid, sexist, or restrictive gender roles, learned during socialization . . . result in restriction, devaluation, or violation of others or self" (O'Neil, 1990, p. 25). GRC results from the heavy competition that exists between rigid, inflexible, or restrictive masculine gender roles and situational demands. Further, "the ultimate outcome of GRC is the restriction of a person's human potential or the restriction of another person's potential" (O'Neil, 2008, p. 362). In other words, strict adherence to masculine gender roles can lead to psychological problems, including *success*, *power*, and *competition issues*; dominating others for the benefit of one's own gain; *emotional restrictiveness*, blocking out all feelings for fear of being vulnerable and looking "womanly," which negatively can affect relations with both women and men; and *conflict between work and family relations*, referring to how men experience restrictions in balancing their work, school, and family relations, often resulting in health problems, working too hard, stress and anxiety, and lack of leisure and relaxation (O'Neil, 2008).

In sum, current thinking among mental health professionals and other social scientists emphasizes how gender and gender roles are socialized in young boys and girls rather than being considered inborn, often resulting in mental health struggles related to rigid adherence of these roles. No doubt, as the songs say, one still can "enjoy being a girl" or accept that "boys will be boys," along with various joys this might give individuals, even their families and communities. Moreover, as some may still believe, adopting gender roles may help the larger society organize critical tasks related to survival (Gilmore, 1990). However, current evidence demonstrates that, in many societies, unquestioned adaptation of these roles, particularly if they are power-based social constructions, also can lead to anxiety, anger, depression, and even poor physical health because of the negative bifurcations that can result not just between men and women but also within individuals regarding their own intrinsic interests, values, and activities. Further, today's world provides a cacophony of images and messages about how men and women should and do behave that may be difficult for individuals to sift through in order to negotiate a consistent or comprehensible sense of themselves as gendered beings.

RACIAL-ETHNIC CONTEXTS OF GENDER AND GENDER ROLES

So far we have discussed gender issues broadly, emphasizing the larger society without highlighting the more specific roles that race-ethnicity can play as well. As with gender, a power-based social hierarchy based on race-ethnicity has been the hallmark of much of the sociohistory of the United States. Multiple forces instituted through laws and social policy (e.g., slavery, school segregation, forced internment, and anti-immigration laws) have led to strong hostility toward and overt discrimination of many people from a number of diverse racial-ethnic groups, including Black/African Americans, Latinas/os, and Asian/Asian Americans (Sue & Sue, 2008). On a side note, in this book, we use those terms that refer to diverse racial-ethnic groups (e.g., "Black" and "African American" are used interchangeably) that remain in common use, both by government sources and well as by our research participants.

The lives of most if not all individuals from these groups, who are referred to collectively as *people of color*, continue to be marked by the effects of racism and discrimination. First it is critical to define *racism*. We use two definitions. Racism is:

> a system of cultural, institutional, and personal values, beliefs, and actions in which individuals or groups are put at a disadvantage based on ethnic or racial characteristics (Tinsley-Jones, 2001, in Miville & Ferguson, 2006, p. 89)

> through the exercise of power against a racial group viewed as inferior, by individuals and institutions with the intentional or unintentional support of the entire culture. (J. Jones, in Miville & Ferguson, 2006, p. 89)

In short, racism is "a systemic and dynamic force that disempowers one group by defining them as inferior, thereby affording another group power and superiority.... Although racism may be expressed in blatant or overt ways, there are many forms of covert racism as well" (Miville & Ferguson, 2006, p. 89). D. W. Sue and Sue (2008) have outlined some specific consequences that result from institutionalized oppression of this nature (i.e., what they call *ethnocentric monoculturalism*):

- Belief in the superiority of one group, where characteristics of the dominant racial-ethnic group (White Euro-American in the United States) are seen as both desirable and normative (e.g., appearance, behaviors, and values)
- Belief in the inferiority of others, where characteristics of nondominant groups are seen as less desirable, even deviant
- Power of the dominant group to impose its standards on less dominant groups—for example, the access to important resources, such as housing, education, and well-paid positions
- Manifestation in institutions via "programs, policies, practices, structures, and institutions" in society (p. 87)
- The invisible veil, or the assumption of a universally shared view on the "nature of reality and truth" (p. 88)

As can be seen, the forces of racism can have a debilitating impact on the mental and physical functioning of many people. We now address how these issues might apply each to women and men of color.

Women of Color

As noted earlier, discussions of gender and gender roles have historically centered on explications of presumably White gendered experiences (Raffaelli & Ontai, 2004; Reid & Comas-Diaz, 1990; Settles, 2006; Settles, Sellers, & Damas, 2002). An early example of this occurred in the 19th-century women rights' movement, which focused on liberation from sexist oppression by emphasizing home and family as a "woman's sphere" (hooks, 1981, p. 47). The critical Seneca Falls Declaration, "the articulated consciousness of women's rights," in the mid-1800s primarily focused on the injurious impact of marriage on women because they were robbed of their property rights (Davis, 1983, p. 53). Unfortunately, the declaration completely ignored the problems faced by poor women as well as women of color. Moreover, although some women's rights activists wisely called for unity between Black Liberation and Women's Liberation movements in the 19th century, others disagreed, believing "it is more important that women should vote than that the black man should vote" (H. W. Beecher, in Davis, p. 72).

Although Black/African American women and other women of color may experience a similar impact of sexism and patriarchy as White women, patriarchy and sexism do not affect these women in the same way, especially since they typically were excluded from political movements, feminist discourse, and psychological theories regarding women's rights and overall disempowerment (Baca Zinn, Hondagneu-Sotelo, & Messner, 2004; Espin, 1997). More importantly, women of color often have labored alongside men of their communities. A stark example of these conditions was depicted during the days of slavery when pregnant Black women were forced not only to continue working in the fields but could be the target of flogging for failing to meet the daily quota:

> A woman who gives offense in the field, and is large in a family way, is compelled to lie down over a hole made to receive her corpulency, and is flogged with the whip or beat with a paddle which has holes in it; at every stroke comes a blister. One of my sisters was so severely punished in this way, that labor was brought on, and the child was born in the field. (Grandy, 1844, in Davis, 1983, p. 9)

Thus, the myriad experiences of women of color cannot be simply divorced or disassociated from that of men from their racial-ethnic background, given their common struggles for survival in an overtly racist environment. Indeed, Davis (1983) argues that by being able to perform domestic duties for one's family "which has long been a central expression of the socially conditioned inferiority of women, the Black woman ... [helped] lay the foundation for some degree of autonomy, both for herself and her men.... She was, therefore, essential to the *survival* of the community" (p. 17).

It is important to contextualize the impact of patriarchy and sexism on women of color within a racial-ethnic framework (Miville & Ferguson, 2006). Several scholars have described how numerous gendered racial stereotypes that today abound for women of color (e.g., sexually promiscuous, docile and obedient) reflect systemic means of gaining dominance or control over them (Greene, 1994; Wyatt, 1997). Moreover, these images also have "served the purpose of masking the social reality of sexual exploitation" of women of color (Greene, 1994, in Miville & Ferguson, 2006, p. 91).

Scholars also have described the intersecting impact of cultural values with sexism and patriarchy on women of color. For example, Gil and Vasquez (1996) delineated the "Maria paradox" for Latina women that arises from conflicts between traditional gender roles, or *marianismo* (i.e., the all-sacrificing wife and mother; Santiago-Rivera, Arredondo, & Gallardo-Cooper, 2002) and the modern world, where women are expected to achieve and, at times, compete with men. *Marianismo* refers to the roles that women play and is based on the religious persona of the Virgin Mary: girls and women "must be pure, long-suffering, nurturing, . . . pious . . . virtuous and humble, yet spiritually stronger than men" (Santiago-Rivera et al., 2002, p. 49). A psychological trap can be laid as Latinas attempt to immerse themselves in traditional cultural norms for women (e.g., not raising their voice in anger) that then can lead to the restriction of life choices and psychological distress, including anxiety and depression (Miville & Ferguson, 2006). Although today many Latinas "report that as a result of acculturation, education, and involvement in relationships, they experience less conflict about not living" according to their racial-ethnic traditions, *marianismo* remains a potent cultural norm according to which many Latinas are socialized (Santiago-Rivera et al., p. 50).

The negative impact of institutionalized racism and sexism also can be turned inward psychologically. Black feminist poet Audre Lorde (1984) poignantly describes the *internalization* of oppression, where an individual comes to adopt the negative institutionalized beliefs about her or his group, for African American women when she asserts, "We are Black women born into a society of entrenched loathing and contempt for whatever is Black and female. We are strong and enduring. We are deeply scarred" (p. 151). Similarly, Hurtado (2003) reflects on the use of Spanish among Latina feminists "as a political assertion of the value of their heritage and the means to create a feminist discourse directly tied to a [Latina] experience" (p. 8). She refers to the work of Patricia Zavella, who studied the discourse of Latinas who expressed fears of "getting burned" if normative social conventions were transgressed, particularly in the face of repressive religious ideologies that may constrict Latinas' self-expression and agency.

Another important aspect regarding racial-ethnic contexts of gender and gender roles relates to their potential for being different from the dominant group's expectations. For example, in Filipino culture, although Filipina American women are expected to be emotional and nurturing, the gender role socialization of Filipina American women is distinctive because they are socialized and recognized as leaders and decision makers within their household. Furthermore, contrary to typical gender role constructions in many Asian communities, women are encouraged to pursue educational attainment and professional development (Pido, 1986). Given the scope of their gender role socialization, Filipina women are commonly viewed as the head of the household (e.g., they manage the household finances, determine which school the children will attend, play the role of disciplinarian of children, and dictate the rules of the household) and are taught to be assertive and independent (Nadal & Corpus, 2012). This is contrary to the more pervasive stereotype that Asian women are submissive, passive, dependent, and subordinate to men (Chinn, 2002).

Similarly, Tafoya (1997) and Garrett and Barret (2003) describe more flexible roles normally present in Native American tribes and nations. For example, Tafoya notes that "most Native communities tend not to classify the world into concrete binary categories of the Western world . . . but rather into categories that range from appropriateness to inappropriateness, depending on the context of the situation" (in Miville & Ferguson, 2006, p. 93). It is the understanding of "the relative nature of opposites (i.e., 'walking in step' within the circle) [that] provides a path toward direction and meaning in life" for many Native Americans (Miville & Ferguson, p. 93).

In sum, to better understand how gender and gender roles evolve, scholars today emphasize the role of the social context rather than biology. Regarding how women of color construct their sense of themselves as gendered beings, it is crucial to understand the role that race-ethnicity can play in this evolution, particularly given the dual impact that sexism and racism may have on their mental and physical health. It is also important to incorporate traditional cultural values, beliefs, and norms when describing the makeup of gender roles within particular racial-ethnic communities. Finally, the conflicts that can arise when traditions meet modernity among women of color can at times lead to mental and physical distress, and further examination is required. We next turn to gender and gender role construction among men of color.

Men of Color

As noted earlier, in many if not most societies, men typically hold a dominant power position relative to women, regarding their social status and what are considered to be their presumably superior native abilities and traits. This remains true for many communities of color, both in the United States and around the world. For example, Chinn (2002) describes how for many Asians and Asian Americans, the social order initiated over 2,500 years ago by the great philosopher Confucius continues to be influential:

> His teachings sought to establish stable, reciprocal, ethical but fundamentally nonegalitarian social relationships based on gender, age, and position in society. Confucian ethics defined relationships between ruler and minister, father and son, husband and wife, elder and younger brother, even those between friends with the goal of establishing a society so just and virtuous it would need no legal system. At the apex of the social hierarchy was the family patriarch. . . . Sons maintained the family lineage, inherited property, worshipped the ancestors, and in turn were worshipped by their descendants. . . . Even as imperial China declined, Confucianism's nonegalitarian ideology gained strength by appropriating Darwin's theory of evolution to justify the low status of women and the lower status of girls. Females were simply biologically inferior and less highly evolved than males. . . . The value of a girl was in marriage to a powerful man. (p. 304)

Many Asian and Asian American parents raise their daughters to be "compliant, feminine, and educated enough to be marriageable" (Chinn, 2002, p. 302), whereas boys are socialized to feel more valued than girls, expecting eventually to be "worshipped by their descendants" (p. 304).

However, in the United States, negative stereotypes for men of this racial-ethnic background often reflect more feminine roles and values, and they can be viewed in the larger society as submissive and passive. Media portrayals have largely made Asian American men invisible; if featured at all, they generally have included "waiters, cooks, servants, laundry workers or martial arts experts" (D. Sue, 2001, p. 787). Asian American men also may experience a type of glass ceiling in the workplace due to institutionalized racist practices as well as their culturally different values and communication styles (e.g., talking less frequently). Moreover, given the newly immigrated status of many Asians in the United States, the family structure may be reversed, with women bringing money to the household equally to or in greater amounts than their male relatives (D. Sue, 2001), thereby causing traditional gender roles to founder.

For many Latino/a communities, gender roles as defined by culture and religion continue to hold sway. These roles typically are communicated by the constructs of *marianismo* described earlier and by *machismo*:

> *Machismo* refers to a man's responsibility to provide for, protect, and defend his family. His loyalty and sense of responsibility to family, friends, and community make him a good man. The Anglo-American definition of *macho* that describes sexism, male-chauvinist behavior is radically different from the original Latino meaning of *machismo* which conveys that notion of "an honorable and responsible man." (Morales, 1996, in Santiago-Rivera et al., 2002, p. 50)

As Morales (1996) and others (Bacigalupe, 2000) have noted, in the United States, the concept of *machismo* as an ideology has perpetuated generally negative stereotypes of Latino men. Negative stereotypical characteristics of *machismo* include male dominance and chauvinism, bravado, womanizing, aggression, violence, alcoholism, emotional restrictiveness, antisocial behaviors, hypermasculinity and excessive masculinity, focus on individual power, sexual promiscuity, extreme rudeness, less education, and lower affiliation to ethnic identity (Arciniega, Anderson, Tovar-Blank, & Tracey, 2008; Casas, Turner, & de Esparza, 2001; Hurtado & Sinha, 2008). For many Latinos, adhering to such characteristics and practices also can validate their masculinity as Latino men, and such devotion may become central to their sense of masculinity. Moreover, Latino men who adhere to these characteristics may be placed at great psychological risk, potentially leading to the development of gender role conflicts (O'Neil, 2008) described earlier. Thus, strict adherence of Latino men to a stereotyped form of *machismo* may have negative implications for their psychological well-being.

Alternatively, the construct of *caballerismo* communicates more positive values associated with masculinity among Latinos and can include protecting and providing for the family and less fortunate members of society; being family oriented; having dignity, wisdom, honor, and responsibility; showing bravery; being emotionally connected to others; being affiliated; giving and showing respect to others; having a strong connection to ethnic identity; focusing on intrapersonal and interpersonal relationships; having a higher satisfaction with life, and having pride in raising one's children (Arciniega et al., 2008; Casas et al., 2001; Falicov, 1998; Hurtado & Sinha, 2008; Villereal & Cavazos, 2005). Wester (2008) suggests that these men are likely to consider and define their masculinity through inner qualities (i.e., integrity, honor) rather than outward qualities (i.e., physical strength) that are more associated with *machismo*.

Regarding Black/African American men, it is similarly important to incorporate the influence of African-centered values, such as a holistic view of oneself, the vitality of feelings, and a collective approach to survival in understanding their gender role constructions (Parham, 1993). Moreover, as with African American women, the stark consequences of racism and racial violence must be acknowledged in the lives of Black men and their sense of themselves as gendered beings, potentially resulting in: "(1) problems of aggression and control, (2) cultural alienation or disconnection, (3) self-esteem issues, (4) dependency issues, (5) help-seeking attitudes and behaviors, and (6) racial identity issues" (Caldwell & White, 2001, p. 738). As with women and other men of color, negative images and stereotypes about Black men abound in the larger society, particularly through the media, including "absent father, pimp, drug dealer, player, gangster, [and] academic underachiever. . . . The obvious problem with media definitions of Black masculinity is that they are admittedly distorted and are predicated on a model of cultural deprivation" (Caldwell & White, p. 745). Unfortunately, many of these images may be internalized by young Black boys and men and may be linked with the psychological problems noted earlier. A number of mental health professionals have developed innovative strategies for combating these issues, many of which involve clients learning responsibility, connecting or dialoguing with members of the community and the extended family as well as learning Africentric values (Parham, 1993; White & Cones, 1999).

Connell (1987, 1995, cited in Miville & Ferguson, 2006) defined the notion of "racialized masculinities" to depict the multiple ways that men of color are marginalized in the larger society, leading to their denigration: "[T]his 'othering' of racialized masculinities helps to shore up the material privileges as part of a system that includes gender, as well as racial, class, sexual, and other relations of power" (p. 92). Many men of color may adopt a "cool" or "tough" persona as a means of combating this process. Sometimes this approach can be successful regarding individual survival; however, many families and communities continue to suffer from the lack of positive role models and other mental health struggles that come from restricting emotions and adhering to rigid behavioral standards (Miville & Ferguson, 2006).

In sum, constructions of gender and gender roles by men of color may be understood best within a racial-ethnic framework that includes the impact of various forms of racism on their mental well-being. Moreover, the role of cultural values and norms in specifying what it means to be masculine may be critical to explore further. Finally, as with women of color, the clash between cultural expectations and modern-world achievements (by both men and women) may create circumstances that could either detract from the constructions of positive definitions of manhood or lead to more flexible understandings of how men and women may behave in multiple settings.

CONSTRUCTIVIST GROUNDED THEORY METHOD

In this chapter we have presented an overview of the current literature regarding gender and gender role construction among men and women of color. Much of the existing research on this topic is in its nascent stages and typically has attempted to apply constructs and measures that do not take into account race-ethnicity directly. For example, most instruments measuring masculinity and femininity still utilize lists of adjectives ascribed as one or the other that individuals decide apply to themselves (Stets & Burke, 2000). Given the dearth of racially ethnically oriented frameworks for understanding gender, the current project undertook to explore the meanings of gender and gender role construction among a sample of more than 60 self-identified participants from Black/African American, Latina/o, and Asian/Asian American backgrounds. Given the long-standing history of oppressive forces of racism and sexism, we wanted to study our topic in a manner that incorporated the unique voices and stories of our participants. These individuals were recruited for our study using a variety of strategies, such as flyers, email announcements, personal contacts, and snowballing (i.e., asking participants if they knew others who might be interested in being interviewed). We interviewed individuals for approximately 45 to 90 minutes, using a semi-structured interview protocol (see appendix), and then had the audiotaped interviews professionally transcribed. The transcriptions formed the bases of the data analyses presented in the subsequent chapters, with some minor editing of quotes for readability. Prior to beginning the interviews, all participants completed an informed consent, a demographic data sheet, and two open-ended questions asking their descriptions of the ideal man and ideal woman. Participants were given $10 for their involvement in the project. The appendix contains demographic information for each participant, categorized by racial/ethnic and gender background (e.g., African American men, African American women, etc.). All participant names used in this book were changed to protect their confidentiality.

We used constructivist grounded theory (CGT) methodology to analyze our findings for common themes among our participants. Because race-ethnicity and the context of social oppression may be important in the constructions of gender and gender roles among men and women of color, we believed this method to be particularly useful for our research. The basic stance of grounded theory (GT) attempts to capture or "see the world as our research participants do—from the inside" (Charmaz, 2006, p. 14). GT is named as such because its purpose "is to produce innovative theory that is 'grounded' in the voices of participants and their own understandings of the complexities of their lived experience within their sociolcultural context" (Fassinger,

2005, p. 156). Theory that emerges from GT generally is meant to explain processes, actions, interactions, or broad experiences.

As noted earlier, a key aspect of GT techniques is their potential to give voice to marginalized people and communities. In particular, a *constructivist* GT approach is useful in this respect because it is assumed that "neither data nor theories are discovered. Rather, we are a part of the world we study and the data we collect. We construct our grounded theories through our past and present involvements and interactions with people, perspectives, and research practices" (Charmaz, 2006, p. 10). In other words, CGT researchers do not assume there is a single objective truth or reality for any one group of people but rather multiple social constructions of reality and truth (Fassinger, 2005). A CGT approach presumes that the theory that emerges "offers an *interpretive* portrayal of the studied world, not an exact picture of it" (Charmaz, 2006, p. 10).

In GT, theory is derived from a rigorous and complex system of coding in order to make sense of participants' meanings and actions (Charmaz, 2006). The use of GT requires active engagement in multiple readings of transcripts to systematically code the major themes that emerge. Analysis entails a number of levels of coding and represents "the interplay between researchers and data" (Strauss & Corbin, 1998, p. 13). Essential components of GT analyses involve "the procedures of making comparisons, asking questions, and sampling based on evolving theoretical concepts" (p. 46).

Researchers' Worldviews

As authors of this book, we recognize that we bring multiple perspectives to our approach to the topic as well as the ways in which we conducted and analyzed this series of interviews. All of us are people of color, including Latina/o, Asian/Asian American, Black/African American, and multiracial, who were socialized both as members of our respective racial-ethnic groups as well as mental health professionals who place great emphasis on being culturally sensitive and aware in our work. Most of us were trained, or are in training, as professional psychologists with strong beliefs about promoting social justice in the ways we do research and practice in our field. We all received formal training (and most of us now are conducting such training) focusing on the deleterious effects that both racism and sexism, in addition to other forms of oppression as based on social class, sexual orientation, and so on, have had on many individuals in the United States.

Our interest in this book project emerged from conversations that began when many of us were part of a research team, led by the book editor, Marie L. Miville, that wanted to explore intersections of multiple oppressions, particularly as these related to men and women of color. We engaged in a variety of readings to immerse ourselves in some of the current thinking about how race-ethnicity and gender might affect each other. A key conversation many of us recalled was a discussion of a seemingly simple topic, hair, and how women of color were often criticized by the larger society, as well as within their own communities, for having anything other than (i.e., less than) straight hair that easily flips with one's hand, what has been called "good" hair. This began our research journey that has now been realized in this book project. We are aware that although multiple perspectives are represented here, in the ways in which we shaped our questions, we interacted with our participants, and we analyzed our data, we likely "did" gender in some similar ways that our participants shared with us. The stories, codes/themes, and theoretical model we present here are based on a great deal of effort, beginning with our participants, yet we recognize that as with any qualitative investigation, this work represents our current constructions of gender roles. Nevertheless, we hope our work can deepen the ongoing discourses on ways that individuals negotiate the multiple complex meanings of race-ethnicity and gender throughout their lives.

CONCLUDING REMARKS

As we have explained here, we developed an interview project as a way of beginning to establish a theoretical model based on the lived experiences of men and women of color regarding their gender role constructions. By using CGT analyses, we hoped to capture the words and actions of our participants to better understand how they construct meanings about their sense of selves as gendered beings. The next chapter presents the poignant narratives of Black/African American men. As these narratives illustrate, Black men often are bombarded with numerous messages regarding the race-ethnicity and gender from a variety of sources, often emphasizing negative traits or qualities. At the same time, our participants identify important people in their lives, such as parents and teachers, who provided positive counter narratives to these negative images, particularly through leadership and role modeling.

REFERENCES

Arciniega, G. M., Anderson, T. C., Tovar-Blank, Z. G., & Tracey, T.J.G. (2008). Towards a fuller conception of machismo: Development of a traditional machismo and caballerismo scale. *Journal of Counseling Psychology, 55*(1), 19–33.

Baca Zinn, M., Hondagneu-Sotelo, P., & Messner, M. A. (2004). Gender through the prism of difference. In M. L. Andersen & P. H. Collins (Eds.), *Race, class, and gender: An anthology,* 5th ed. (pp. 166–174). Belmont, CA: Wadsworth/Thomson.

Bacigalupe, G. (2000). *El Latino*: Transgressing the macho. In M. T. Flores & G. Carey (Eds.), *Family therapy with Hispanics: Toward appreciating diversity* (pp. 29–57). Needham Heights, MA: Allyn & Bacon.

Caldwell, L. D., & White, J. L. (2001). African-centered therapeutic and counseling interventions for African American males. In G. R. Brooks & G. E. Good (Eds.), *The new handbook of psychotherapy and counseling with men: A comprehensive guide to setting, problems, and treatment approaches* (Vol. 2, pp. 737–753). San Francisco, CA: Jossey-Bass.

Casas, J. M., Turner, J. A., & de Esparza, C. A. R. (2001). Machismo revisited in a time of crisis: Implications for understanding and counseling Hispanic men. In G. R. Brooks & G. E. Good (Eds.), *The new handbook of psychotherapy and counseling with men: A comprehensive guide to setting, problems, and treatment* (Vol. 2, pp. 754–779). San Francisco, CA: Jossey-Bass.

Charmaz, K. (2006). *Constructing grounded theory: A practical guide through qualitative analyses.* London, United Kingdom: Sage.

Chinn, P. (2002). Asian and Pacific Islander women scientists and engineers: A narrative exploration of model minority, gender, and racial stereotypes. *Journal of Research in Science Teaching, 39,* 302–323.

Davis, A. Y. (1983). *Women, race, and class.* New York, NY: Vintage.

Enns, C. Z. (2004). *Feminist theories and feminist psychotherapies: Origins, themes, and diversity,* 2nd ed. Binghamton, NY: Haworth Press.

Espin, O. M. (1997). *Latina realities: Essays on healing, migration, and sexuality.* Boulder, CO: Westview Press.

Falicov, C. J. (1998). *Latino families in therapy: A guide to multicultural practice.* New York, NY: Guilford Press.

Fassinger, R. E. (2005). Paradigms, praxis, problems, and promise: Grounded theory in counseling psychology research. *Journal of Counseling Psychology, 52*, 156–166.

Garrett, M. T., & Barret, B. (2003). Two spirit: Counseling Native American gay, lesbian, and bisexual people. *Journal of Multicultural Counseling and Development, 31*, 131–142.

Gil, R. M., & Vasquez, C. I. (1996). *The Maria paradox: How Latinas can merge Old World traditions with New World self-esteem.* New York, NY: Perigee.

Gilmore, D. (1990). *Manhood in the making: Cultural concepts of masculinity.* New Haven, CT: Yale University Press.

Glaser, B. G., & Strauss, A. L. (1967). *The discovery of grounded theory*. Chicago, IL: Aldine.

Greene, B. (1994). Lesbian women of color: Triple jeopardy. In L. Comas-Diaz & B. Greene (Eds.), *Women of color: Integrating ethnic and gender identities in psychotherapy* (pp. 389–427). New York, NY: Guilford Press.

Heppner, M. J., Davidson, M. M., & Scott, A. B. (2003). The ecology of women's career barriers. In M. Kopala & M. A. Keitel (Eds.), *Handbook of counseling women* (pp. 173–184). Thousand Oaks, CA: Sage.

hooks, b. (1981). *Ain't I a woman: Black women and feminism.* Boston, MA: South End.

Hurtado, A. (2003). *Voicing Chicana feminisms: Young women speak out on sexuality and identity.* New York: New York University Press.

Hurtado, A., & Sinha, M. (2008). More than men: Latino masculinities and intersectionality. *Sex Roles, 59*, 337–349.

Institute for Women's Policy Research. (April 2011). *The gender wage gap: 2010.* Downloaded from http://www.iwpr.org/publications/pubs/the-gender-wage-gap-2010-updated-march-2011.

Jones, L. S. (2003). Power and women in the counseling relationship. In M. Kopala & M. A. Keitel (Eds.), *Handbook of counseling women* (pp. 31–39). Thousand Oaks, CA: Sage.

Lorde, A. (1984). *Sister Outsider*. Berkeley, CA: Crossing Press.

Lucal, B. (1999). What it means to be gendered me: Life on the boundaries of a dichotomous gender system. *Gender and Society, 13*, 781–797.

Mahalik, J. R., Cournoyer, R. L., DeFranc, W., Cherry, M., & Napolitano, J. M. (1998). Men's gender role conflict and use of psychological defenses. *Journal of Counseling Psychology, 45*, 247–255.

Miville, M. L., & Ferguson, A. D. (2006). Intersections of sexism and heterosexism with racism: Therapeutic implications. In M. G. Constantine & D. W. Sue (Eds.), *Racism as a barrier to cultural competence in mental health and educational settings* (pp. 87–106). Hoboken, NJ: Wiley.

Morales, E. (1996). Gender roles among Latino gay and bisexual men: Implications for family and couple relationships. In J. Laird & R. J. Green (Eds.), *Lesbians and gays in couples and families: A handbook for therapists* (pp. 272–297). San Francisco, CA: Jossey-Bass.

Nadal, K., & Corpus, M. (2012). "Tomboys" and "Baklas": Experiences of lesbian and gay Filipino Americans. *Asian American Journal of Psychology*. No pagination specified. doi: 10.1037/a0030168

O'Neil, J. M. (1990). Assessing men's gender role conflict. In D. Moore & F. Leafgren (Eds.), *Problem solving strategies and interventions for men in conflict* (pp. 23–38). Alexandria, VA: American Counseling Association.

O'Neil, J. M. (2008). Summarizing 25 years of research on men's gender role conflict using the Gender Role Conflict Scale: New research paradigms and clinical implications. *Counseling Psychologist, 36*, 358–445.

O'Neil, J. M., Good, G. E., & Holmes, S. (1995). Fifteen years of theory and research of men's gender role conflicts: New paradigms for empirical research. In R. F. Levant & W. S. Pollack (Eds.), *A new psychology of men* (pp. 164–206). New York, NY: Basic Books.

Parham, T. A. (1993). *Psychological storms: The African American struggle for identity.* Chicago, IL: African American Images.

Pido, A. (1986). *The Pilipinos in America: Macro/micro dimensions of integration and immigration.* Staten Island, NY: Center for Migration Studies.

Raffaelli, M., & Ontai, L. L. (2004). Gender socialization in Latino/a families: Results from two retrospective studies. *Sex Roles, 50*, 287–299.

Reid, P. T., & Comas-Diaz, L. (1990). Gender and ethnicity: Perspectives on dual status. *Sex Roles, 22*, 397–408.

Santiago-Rivera, A. L., Arredondo, P., & Gallardo-Cooper, M. (2002). *Counseling Latinos and la familia: A practical guide.* Thousand Oaks, CA: Sage.

Settles, I. H. (2006). Use of an intersectional framework to understand Black women's racial and gender identities. *Sex Roles, 54*, 589–601.

Settles, I. H., Sellers, R. M., & Damas Jr., A. (2002). One role or two? The function of psychological separation in role conflict. *Journal of Applied Psychology, 87*, 574–582.

Stets, J. E., & Burke, P. J. (2000). Femininity/masculinity. In E. F. Borgatta & R.J.V. Montgomery (Eds.), *Encyclopedia of sociology*, rev. ed. (pp. 997–1005). New York, NY: Macmillan. Available at http://wat2146.ucr.edu/Papers/00b.pdf

Strauss, A. L., & Corbin, J. (1998). *Basics of qualitative research: Techniques and procedures for developing grounded theory*, 2nd ed. Thousand Oaks, CA: Sage.

Sue, D. (2001). Asian American masculinity and therapy: The concept of masculinity in Asian American males. In G. R. Brooks & G. E. Good (Eds.), *The new handbook of psychotherapy and counseling with men: A comprehensive guide to setting, problems, and treatment approaches* (Vol. 2, pp. 737–753). San Francisco, CA: Jossey-Bass.

Sue, D. W., & Sue, D. (2008). *Counseling the culturally different: Theory and practice*, 5th ed. Hoboken, NJ: Wiley.

Suzuki, L. A., & Ahluwalia, M. K. (2003). Gender issues in personality, cognitive, and vocational assessment of women. In M. Kopala & M. A. Keitel (Eds.), *Handbook of counseling women* (pp. 119–130). Thousand Oaks, CA: Sage.

Tafoya, T. (1997). Native gay and lesbian issues: The two-spirited. In B. Greene (Ed.), *Ethnic and cultural diversity among lesbians and gay men* (pp. 1–10). Thousand Oaks, CA: Sage.

Tinsley-Jones, H. A. (2001). Racism in our midst: Listening to psychologists of color. *Professional Psychology: Research and Practice, 32*, 573–580.

Tryon, G. S., & Winograd, G. (2003). Developing a health identity. In M. Kopala & M. A. Keitel (Eds.), *Handbook of counseling women* (pp. 185–197). Thousand Oaks, CA: Sage.

Villereal, G. L., & Cavazos, A. (2005). Shifting identity: Process of change in identity of aging Mexican-American males. *Journal of Sociology and Social Welfare, 32*, 33–41.

Wester, S. R. (2008). Male gender role conflict and multiculturalism: Implications for counseling psychology. *The Counseling Psychologist, 36*, 294–324.

Wester, S. R., & Vogel, D. L. (2002). Working with the masculine mystique: Male gender role conflict, counseling self-efficacy, and the training of male psychologists. *Professional Psychology: Research and Practice, 33*(4), 370–376.

White, J. L., & Cones, J. H. (1999). *Black man emerging: Facing the past and seizing a future in America*. New York, NY: Freeman.

Wyatt, G. (1997). *Stolen women: Reclaiming our sexuality, taking back our lives*. New York, NY: Wiley.

Chapter Two

GENDER ROLES AMONG AFRICAN AMERICAN MEN
Marie L. Miville and Joel Sahadath

The experiences of Black/African American men in the United States historically have been characterized by scholars as a "plight" because, in essence, "manhood has not been a birthright for Black males, who have not generally been granted traditional masculine privilege or power in the United States" (Mincy, 1994, in Gayles, Alston, & Staten, 2005, p. 50). U.S. Census statistics bear out the harsh realities that Black men continue to face growing up today: Currently, more African American males are incarcerated than were enslaved in 1850, a staggering 846,000 (Alexander, 2010). Moreover, according to Alexander (2010), although African Americans make up approximately 13% of the U.S. population, they represent 40% of the prison inmate population. African American men also have the lowest life expectancy of any racial-ethnic and gender group in the United States, with homicide being the lead cause of death among Black men between the ages of 15 and 34 (Gayles et al., 2005). Moreover, although African Americans have similar rates of mental illness as compared with Whites, Black men are overrepresented in several at-risk populations, including the homeless, inmates and juveniles in custody, traumatized individuals who have been exposed to violence, and active military service members (Gayles et al.).

At the same time, other statistics point to the increasing success and mobility of Black men in the United States. For example, African American males, along with their female counterparts, have attained their highest educational achievements ever in U.S. history (Virella, 2011). Between 2000 and 2010, the number of African Americans with a bachelor's degree substantially increased; Black men now have a ratio of 15.7 per 100 individuals who are college graduates. In total, the current college graduation ratio for African Americans stands at 18.2, as compared with 28 out of 4 million individuals after the Civil War and 1.3 in 100 in 1940 (Virella, 2011). The election of the first African American man, Barack Obama, as the U.S. President further indicates, if not the complete removal of longtime racial and gender barriers in the United States, at least some measure of success in the long fight toward social justice and civil rights for African Americans and Black men in particular. Moreover, a number of Black scholars (e.g., Harper, 2012; Rice, 2008) have called for an "anti-deficit" approach to understanding the successes and accomplishments of Black men today. Rice writes: "As a rule, the way we understand Black males in American society is not in terms of success, at best it is in terms of survival. I argue . . . that within survival are abilities and attributes that mirror those found in the very best kinds of successes" (p. xv).

Essed (1991, in Thomas, Witherspoon, & Speight, 2008) coined the term *gendered racism* to describe how the effects of both racial and gender discrimination can "narrowly intertwine and combine under certain conditions into one, hybrid phenomenon" (p. 307). Although much of the focus of research and interventions on the effects of gendered racism has been on women of color, Schwing, Wong, and Fann (2012) have identified how the dual status of being Black and male also can lead to psychological distress, primarily resulting from negative stereotypes reflecting violence, absence in the family, and presumed athletic proclivities. Yet, in line with the anti-deficit tone of many African American scholars, we believe it is important to explore how constructing one's sense of manhood and the roles involved in being a man also create the potential for opportunity and success for oneself, one's family and community, and the larger society (Franklin, 2004).

How do Black men negotiate their sense of manhood in the face of contradicting stories of success and tragedy? In this chapter, we explored the meanings of gender roles and masculinity/femininity among a group of eight Black/African American men (see Table A.1 in the appendix for demographic information about our participants). We identified a core theme reflecting constant negotiations of gender roles related to being a Black man, with a number of key subthemes, including (a) responsibility and leadership, (b) evaluating multiple messages from multiple sources, (c) negotiating stereotypes, (d) navigating privilege and oppression, and (e) developing flexible gender roles and styles (see Table A.2 in the appendix). The next section explores these themes in depth, incorporating the personal stories of our participants. A final section describes potential applications of these themes for mental health professionals and educators.

NEGOTIATING GENDER ROLES

Our participants often emphasized that they were in constant negotiation about their gender roles and what it means to be a man. These young men perceived the ongoing struggle or evolution, in essence, in becoming or "being a man" as a process embedded within the social context and the network of relationships a man negotiates with others, including oneself, as well as with one's partner or spouse, one's family, especially one's children, the larger Black community, and society as a whole. Many of our participants used the term *responsibility*, which we now describe.

Responsibility and Leadership

A key theme of being a man reflected by nearly all participants centered on responsibility and being a role model or leader for others. As Michael noted:

> Being a man is [*pause, sighs*] knowing who you are, and taking responsibility for what all that entails. Knowing who you are helps me help other people figure out who they want to be. So in being an ideal man, for example . . . it may help younger adults who are guiding themselves in a specific direction look to you as a role model. So an ideal man, in my point of view, would be a role model. . . . But as far as what a real man is supposed to be, I guess I would say—the first word that comes to my mind is responsibility, and I think it comes from the idea of role model, and knowing that you have a responsibility that people are looking up to you, you know. There's a quote that I used to hear a lot, which is: *To the world, you just may be one person, but to one person, you may just be the world.* (emphasis added)

Michael found the key role undergirding his sense of maleness is in what he can teach to others. The impact of this role, he felt, cannot be underestimated in terms of its place in sustaining one's family and community. He further noted that the importance of becoming conscious, being mindful, of one's role as a man and making decisions about how to act within society, particularly the consequences of one's actions, is what distinguishes him from being a child:

> A man who understands his place in society . . . [knows] that in being a man, there are certain things that are expected of you, but that it is ultimately your decision, that your actions actually influence—may influence others basically . . . being a man and not a child, you have to take responsibility for your actions. And so why I keep thinking about the word *responsibility* as the most important thing that goes—it ties into every aspect of a man.

Terrance similarly noted the evolution of his perspective of becoming a man as being observant of one's impact on others:

> In comparing to being a boy or being a teenager, it's you become more respectful, you become more understanding of what life is about. You become more caring and loving and less selfish. And you feel some responsibility for your role in society. You don't feel like you're just here to do whatever it is you want to do and live haphazardly.

Our participants also discussed their strong reactions toward notions or images that ran counter to being responsible—that is, what a man should *not* be. For example, in response to an interviewer question about what he could not tolerate in other men, Sam stated,

> Irresponsibility. One that's not working [*laughs*], you know? One that's not taking care of himself or taking care of their family, whether it be children or if they're married, you know. One that is just making excuses all the time . . . one that doesn't respect others, that doesn't respect the law, that doesn't respect themselves, period.

Similarly, Taj expressed frustration at seeing other Black men acting irresponsibly by, for example, leaving their families uncared for:

> I could just be speaking from living in [city], but I think that from a general standpoint, Black men tend to walk out on their families, they tend to [*pause*] to use, to make excuses as a way to escape from things that they should do. Again, going back to

what the ideal man is, I used being a provider. A provider means to do what it is that you have to do to make provisions, to provide for your family, your friends, yourself, and I think that Black men use scapegoats such as slavery or the way that they were raised, not having parents involved or other supportive figures in their life, and they use that as an excuse. And so what happens is that they won't go to school, they find trouble as a way of expressing themselves, trouble meaning joining gangs or dealing drugs, robbing and stealing, doing things that are unlawful.

At some level, Taj's frustration reflects an internalized stereotype of Black men as absent fathers without sufficient recognition of the impact of racial barriers or overwhelming poverty or hopelessness on other Black men. Perhaps another way of understanding his frustration might be as reflecting a "take no excuses" attitude in connection with being responsible for oneself and others, including the importance of Black men adopting constructive strategies in their response to the harsh impact of racially and economically oppressive experiences. Derrick explained:

A lot of Black men turn to—you walk down the street and you hear them . . . downgrading Black women, and if they knew their history. . . . How could you do that, you know what I mean? If you knew your history and knew where you come from and if you really understood it, you would not do that. So a Black man, I definitely believe, I would add, that they need to know where they come from and know how to carry themselves in general. When you're a Black man, you deal with other races every day. If you're, you know, working towards your goals, i.e., work or school, you're going to be interacting with other nationalities and ethnic groups or what have you. Just know how to carry yourself and don't come off ignorant, but yet still don't let no one degrade you in a certain way.

As Derrick poignantly highlighted, knowing oneself in the context of accurate positive knowledge about oneself as a racial being (i.e., knowing where one comes from historically, culturally, socially, and politically) is essential to becoming a man, particularly as a Black man, and to taking on responsible adult roles.

Other participants noted the positive impact that role models already had in their lives by their embodiment of leadership. For example, a major role model for most of the participants was President Barack Obama. Norris emphasized that President Obama's "charisma, leadership, commitment to family and heritage, and his self-motivation are an inspiration for me." He further noted that reading Obama's autobiography, *Dreams from My Father*, pointed out how the road to becoming a man is not always straight and narrow:

> Hearing about how he did not have this, this, I guess a glorified upbringing in the sense that he made mistakes along the way in terms of disregarding his education at first or questioning the purpose of education or experimenting with alcohol at times when, you know, he was underage. Working through, negotiating his own racial identity when given kind of this polarized community of Black people.

And further, Norris learned the importance of being firm regarding his principles from the president's beginnings as a community organizer:

> Despite the negativity, really sticking true to his core values in terms of not getting caught up in conversations about [*pause*] things that might deter from the issues at hand and really sticking to his guns. I think that's something where for me, as I was growing up and understanding and still understanding what it means to be a man, I think that there is this level of, of being firm in your principles and values, and being open to, to changing your beliefs when given, I think, sufficient information or sufficient reason to do so.

A number of participants also highlighted the importance of role models closer to home. For example, James emphasized how a former president of the historically Black college/university (HBCU) he had attended as an undergraduate had taught him the meaning of being a man:

> He grew up, of course, during segregation in . . . South Carolina, so it was moments where he refused, as a young boy, to be treated any different, differently than anyone else. So it was moments where his family told him that he always had to go to the back door when he went to a White person's house, and he was adamant about going to the front door and being treated equally. And I think it was stories like that that really—I was able to connect and identify with a man who was struggling with this idea of integrity and what he stood for, and taking a stand for what he stood for. And I see that parallel in my own life.

As James, Norris, and others described, being a leader means not allowing difficult circumstances or events to stop Black men from pursuing their dreams and visions about what success, such as pursuing an education, might be for them and their families. However, learning how to do this is a process that for many Black youth often is fraught with a mixture of messages about their traits, abilities, expectations, images, and values, as we see in the next subtheme.

Evaluating Multiple Messages from Multiple Sources

Throughout childhood and youth, participants learned about being and becoming a man through many messages heard from a variety of racial and gender socialization sources, including parents and other relatives; church members and religious beliefs; schools settings, particularly teachers and peers; racial-ethnic communities; and the media. These messages were expressed in many ways, ranging widely in tenor from negative to positive, rigid to flexible, and punishing to rewarding. As they grew older, participants carefully sifted through many of these messages as well as the sources from which they came, attempting to identify those that rang of truth for themselves, their communities, and the larger society, and those that did not.

Parents were, without a doubt, primary socializing agents regarding participants' gender role constructions about how both boys and girls "should" act. As Sam noted:

> Well, I think, first of all, it starts from the home. I think whatever they see in the home, that's what they will, I guess, determine what is masculine, what's feminine. I know, for instance, for me, in my household, it was always pointed out when someone was masculine or what was considered to be feminine.

Parents also played a significant role in highlighting the role of responsibility, for example, in seeking an education or being employed, as part of being male (or female). Derrick noted:

> As a Black male growing up, my parents expected me to go to school. They expected me to be responsible. They wanted me to go

to college but . . . they didn't really stress me in terms of like, okay, if I chose not to go, then they wouldn't look down on me as long as I went out there and got a job and I was doing well.

Fathers in particular played crucial roles for participants, by the examples they set, either by what they did or did not do, and the qualities they exuded to participants in their roles as fathers and providers. Michael recalled,

> I think a lot of my ideas about what a man should be comes from my own father, and my view of my father as a child, and my view of my father now. . . . As a child, my father slept during the day and worked at night. So when I was awake, he would sleep. When I would sleep, he was awake. I never thought of my father as being an absent father, although he would sleep most of my life growing up. My dad was always around whenever he could be. Never thought of him as being absent. But when I got older, I started to hear stories about people with their dads . . . and I started to realize that my father wasn't as present as a lot of other people's. But it was because my dad had to do what he had to do. . . . And I remember my dad always—never complaining, and at the end of the day, my childish view of him maybe being asleep all the time and my manly view of him doing what he had to do and take responsibility and be the man to make sure that I could have the future that I have is very admirable. I also think it's admirable that he's humble about it. He doesn't want anything in return but to see me be happy and to see me succeed, whatever that means.

As Michael stated, for the most part, he viewed his father very positively as a role model. Only on hearing about the stereotype of absent fathers from others did he begin to question his father's real presence in his life. However, Michael ultimately felt admiration for his father's self-sacrificing decisions as he gave up actual time with his son in his efforts to provide for him and help him succeed.

Participants also shared that their fathers often played the gender-stereotypical role of provider only, as Sam noted:

> He was the one who was fixing things in the house. Whenever things were broken, my mom would turn to him. He was the one that was the main provider in the household. He didn't really do the nurturing part. He was more the worker.

Sometimes immigration or other institutional concerns interfered with the physical availability of fathers during the participants' boyhoods. Such was the case for Derrick:

> As far as masculinity is concerned, my father wasn't there always when I was younger and when he was around, he was a kind of take-charge kind of man. His line of work, when he lived in the United States, wasn't legal per se, but his masculinity showed through everything he did, as far as being controlling, taking charge of what he had to take care of, being the man basically of the house when he was around. He took care of bills, he took care of food supply. He spent time with the kids, he had a lot of kids, so he spent time with me when I was younger. He just knew when to take charge when he had to.

Because of his father's absence throughout much of his childhood, Derrick also viewed him more complexly, not just by what he did when he was present but also through the emotional impact of his absence:

> Now, when I say my father contributed to my masculinity is, yes, when he was around, he took care of things and was very dominant and compassionate, yes, but still he took care of things and that's what a man is supposed to do, quote-unquote, in today's world. But where it really contributes to *my* views as I got older and I came to my own conclusion as a masculine man is because the operative word was *when he was around* . . . if you're going to have kids, that's a responsibility issue. That's some sense of responsibility you should always have, and if he's not around, that's something I would not do if I had kids, you know? . . . I've always said when I got older, that if I had kids and if I was really sure that they were my kids, that I would be a very active father. So that's something that he [my father] did not do when I got older, [and] I felt that that wasn't part of being a masculine man.

As Derrick noted, his father not being able to be around affected his own constructions of being a man; as a result, Derrick noted that if he himself were to have children, he would do so only if he was able to be present and active in their lives. That is, in addition to providing material things to his family, such as money and housing, Derrick came to define the provider role for himself as necessarily providing love and attention to children on a regular, if not daily, basis.

Other participants also highlighted their fathers' impact on their gender role constructions. For example, Norris grew up with a mostly absent father, although with a different impact than Derrick. In a critical incidence, his father taught him the importance of being true to one's feelings, even if these might make him appear weak in the traditional gender role sense of how men "should" act:

> I think I got to know my dad kind of late. The relationship was fine, we just weren't close, and I would see [him] maybe a couple times a year. Now that I'm an adult, I see him more frequently, but you know, it's still a little strange. But I do remember one piece of advice he gave me that I still remember to this day. He said, "Don't be afraid to say 'I don't know'" . . . And I think that stood out to me so much because it in some ways, it—when I'm also, when I'm reading between the lines, he was also saying that some men are afraid of something and it is to admit what they perceive to be a fault of not knowing. And to hear, I guess, another man speak about fear is always memorable. Now did he give me any stories or anything about that? No, he didn't. But I think it was a moment where he recognized there is a vulnerability in [*pause*] taking on this identity of being a man. . . . His sister passed away in a car accident, and I remember how, you know, emotionally distraught he was over that and verbalizing that. And I think a lot of—now this kind of conflicts with what you see on TV in terms of manhood, right? Men aren't supposed to talk about these sorts of things or you have to pry it out of them, but for him it wasn't like that. He loved her, he was willing to share that.

Although his father may not have been around on a daily basis, he nevertheless taught Norris a critical lesson: Counter to traditional notions of masculinity as being invulnerable and not showing weakness, it was important to recognize how important emotions, including fear and grief, are in defining oneself as a Black man.

In contrast, Taj poignantly shared the emotional impact of his father on his gender role constructions, embodied as the traditional unemotional male role:

> My father worked a 40-hour plus job. He always made good money and I grew up in a two-family, two-story home . . . I was privileged. I never really saw the effects of poverty until I was of age to visit outside of my home, to maybe friends or family,

family members who lived in [*pause*] what we called the projects, housing developments. So I say all that to say that my father was, he was about maybe five eight, a dark-skinned guy [*pause*], deep voice, you know, you would consider him to be very masculine. He has no signs of any emotion, you never would ever see him in a vulnerable state. He would never cry in front of us or anything like that. He used his hands and his belt as a way to discipline us as children. So he would of course be defined as . . . "the norm," if you will, for masculinity. He's like, most would say, Well, he's very masculine. But his actions to me show femininity, someone who's feminine, because he ran away from his responsibility, he took a very passive role in taking care of his children, the upkeep of his home. He didn't do any of those things. He didn't go out and mow the lawn and cook meals, or he didn't [*pause*] give us hugs or anything. He was a very hard man.

However, despite this presumably "tough" image, Taj observed of his father:

I believe my father was afraid of—this goes back to me saying not being afraid. He was afraid of life, afraid to really travel and explore [*pause*], being stuck in his own way of thinking, not being responsible, not being the caretaker, not being loving, those things, and I think that that's very important for a young man and a young woman to have, especially when I didn't grow up in a single-family home, so to speak. . . . There was my father as well, but he just wasn't active.

As Taj learned, simply acting the traditional tough stance as a male does not necessarily translate into actual courage or responsibility; instead, Taj came to define being a man as necessarily involving facing one's fears, taking chances, and seeking opportunities where these may not seem obvious or easy.

Mothers also played critical roles for most participants in providing a number of gender-relevant messages as well as reinforcing gender-linked behaviors and styles (i.e., how to be or act "masculine" or "feminine"). At times, to some participants, mothers also modeled what it meant to be masculine through their example, in the sense of "doing" or being responsible for the family, home, and children. As Sam stated:

If we had any issues or anything of that sort, it was my mom. So that's where the femininity I saw in her, because she was the nurturing type, she was the one that was basically maintaining the household. She worked but she still came home and did that. She basically—anything that has to do with us, she was the one that was the main person over it. Anytime we had—again, anytime we had any problems, we turned to her.

Moreover, as Marquis noted, mothers and other female relatives also played the role of reinforcer of presumably gender-appropriate behaviors—that is, how boys and men "should" behave:

One thing I do remember, you know, growing up with my mother and particularly my grandmother was that—and I would watch it on these shows, particularly talk shows, where the men would cross their legs and they would talk with their hands. Even though they were clearly heterosexual, they would cross their legs, you know, very much like a lady and they would talk with their hands, and she told me not to do that, at least not here. She said that men do not talk with their hands, men do not cross their legs.

James recounted similar experiences:

I think in my own experience, my mother was key to, in terms of how she modeled what or projected what—she had three boys and one girl, so she spent a lot of time raising boys. So it was different traits and characteristics that she constantly instilled in us, and having manners and presenting yourself well. And we definitely can't sag our pants. Your shirt—I can even remember in first grade, your shirt always had to be tucked in. Like if you came home with the shirt, you know, hanging out of your pants, she sort of disciplined you for it, so and I think it came primarily from her.

Mothers and other female relatives also at times privileged their sons, relative to their daughters, by allowing them not to do certain household chores and giving them certain liberties not given to girls. As Norris said:

They spoiled me in a certain way that I think was unique to me being a boy for one . . . if I wanted a toy and I made enough noise about it, I would get it. If I, you know, I think I had a cell phone before my sister did and she's older. I got to stay out a little bit later when I was in high school and go to these parties and not be questioned as much. As I got older, you know, stuff like washing the dishes wasn't—I didn't get yelled at for not doing it anymore.

Mothers and other female relatives sometimes provided mixed, even confusing, messages about how to behave as a boy or man, presumably based on their own negative experiences with men in their lives. Norris shared:

Family is complicated because I grew up in a house predominantly with women. There was my grandmother, my aunt, my mother, my sister, my older sister, she was—she is four years older than me, and my uncle who's handicapped. So the influence of women, as you can imagine, was very strong. From them, I think I got a slightly different take on what it means to be a man. From them, I would say to be a man meant [*pause*] being, being a person of your word, following through on—again, following through on all your promises. . . . It meant being patient. . . . In terms of being patient, I think, you know, for example, my grandmother separated from my grandfather in Jamaica and she came to America with my aunt, mother, and uncle. And they used to argue a lot, from my understanding, stories that I've been told, and I think, you know, he—I don't even know who to—I'm trying not to place blame on either of them, but one of the faults that I heard was that he wasn't patient, and you know, pretty much wanted things his way when he wanted it, and being argumentative. And so my family, my immediate family, did not want me to, I guess, follow those footsteps. On the same lines, though, I think being a man was also a series of contradictions for me growing up in the household because, at the same time . . . so yeah, the household for me was not necessarily conducive for me to really figure out what it meant to be a man, I would say. There was just too much contradictions [*laughs*] going on.

Contradictory messages again were present for Norris from his mother when he wanted to play football in high school, with the effect of him feeling somehow less than a man:

I remember even asking my mom, even bringing up the subject of football. "No, no, don't want you to do it," and she wouldn't sign the papers. So in some ways, right? that was demasculinize—is that even a word? I don't even know. Demasculinizing. . . . kind of taking away an aspect of my malehood.

As Boyd-Franklin and Franklin (2000) sagely observe, African American mothers have known for more than 400 years that "the deck [is] stacked against their sons from birth" (p. 18), leaving mothers at times to overcompensate in protecting them from the many risks they face. Our participants' stories clearly indicated just how important, and sometimes confusing, their mothers' impact was in how they defined themselves as men.

Extended family also played a critical role for participants in negotiating their gender roles. For example, Derrick attributed learning about being masculine from his uncles:

> My uncles, they associated masculinity with being a thug and being on the streets and hanging with your boys and so forth and so on. So growing up, at a young age, I felt that that was the meaning of masculinity.

Marquis similarly noted how his grandmother was impactful during his childhood:

> Growing up and living with my grandmother, you know, being a vivacious woman of the quote-unquote old school, a lot of those teachings are not really taught together because a lot of them are very old and many of them have passed away. However, her teachings have always been, you know, that a male is always respectful to a female. He's never, you know, somebody that's a pushover. He's somebody that commands attention. . . . So I got those teachings from family.

Finally, as Norris recalled, messages could at times be conflicting in the larger family context, as based on how different relatives behaved with each other:

> Within the family structure, where I saw kind of the conflicts where, again, at these large family gatherings where the jokes sometimes, what I'd overhear among the men, would be kind of flirtatious and sexual in nature, and [*pause*] I, I think I was confused because I thought that's not what a man should be about, at least, you know, what I was taught by my mom and aunt and grandmother. But within these larger family gatherings, that's how the other men were and I didn't—I mean, these, they're family and they seem like good guys, right? So why should I not be like them? And even my own father, you know, like well, I kind of look like the guy, so why didn't I—why was it frowned upon, you know, that he, he drank a lot? Isn't that what a lot of guys do?

Michael poignantly highlighted the complex impact of the family setting not only in reinforcing gender roles but in the challenges of becoming a role model for others.

> A young cousin of mine . . . I hadn't seen him in so long, comes running in the house with his bookbag, just coming from school. He doesn't really know me because I'm hardly ever down in South Carolina, but he knows of me. So we're playing cards. The little cousin—let's say his name is Tim—comes in and I say, "Hey Tim, how was school?" [*pause.*] So I want to further engage this young Black man—because he is a little boy now, and I could see everyone just not really paying any attention. So I say, "Tim, what kind of—what's your favorite subject in school?" "I ain't got none." Everyone laughs in the room. I'm not laughing because I don't think it's funny. So everyone—and everyone looked at me like "What's wrong? Why are you asking him these questions?" And I said, "I just want to know what his favorite subject is. What is the—what's the problem with asking that?" And they're like "He don't have a favorite subject, he ain't got no favorite subject, whatever." And so I'm like "You have"— I look at him, I say, "You have to have a favorite subject, there's got to be something you like. Art, anything, math, science." And you know what this little boy said to me, who is my cousin? He said, "I like recess because I get to shoot little boys in the butt with my BB gun." And it was serious. And everyone in the room laughed.

This incident points out how families can both add to and subtract from young men's efforts to be positive role models for younger relatives. Michael struggled to figure out how he might fulfill his role as a mentor while at the same time still feel accepted by his larger family:

> So here I am in this situation. Nothing's being done, and I clearly see the road he's going down. And because I'm in my own studies mainly, I'm up here in [city], I don't have time for him as much as I would like to, so I can't have that constant connection with him like I would like. So do I sit there and not say anything and just let this behavior continue? . . . He has no idea of how many people fought for him to even be in a school to learn the things that he's learning, because these are the things that I understand now as a man that I didn't understand when I was a little boy. But here, no one is taking responsibility for his answers and for his future.

For Michael, this incident painfully highlighted his growing distance and alienation from his family of origin as a result of moving away to seek an education in a predominantly White university as well as his current struggle to define himself as an educated Black man in the context of internalized racism:

> And if I said something, then I'm the "White boy" from [university] that's trying to like be White. And so if it becomes a thing to me, why does everything that has to be futuristic or positive or educational or informational, why does all of that have to be White? And these are the things that stereotypically have become internalized in the Black community so much so that you can't even look at this little boy and engage him in such a way just to ask him what does he like to do in school, and the answer not be something as ridiculous as the answer he gave me, and it not be reprimanded—him not be reprimanded for it. So these are the little things that, within my own family, I can't specifically change, so I decided not to say anything clearly.

Michael feared for his cousin and wondered how he can better intervene with him in the future while struggling with the impact and meaning of his own education:

> But it hurts me in such a way to know that when I do get the phone call of him being in jail, or . . . dead, . . . I'm not going to be as shocked as I would when I get the phone call that he graduated from high school, or . . . that he is going to college. . . . And as a Black man, I feel it's my responsibility to try to lead him down the right road, but without the connection, I can only do but so much.

Participants also highlighted the role of *religion* as well as interactions with *church members* as helping negotiate their sense of manhood. For example, Michael ascribed the age-old division of work by the sexes to religious beliefs:

> Especially in the church, you have the old famous saying in the Baptist church, you know, Adam and Eve, not Adam and Steve. So you always are having this dichotomy from just the beginning of time, it was always [*snapping fingers*] man, woman, boy, girl, always, always.

Taj similarly attributed the source of strict gender roles to religious beliefs:

> Gender roles I feel are defined based on the Bible. And to me, it's relevant, it's very relevant. To me, it's true. I believe in God, I believe in the Bible. I believe that men are supposed to be the leaders of a family. They're supposed to be leaders of our country. And I'm not saying that women can't do it, and they have been doing it for quite some time, but I believe that the man is supposed to do these things..

Whether they were deeply religious or not, several participants viewed the church as a key social institution that instilled values and provided important role models. As Terrance explained:

> I think church is just a positive institution. I'm not deeply religious or deeply anything. I just see church as a positive institution. . . . Seeing a Black man in the church, that's a positive. Seeing them in that positive institution, as opposed to seeing them on a street corner or seeing them [*pause*] seeing them only in sports or seeing them only on a music video, and just having direct contact with those men in church was a positive thing. . . . I just had a great—a good example of seeing Black males in a social setting.

As some African American scholars have noted (Boyd-Franklin & Franklin, 2000), spiritual communities have a critical influence in how young African American boys construct a positive sense of manhood. A number of participants clearly indicated that this was the case in their own emerging definitions.

School settings formed another set of primary socializing institutions, especially through interactions with teachers and peers. Norris recounted:

> Because I went to a Catholic school, they adhered to some of the more traditional roles of men and women. Guys, you always have to come wearing a shirt and tie, holding the doors for women as teachers or classmates. . . . It set, I guess it [holding a door open] set up a [*pause*] I guess the message they were trying to send was humility, having humility, and I think I bought that for a long time [*pause*]. And I think it also meant that a lot is expected of you as a man and you need to—in order to show

that you are a leader, you needed to know when to, you needed to—you also have a social responsibility as a leader or a responsibility to others, especially to women in that sense, being sensitive to their needs and knowing when to [*pause*] knowing when or how to be supportive to them.

He further described the powerful impact of male school teachers as positive role models:

The teachers are West Indian [*laughs*] . . . the male teachers were the ones who I guess were strict disciplinarians, kind of did the, did the heavy stuff, the dirty stuff, you know, taking the trash out or moving the boxes. . . . I remember one time, I think some students from the local public school went in our building, our school building, and this was before classes started so we were still in the schoolyard, and so the male teachers, you know, went in the middle of the building and kicked them out and searched the other building and kicked them out. So you know, they were the protectors. They were fearless.

Teachers at times also had a confusing, even negative, impact on students regarding mixed messages about gender roles. For example, Norris observed the confusing impact of a teacher he had viewed as a mentor when the teacher spoke in objectifying terms about a female parent:

I had one teacher, I loved him, but he seemed flirtatious with the female parents, and I remember one time he was over kind of talking to another male teacher about a parent or something. And I didn't hear exactly what he was saying, but it was—you could tell it was some sort of flirtatious or kind of looking—now that I look back at it, it's probably looking her up and down and that kind of thing. And this is a teacher, mind you, and I honestly at the time saw [him] as a role model. So I thought, well, if he can do it, then the rest of us can do it, I guess, but it never felt right for me being that way. So I was like, okay, is there something wrong with *me*?

Peer influences also played a major role for participants in teaching both values and behaviors linked with being a man. As with role models and parents, messages were often mixed, and participants carefully reflected both their impact and their take-away message. Norris discussed when he began thinking about dating and viewing girls as sexual objects and feeling heavy peer pressure from other boys:

> I guess in middle school from peers, which is not surprising, right? Where, you know, a lot of the guys would talk about, began to talk about the girls, our classmates in a very sexual way. And whether or not they experimented with sex I think didn't come into too much play just yet because I went to a small school, but to begin to see their bodies in, in—to see these girls I grew up with and went to school with as women now, and not in a respectful way. To talk openly about kind of—you know, in a derogatory way. And as a guy, if you're not with that or not with that conversation, then you're not really—then it became a question of what your sexual orientation was. . . . And [*pause*] you have to, I guess, be willing to accept dares and take risks, I think where for me the more salient things that I got from what my classmates thought, the guys thought what it meant to be a man.

Experiences with particular peers also had tremendous impact on participants, both in terms of positive and negative modeling as young Black men, as Norris indicated:

> Unfortunately, some of them played into the stereotypes that were expected of them as Black males. . . . Case in point: One guy, he was two years above me . . . he's taken on this whole new identity. You know, wearing the big gold chain. In his backpack, he had this like this mesh pocket, he would put condoms in there . . . he wanted everyone to see that he was, you know, whatever he was. You know, going to a lot of parties, just being very social. And I found that to be, you know, I found that to be a problem. Some of them, again, playing into the stereotype of being very funny. I found that to be a problem.

Attending an HBCU had a powerful positive impact on James. Teachers and mentors provided very clear demarcations of traditional gender role behaviors and traits that clarified how best to behave and interact with the larger world:

> When I went to [HBCU], it did become very visible, the lines and the boundaries and what's expected of a man and what's expected of a woman and how you interact, you know, considering that you have these gender roles now. So I think, and still to this day, my mentors really strive to mold me like into this, I guess this, this person who's very clear on the expectations of

the larger society and his own immediate environment of what, what's expected of a young man. . . . So like we started to use that as the standard when we go out into the world.

James contrasted his positive experiences at an HBCU with his current experiences at a predominantly White university:

I will say that this experience at [school], as I've mentioned before, is my first real experience like in navigating an institution that's primarily driven by the White race and a lot of students are of the White race. So I think for me, this has been a real test in terms of my idea of what a man should be and especially a Black man, and the expectations and boundaries. I was just reading some literature by a guy whose name—I know one book is by Lena Wright at Ohio State University, and she's writing about the Black male socialization and how sometimes mainstream institutions can sort of like emasculate Black men. And so I've been thinking about it and considering what they're saying about how the Black man engages with the mainstream institution as I navigate through.

As a result of his interactions with this mostly White institution, James found himself consciously readjusting his behavior to project what he believed was a more positive image of himself as a Black man that sometimes seemed a stranger to others from his own background: "In most of my interactions, I really try to project a sincerity and be compassionate and, you know, those aren't normally associated with Black guys. So it's—even some Black women here are like kind of confused or thrown by it."

James's experiences with both institutions highlight the role that active, knowledgeable, and sensitive teachers can play in facilitating positive constructions of oneself as a Black man. For James, being in a cultural milieu that overtly reflected his racial-ethnic values and norms, such as an HBCU, prepared him to go out and effectively interact with the larger social world, even in a setting that was not welcoming to him.

Yet another primary socializing source regarding gender roles and being a man was the *racial-cultural background* and originating region of participants. For example, Sam credited his West Indian/Jamaican background as being a major force in shaping both his behaviors as well as his overall path in life:

'cause I come from a West Indian background, so it's like if you even show the slight sign of femininity at all, you were quickly reprimanded for it. . . . I think if I compare myself to Americans out there, I think my family was much str—appeared to be much more stricter than the ones that are there, so they kind of like—how do I say it? They kind of—like my family kind of mapped out, in a way, my life, in a way, like they kind of like—they have this whole idea of—what I should be, and I think some American families don't really do that to that extreme because I think my parents wanted me to be better than they were. So even though they didn't push me to go to college, like they kind of expected me to and I kind of knew I had to go, but they never really said it, but you know, you can feel that they really wanted me to. . . . So things were a little bit more guided.

James noted how critical being raised in primarily African American settings was to his sense of confidence about his manhood:

Growing up in the South and the path I took for college sort of put me in a bubble to be removed from the mainstream. So I had these bits and moments where I engaged internships, jobs, but most of my interactions have taken place within Black institutions, Black churches. I grew up as a Catholic but it was an all-Black Catholic church. . . . So I guess that's why internally, I'm configured to be more affirmed of myself than to question and to really consider other people's perceptions. So I don't spend much time considering how people are treating like Barack Obama.

Thus, as has been noted by many scholars (Franklin, 2004), being aware of one's racial-ethnic heritage is central to constructing positive definitions of one's roles as a Black man.

The role of the *media* also played a powerful role as a socializing agent both of traditional gender roles (what it means to be a man or a woman) as well as negative stereotypes about these meanings for both Black men and women. Michael summarized the most common viewpoint about the role of the media in promoting racist images of Black men: "[W]hat we see is the angry Black man. We see robbers, we see gangsters, we see men shooting guns, we—we hardly ever see a lawyer, a judge, a doctor." Terrance further identified how the media helps shape the social locations of both Black men and women:

[W]hat's in the media and that being what's kind of fact, Black males are viewed, you know, lower than Black females, lower than White females, lower than White males . . . but just the dominant portrayal of Black males is more so negative than positive. There's no balance.

Taj suggested a purposefulness in the negativity of such portrayals in maintaining marginalized positions of people of color:

> When we go into the deeper parts of the South, when we look at the Jenna Six, we look at these things and we see how there's not a big reaction. It gets little media attention because who's behind the switchboards, and who's behind—who's the owner of CNN? Who's the president and the chairman? They're White, they're White men who helped to control what it is that we see, the images that are put into our minds.

Participants also discussed the complex impact of media—for example, particular television shows, such as *The Cosby Show*—in demonstrating both positive and negative images of Black men and women, as well as famous TV personalities, like Oprah Winfrey. Marquis noted:

> I had good media that showed many respectable male figures. The Cosbys, for one. And there's definitely like a lot of great family programming that allowed me to understand what it means to be a man and carry that on throughout my life.

And further, Taj observed:

> Let's just look at Oprah Winfrey. Oprah has changed the way people all over the world think. She's brought so much empowerment to the African American community and culture, to the—she's brought empowerment and change to Africa. She's done so many, so many great things.

However, Taj also lamented that even Black-owned media provide confusing and ultimately negative messages for young people:

> When we have TV shows such as the *Keisha Cole Show* showing—that's on BET—showing [*pause*] that riches and fame doesn't really change you, it makes you a little bit worse. You know, it shows you that, that being disrespectful and, um, partying and drinking is what life is supposed to be at, be about. And so . . . the

young Black women that are growing up, they don't have anyone to look up to because if they're living in a ghetto, and they see that their mother may be doing drugs or they don't have a father or their grandmother is taking care of them, and they're watching TV to try to find some kind of escapism from their situation, or they can relate, or they can see is, is, is what they're living in, how can you—how can one change?

As we discuss in the next section, actively responding to, rather than unconsciously internalizing, these many negative stereotypes is critical to negotiating gender roles.

Negotiating Stereotypes

As we just observed, a theme critical to gender and gender role construction is becoming aware of and actively responding to the enormous array of racist and sexist stereotypes to which young Black men are exposed daily. As noted, many of these stereotypes are transferred through a variety of media, often with the effect of communicating the hierarchical social positions of men and women from different racial backgrounds. Marquis's perspective on how White Americans view African Americans is illustrative of participants' general perceptions of these stereotypes:

> I think [Whites] overgeneralize, I feel. I feel like they see a small sector of Black men who are not doing anything, who are again not being responsible, who are just on the street corner selling drugs and sleep all day and run the street all night, having babies here and there. And they're not looking at the ones which I think the majority of Black men are doing their thing, and they're not looking at them. They act very surprised.

Marquis also discussed how this stereotype affected him while he seeks an education:

> For instance, when I went to school, they [White students] were surprised that I joined the program that I was in, and when I became what I am now, it's a big like surprise, like wow, you really did that? Wow. It's like they didn't expect that. They expected me to, what I'm gathering from them is they expected me to be at a lower place, to be struggling, to be just living from paycheck to paycheck, not able to maintain, you know?

Sam recalled a traumatic incident with a White female instructor at his university who perpetuated negative racist and sexist stereotypes:

> It was a sociology class and we were talking about race and how different races, different genders, they receive different types of pay, whether it be as a psychologist or a teacher or whatever. And I remember going up to my teacher—I'll never forget it—and it was so—I kind of wanted to say something about it, but I didn't want to be like the quote-unquote "angry Black man," so I remember she kind of broke it down, and when—it was four of us, it was literally a Black man, which was me, a Black female, a White female, and a White male, and she informed us that the White male would make more, and then she informed us that maybe the White female and the Black male would be on the same, and the Black female would be the lowest. And like it kind of upset me that she even said that because I don't think that that's, first of all, appropriate and I didn't think that that was accurate. . . . I was mad! [*laughs.*] I was very, very upset. I went home and I spoke to my family about it, and I was just like upset. . . . But that just kind of disgusted me because I know I have my family members who are actually doing things and who are actually progressing, whether they're Black men and Black women, that are progressing in life, and for that old mentality to still be around is kind of sickening to me, to be honest.

Sam's experience with his White professor brought home to him the message that others still viewed African Americans, particularly Black females, to be at the lower end of the social strata, a notion to which he responded with disbelief, anger, and disgust. Sam took an active step toward combating this view from a presumably knowledgeable and powerful person, a university professor, by seeking support and advice from his family as well as reaffirming his own belief that social progress is the common theme for both Black men and women rather than a presumptive racist social hierarchy not of his or his community's making.

Other participants observed how many within the Black community internalize racist and sexist stereotypes, sometimes with disastrous results, as in the example of Michael and his younger cousin. As Michael later noted:

> And people don't even understand within your own culture, within our own Black community, you're saying that the lighter

you are, the prettier you are. So what's the lightest color there is? White. So you're trying to automatically say: "Positive, White. Negative, Black." And then it just gets into this whole thing where you internalize it. And then what is the Black girl, the dark-skinned girl to think growing up her whole life? Like, I'm ugly. Now I have to prove myself. Let me put on two thousand tons of makeup, let me put on the shortest dress, let me do all these things just to feel pretty. But what ends up happening is, she doesn't look pretty . . . so it's just this whole thing of just misinterpretations, internalizations, all being misguided in finding your own identity. And I think our community struggles *so* much with it because not only is it perpetuated [*pause*] in the minds of other cultures, but it's reproduced in our own culture.

Many of the participants recognized the effects of internalizing these stereotypes in themselves and other young Black men as they approached adulthood. For example, some participants, such as Derrick, spoke of having to "prove" themselves as a result of their awareness of negative stereotypes of themselves as based on both race and gender:

Black men and Black women in today's society have to work a lot harder . . . I think that they have to work hard anyway, because they're already looked upon like they don't know much or they're not made for certain positions or they're not smart enough to hold certain positions.

Norris poignantly recounted the impact of acting out on the basis of these stereotypes:

So some of the boys at the all-boys school, you know, were very proud of who they were. And I think they felt more affirmed because, you know, eight hours in the school day they're together, so now when they go to these conferences or things and stuff like that, they—collectively they're very strong. But still, they would [*pause*] . . . knowingly adopt the stereotypes that the media portrays or portrayed them to be [*pause*] for two reasons. One, because they really believed it. But the one that I believe most is that it was their way of rejecting it. So they knew that wasn't them. Therefore, they felt okay to dress up as them.

Unfortunately,

the end result was the same. . . . [A] lot of people, I think, downplay their intelligence because they were afraid to be labeled as a sell-out or because they felt so far above it, they wouldn't—they didn't have the language or didn't even care to break it down for everyone else. And I'm hoping it's that. And I do think it is that. People are so far, at such an earlier age, having been exposed to, you know, a lot of racial nonsense, if you will, that when it came down to a moment where they can speak on this or should speak on this, they're just like "You know what? No one's really ready for the truth, so I'm just going to keep the truth to myself." And, which is unfortunate, to some extent, that we felt that way.

Franklin (2004) writes how young Black men, while prized within the family, become objects of hate, fear, and derision in the larger society. As a result, some become "one of the boys" as a matter of survival: "the 'distinct walk,' the ability to rap and communicate as only 'brothers' do, our distinguishing dress styles, athletic prowess, an unsubmissive, noncommittal, but highly sexualized attitude toward Black girls" all become a means of paradoxically becoming at once visible, yet invisible, by the attentions these actions garner (p. 83). As Derrick sagely observed, becoming visible in this way may actually sow the seeds of silence and subjugation for many young African American men.

At the same time, Derrick spoke of his admiration of those who were able to resist, even defy, the difficult odds of achieving success in the face of racist and sexist stereotypes:

> As I got older and was exposed to different views, or even today, like watching the hearing for Sotomayor becoming the Supreme Court justice, it's just enlightening. Like this is a minority woman who is going to sit at the top, you know, she's going to sit on the Supreme Court, which is phenomenal and she defied all odds. A lot of people—well, she's the first Black—not, well, Black, Latino woman up there. So just different events as I've gotten older makes me—that contribute to my ideas of the Black man and woman and what they should be.

Growing older and observing the success of others despite the odds helped contribute to Derrick's own sense of what was possible to achieve as a Black man living in the United States.

Another helpful strategy in negotiating the impact of stereotypes is the ability to stand back and observe how people who are not of African descent might develop distorted views of Black men. Michael explained:

> I think the overall view is very distorted because a lot of upper-class White Americans don't understand Black Americans because of the cultural differences, because of the hostility between the two groups. Because it's hard to have a dialogue. For instance, if a White man asks a Black woman, "Oh, is that your real hair? What is this weave?" The Black girl might get extremely offended and get upset because, "How dare he ask about my hair?" When really he has no idea from nothing, he's never encountered a Black girl, he never encountered a weave, he has no idea whatsoever. So the offense comes in when really the ignorance is being shown, so the ignorance turns into offensiveness, and there's hardly any cultural dialogue going on. . . . It's hard for either one to correctly and accurately interpret the other without there being any confusion.

As Michael noted, putting oneself in the place of someone who holds negative stereotypes and racist attitudes sometimes can help explain the inexplicable. Of course, public discourse involving individuals in the more dominant social position doing the same would also greatly affect the presence and impact of these stereotypes (White & Cones, 1999). However, Michael displayed courage and insight in understanding the nature of negative stereotypes, attributes that serve as powerful means of resisting the negativity and helping him construct a more positive sense of himself as a Black man.

Navigating Privilege and Oppression

Another important category that emerged regarding participants' negotiations of their gender roles was how they viewed themselves in relation to women or, more generally, how men and women "should" interact with each other in a broader sense. Most participants expressed ambivalence about these relations. Many participants clearly believed that the suppression of rights of women as well as the subjugation of Black women, particularly in the larger society, was wrong. This awareness of the negative treatment of Black women often hit close to home for many participants in terms of their own childhoods since mothers had played a prominent role, as Terrance stated:

> I've had very strong women in my life just as I've, you know, seen strong men. I think in the Black community, African American community, you see more women doing the right thing, so they tend to be—they end up having that father–mother role. I was fortunate I had, you know—sad to say the fortunate thing, but you know, over 52% of Black children live only with their mother, so they take on a role of having to be both the male figure and the mother.

At the same time, Terrance noted the complexities of how women and men interact in terms of dominant and submissive roles, even in terms of what he perceived as what women themselves may want or prefer:

> I've dated women who do make more money than me. I'm a student right now, so that's obvious, but they, they still seem to want to take on a role—I don't know, the word isn't submissive, but I mean there's always dominant and submissive. So it's not about money, it's not about education level, 'cause I would say they make more money and they've already achieved the degrees that I'm working on achieving. But they still, they have something, have something ingrained where they'd still rather be kind of submissive as opposed to the dominant person. . . . I just assume it's by nature almost [*laughs*] that women want to be submissive to a male.

Derrick best expressed the ambivalence many participants felt about being supportive of the rights of women to be independent or have a voice in the larger society yet, at the same time, believing that there should be clear delineation of roles for men and women in order for families to function effectively:

> A woman's place. Um [*pause*] I have different feelings about that as far as a man's place and a woman's place. In certain aspects, I feel like a woman's place is—she should be independent and she should know how to take care of herself on her own, but if you're in a relationship with a man, I believe that a woman should know when to be submissive to her husband. She should know her place in marriage, and I'm not saying that means cooking and cleaning and doing all that stuff, because . . . that was so 1930s and '40s. But just know when to be submissive,

know that, okay, if my husband is taking care of X, Y, and Z, then I can do A, B, and C, because it's a 50–50 thing.

Derrick, perhaps unknowingly, expressed his ambivalence by first noting the importance of women being submissive to men but then states the reason being "because it's a 50–50 thing." Taj similarly stated, "Women are the backbone to men, and when the man is down and out, the woman is supposed to step in." Both of these participants capture the mixed views that many participants expressed toward the rights versus responsibilities of women, particularly women in their families. At the same time, it is also important to point out that most participants presumed that men had as much to be responsible for in the family. Moreover, Willie and Reddick (2010) suggest that, for many generations—indeed long before their White male counterparts—Black men have supported both the education of women and their entry into the workforce, basing these views on the belief in the "equalitarian family in which neither partner prevails" (p. 90).

Regarding the struggles of African American women as targets of both racist and sexist beliefs, Norris recalled the struggles of Black females in social settings, when he attended a predominantly White high school, in contrast to Black males, who were valued for their athleticism:

> Black girls kind of felt they lacked social capital, you know. No one would ask them out to the dance as quickly unless they were—then you get into the color complex, unless they were light-skinned. Having different hair textures meant [*laughs*] different experiences. Playing sports or having braids, you know, people questioning, "Oh, what is it like?" All the questions about that sort of thing. [*pause*] Black girls feeling that they had to sometimes kind of suck up their gender concerns in order to confront the larger or to team up with the guys to confront the racial problems.

As a high school teacher, Norris continued to sift through his own definitions of masculinity in the context of hierarchical or nonhierarchical gender relations: "So my question for myself, I guess, mainly for the last two years was how can I be an ally, be supportive of their needs as Black women on campus, while still being able to create an identity of masculinity, Black male masculinity for myself?"

Perhaps, as Boyd-Franklin and Franklin (2000) suggest, a third "R" may be the most important in navigating the divide between privilege and oppression among men and women in the Black community: respect, as in the old adage, "If you want respect, you've got to give respect" (p. 143). As Norris demonstrated, part of understanding and defining one's own masculinity can involve serving as an ally to Black women and others who may be similarly oppressed and seek social justice.

The next and final theme of the chapter addresses this process of constructing gender roles that are complex yet communicate one's cultural values and beliefs in ways that uphold one's family and community while positioning one to seek opportunities and achievement at all levels.

Constructing Flexible Gender Roles and Styles

As we have written, all participants were well aware of traditional gender roles—what has been termed masculinity and femininity—as well as culturally based expressions of these roles (e.g., "thug is a style"). Most of these roles were rigidly enforced during their youth, and young African American boys who violated these roles often faced embarrassing consequences. Michael recalled:

> There were certain things that boys just did not do. In order for me to do anything that was considered feminine, unless I was absolutely excellent at it, then it was okay. For instance, jump-roping. I could jump rope like anyone's business, but because I was incredible at it and I made it look crazy interesting, it was okay in the Black neighborhood. It was okay to see me jump-roping. People just kind of got used to it. But it wasn't that I was trying something new. It was because I was actually really good at it.... If I weren't good at [it], I would have been told to stop, I'm pretty sure, because ... not being good at it embarrasses not only myself but embarrasses my family because the embarrassment comes from the connection of the jump rope being feminine.

Most participants viewed masculinity and femininity on opposite ends of the spectrum, as embodied in the traits Taj described for femininity and its association primarily with women:

> Femininity is normally related to a woman, and I think that it should. [*pause*] It's to me ... all about how the person, the female

nurtures herself and her family and how caring she is . . . If she's lovable, if she's likable. It's in her poise, it's in her body language, it's in her diction. It's in her [*pause*] in her smile. It's in her touch. It's, to me, softness, it's . . . we think of mothers, we think of them as being loving. . . . So to me, the definition of femininity would be a very passive role, a person who's very passive or someone who is able to be very caring, but aware of what she is doing, aware of what she gives off to society, aware of who she is.

Terrance stated succinctly, "Men are naturally stronger. That's biology." Yet, at the same time, in constructing their own definitions of masculinity, participants resisted equating traditional gender styles or traits with these definitions. Instead personal definitions of masculinity were more generally linked with being responsible to others:

I definitely don't—and I said it earlier—don't attribute thug as being a masculine man. You have a thuglike style. If that's your style, that's your style, but that doesn't make you a masculine man. It's just a style that I feel. Nothing to do with your masculinity. When it all comes down to masculinity for me, it's about how you carry yourself and how you contribute to your race, your family or your partner, or whomever or whatever is important in your life that at the end of the day, when you close your eyes in that box, your life would have some sort of meaning. That's a masculine Black man to me. Thug is just a style.

Moreover, masculine and feminine traits could be viewed as being embodied within either a man or a woman, as Taj observed:

[F]ollowing my mother and seeing how she had to take on such a responsibility [*pause*] as being the sole provider in our family, and my father lived with us and worked, he worked, but he was—never contributed to the household. So that's why I know that it's not in the sound of one's voice, it's not in the height of how tall you are or, or how big your hands are or all of those things. I know that masculinity, masculinity and femininity, it's all in one's action. I don't, I don't classify any other way, personally.

Michael further stated:

[M]asculinity is a man who knows who he is and is comfortable sharing that with the world. So I think a feminine [*pause*] guy in some ways can have a lot of masculine qualities. I don't think masculine has to be just the way you walk or just the way you talk. I think a drag queen that works in—as a CEO of a company could be considered masculine in his or her profession and what it is that he's actually doing, more so than what he or she represents as far as a drag queen. So masculinity extends beyond behavior or it extends more in the mind and how you view yourself and being comfortable when sharing that. I think that's masculine.

James similarly viewed femininity as reflecting strength and leadership, albeit embodied in more traditional ways:

I also think about that individual being a person of power and authority as well, because they've mastered the social graces for women. You know, the epitome of what women should strive to be. So in their own sense, they're a leader, yeah.

As James, Michael, and Taj pointed out, negotiating gender roles as an African American man (and woman) necessarily involves constructing one's own expressions of these roles, but they saw these expressions as potentially varying across people and settings. Moreover, for many participants, negotiating gender roles ultimately related to what one could provide to others, how one accepted responsibility and leadership in the service of one's family and one's race, rather than in what clothes one wore or the language one used.

NEGOTIATING GENDER ROLES REVISITED

As we stated earlier, negotiating gender roles is embedded within a complex of social relations. It also is part of a larger process of negotiating self as more than the sum of multiple "parts" or social group categories (race, gender, sexual orientation). It was clear from participants' stories that in order to construct a more positive sense of self as an African American man, socially oppressed and marginalized aspects of oneself must *not* minimized, denied, or forgotten but rather embraced, understood, and shared with others. Indeed, as several participants emphasized, it is important to understand both the history and the impact of racial or gender oppression on oneself and one's communities as well as the cultural values imparted by one's racial background. Many felt that doing so would enable young boys and men to seek and find opportunities for learning and success, thus freeing young Black men to reach out to others, both within their communities and beyond, as Michael contended:

> Being Black in a Black neighborhood versus being Black in a White neighborhood versus being Black in a school that's—you know, all these different things. It depends on where you are. But the ideal Black man would be one who can transcend cultures, who can [*pause*] who can feel comfortable in a Black environment and feel comfortable in a White environment and feel comfortable in an Asian environment, whatever. An ideal Black man would have to be open-minded still.

Michael further suggested that an effective Black man is able to size up a situation and respond as the situation demands while being cognizant of the impact of doing so on himself:

> So like in a specific venue, in a specific arena, I might speak a certain way or I might dress a certain way, or—and it might seem as if I come from a different place, and it might be done on purpose, and that's covering who I really am in order to fit into an arena, to be able to adequately respond to what's going on in that environment. And these are things that we have to do to cover, and it's not even about giving up who you are, but it's just covering that little part of you in order to not be associated with that thing, because what happens when you're associated with it is all the different assumptions that come along with it. And in covering, what are you saying? You know, are you saying that you don't care about where you come from? Are you saying that it's not valuable? That you can just put it on a shelf whenever you don't want to? You have to think about all these things as you get older, as you tend to categorize every single action that you do . . . so it goes back to never knowing and always willing to learn, and constantly engage in yourself with other cultures in order to gain full understanding.

Finally, Norris summarized his evolution of self-understanding as a Black man by posing a "Who Cares!" question, generated after reading Ralph Ellison and Dostoyevsky:

> And I realized . . . that what you see is not even the beginning of the story and that everyone has at some point grappled with

these same things that I grappled and continually wrestle with in terms of identities and social categorizations. But who cares! [*pause*] And it's who cares with an exclamation, you know? . . . I want to be a writer. And these are roles that typically, you know, I assumed were not assigned to men. Men want to write? Really? I thought they wanted to be scientists and that sort of thing. The girls were good in English, right? The girls were good at history you know? And granted, I was always good at math and science, but I realized something else and it's a passion. And so I adopted that "who cares" kind of attitude. . . . Who cares about [*pause*] what I identify myself as, you know, how people identify—because people are going to—when I walk in a room, I know they're going to see a Black man, and some might be surprised, some might feel relieved. But at the end of the day, I want to be known for more than that. You know, who cares until you begin to deny me access to things based on my identifier. . . . and then *you* have a problem, right?

As Norris so effectively observed, it is finding passion—for a cause, a profession—that drives his self-understanding and sense of purpose. He feels pride and acceptance as a Black man and challenges anyone to see him differently. At the same time, Norris feels confident in his abilities to pursue what he wants to be or do because it is what he believes in, not because he fears it is what he is limited to.

APPLICATIONS FOR MENTAL HEALTH PROFESSIONALS AND EDUCATORS

Our findings provide a rich source of information for both educators and mental health professionals about interventions with African American boys and young men. We discuss several themes in light of their potential applications for both counselors and teachers.

Leadership Development

As clearly indicated by all participants, a key theme is that strong efforts to promote leadership development among young boys and men will greatly enhance their chances for success overall. Participants' stories clearly conveyed that African American boys and young men must feel they have a serious purpose in life and a meaningful impact on others, especially by serving as leaders to others, particularly younger generations. As many activists, scholars, and practitioners have noted, a major impact of centuries of racial and gender oppression has been to diminish young Black men's sense of purpose and presumed value to themselves and others. Developing leadership skills and opportunities undoubtedly will provide a clear trajectory toward enhancing these skills.

Boyd-Franklin and Franklin (2000) identify a number of excellent programs that promote and enhance leadership skills. One is the Onis Program, developed by Dr. Vernon Allwood in Atlanta, GA, which is a church-based rites-of-passage program facilitated by a group of respected older men who train young boys in African-based traditions and values over a series of group meetings. Courtland Lee also has designed a "manhood training program" for preadolescent and adolescent boys that emphasizes motivation and skills needed for both educational success and taking responsibility (White & Cones, 1999). Major organizations that promote the interests of African American men include the National Council of African-American Men (NCAAM), which was organized in 1990 as a nonprofit organization that serves to build coalitions, provide advocacy, and initiate self-help directives, and 100 Black Men in America (http://www.100blackmen.org/home.aspx), founded in 1967 in New York City, which helps young Black men focus on long-term goals and clean living (White & Cones).

A major component of leadership is having accurate and positive knowledge of oneself as a person of African descent (e.g., knowing one's history and who had fought for freedom and civil rights before them) in order to understand one's overall roles in society. Such knowledge buoyed the abilities of many participants to withstand difficult times and negative experiences and positioned them to negotiate instances of both overt racism and internalized racism more effectively. Numerous educational programs focusing on Afrocentric history, cultural values, and practices have been suggested that incorporate music, dance, and storytelling to best fit the learning styles of young African American males. Teacher education programs to help build skills for instructors of African American boys have also been developed (White & Cones, 1999).

Finally, it remains critical to provide multiple examples of role models of positive leaders to African American boys and young men as well as the teachings of scholars, educators, professionals, and writers of African descent. Moreover, finding role models in one's life, whether national leaders such as the president or Malcolm X, or someone closer to home, such as one's father or pastor, is an important activity during the course of one's youth. Sponsoring activities, classes, and programs that help develop leadership skills will enable African American boys and men to achieve their potential as leaders of the future in a variety of ways: spiritually, socially, politically, and professionally. Boyd-Franklin and Franklin (2000) suggest a number of ways to find mentors for a young African American boy: These include school guidance departments, local Black churches, local chapters of Black fraternities, national organizations such as NCAAM, local colleges, and community youth programs.

Mitigating the Impact of Negative Stereotypes

Without a doubt, negative racist and sexist stereotypes, or some combination of both, had great impact on nearly all participants. These stereotypes were heard and felt on a daily basis, particularly through the negative images trumpeted through the media. These negative stereotypes also were made transparent in the social worlds of participants via the expression of "surprise" by others, most often Whites, for participants' achievements in education or their chosen professions. Moreover, some participants seemed to struggle with their own internalizations of these stereotypes, commonly heard as frustration toward other Black men whom they felt were being "irresponsible" to themselves and their families. Finally, some participants experienced themselves as targets of the internalization of negative stereotypes by family and community members; for example, some believed they were viewed as "acting White," because they were seeking an education in a predominantly White institution. Michael's attempts to mentor his younger cousin regarding educational achievement led to his being rebuffed by other family members, a situation that clearly impacted his emerging identity as an African American man. As we noted earlier, the effects of gendered racism can be seen on multiple levels in the personal narratives of the young men interviewed.

Educators and mental health professionals can apply these findings by helping boys and young men to articulate what stereotypes they have heard about (via movies, TV shows, blogs, music, even sports heroes). As other scholars have noted, common stereotypes about Black men and women are known to exist: for example, the absent father or violent criminal (Thomas et al., 2008). Recent research has led to the development of a psychological instrument (Schwing et al., 2012) assessing African American men's experiences with gendered racism, focusing primarily on the negative impact of exposure to these kinds of stereotypes. Thus, educators and mental health professionals might initiate dialogues and other interactive activities with young men about their exposure to these stereotypes and frame these images as stereotypical rather than realistic. Moreover, White and Cones (1999) call for a frank dialogue between Whites and Blacks about the continuing role of race in the United States. In particular, confronting the vast perceptual gap regarding racial concerns between Whites and Blacks, and renewing efforts for Whites to "go beyond the words and learn to feel what it's like to be Black in America" remain critical for negative stereotypes to lose their impact on African American youth (p. 292).

It also is important to provide sufficient space for boys and young men to articulate their perceptions of societal images of Black men and women in order to help them see how these images already may be affecting their lives. In other words, the internalization of these stereotypes, often at an unspoken or unconscious level, must be brought in the open so that interventions can be made to combat their potential effects. As Speight (2007) notes, "internalized racism is not so easy to see, to count, to measure, and does not involve one perpetrator and one corresponding victim, but instead has been adopted and resides in the psyche of targets" (p. 131). Speight calls for better understanding of the psychological injuries that can accrue from "the shame of being shamed" (Watts-Jones, in Speight, 2007, p. 131).

Similarly, experiences that boys and young men have had with others in their lives, including family and community members, also can be brought forth. For example, opportunities can be provided that allow boys and young men to discuss their experiences with covert racism, such as their observations of people acting surprised as they seek out educational opportunities with each other. A number of participants discussed their need to *prove* themselves to others as being deserving of opportunities, perhaps setting a stage for success, but also burnout, depending upon to whom they wish to prove themselves.

A related topic centers on boys and young men who may be acting out the stereotype of a stereotypical Black male as a way of "rejecting it," as Norris said. Finding role models, especially family members, whom these young men can emulate would be an ideal way of ensuring that they do not fall into the trap of becoming the stereotype they are seeking to reject. Moreover, Franklin (2004) identifies 12 lessons that focus on empowering young Black men to move beyond racist and sexist beliefs, such as knowing the deal about racial disparities in the larger society and being prepared, taking advice from elders, getting past being embarrassed, and risking change.

Negotiating Positive and Flexible Gender Roles and Identities

Most participants rejected traditional gender role traits and behaviors (e.g., the way someone walked or talked) typically associated with masculinity and femininity as being genuine indicators of either. Indeed, as participants observed and evaluated the multitude of often conflicting messages from people, institutions/settings, events, and the media, many came to reject the original rigidly enforced traits and behaviors typically associated with masculinity and femininity that they learned in their youth. This was particularly true regarding the relations of gender "styles," as one participant called them, with their own evolving personal meanings of what it means to be a man. To be sure, many participants continued to express themselves along these traditional lines and expect others to do the same, especially girls and women. Indeed, most still conceptualized masculinity and femininity, particularly the latter, as being specifically embodied by either men or women, most typically as polar opposites. However, participants stopped short of linking these gender role traits and behaviors with what they had come to believe was being or becoming a man, particularly a Black man, or a woman.

One key issue was the role of conflicting messages in the participants' gender role constructions. These conflicting messages might, for example, be expressed by the same individual, as Taj observed of his father who was, by traditional male standards, an excellent provider but ultimately ran away from his responsibility as a loving, attentive parent. This was in contrast to Norris's relationship with his father, which was generally distant although his father taught Norris a very critical lesson about the importance of being vulnerable and open to his feelings.

Mothers and other female relatives similarly played an impactful role. Mothers were very present and often were primarily responsible for taking care of the children, strictly enforcing traditional masculine behaviors, and even giving their sons liberties not afforded to their daughters. At the same time, some of the mothers did not want their sons taking on what they viewed as more negative aspects of male role models, particularly in disrespecting women. Moreover, the interplay of various people in participants' lives (male and female relatives, teachers, peers) likely provided more conflicting information, through observation rather than direct teaching.

Thus, it is important for educators and counselors to be aware not only of the very rigid rules that govern gender role behaviors (as most already are) but that young boys and men—indeed all young people—are being exposed to a wealth of often-conflicting messages about how they "should" act. In short, teachers and mental health professionals must openly recognize both the "should" of being male and female as well as the "could" or possibility of being different in order to affirm both young people's observations as well as their right to be who they want to be. Separating styles of masculinity from being a leader in society, and focusing on the latter, may help young boys and men focus on the possibilities and opportunities available to them rather than on the punishments of being different.

Negotiating Relationships with Others

Gender roles were helpful in establishing how individuals should and could behave with one another. That is, a main takeaway message about African American notions of masculinity, whether it is traditional or more flexible, was that it somehow reflected being responsible, not only for oneself but for others. For this reason, it is critical to encourage young boys and men to explore what masculinity means to them and how they see themselves and others within the social context. For example, according to some participants, establishing relationships with other boys and young men often centers on observing who is a leader within a group. James referred to these as "man laws" that help communicate ascribed leadership roles among a network of men, such as a high school or college campus, and are based on who commands the most respect or is viewed as a model by others. James also suggested that such laws or styles of behaving also communicated "your own swagger ... how you present yourself and deal with yourself in those settings," setting the stage for a young man to be either accepted or rejected by peers. James further acknowledged that, at least among the male students at his HBCU, many different styles of maleness were accepted. Thus, it is critical for educators and mental health professionals to recognize that such laws or norms may exist in their school setting or for their clients. Intervening with individuals who are perceived to be leaders might be an effective way to promote healthy relationships among young boys and men—if the leader is open to this approach. Identifying the leaders within a social setting also might help delineate what behaviors are being rewarded among young men within that setting. In addition to approaching young leaders, the rites-of-passage mentoring programs mentioned earlier are excellent ways of providing positive and productive role models of what it means to be a leader within an African American community (White & Cones, 1999).

Participants had mixed views about the different roles of men and women, both in their families and in the larger society. As noted earlier, most strongly believed in the rights of women to be independent people who should have their own voices and careers. However, many also had conflicted feelings about how men and women should interact with each other, particularly in the context of the family setting. Participants seemed to subscribe to fairly traditional leadership roles within the family, believing this arrangement to be tied to or driven by biology; many also ascribed these views to religious/spiritual beliefs. It seems that the delineation of tasks within a family was viewed as crucial for the overall functioning of the family. As previously noted, one effective way to frame these concerns is within the context of respect and mutuality. As Franklin (2004) writes:

> Each of us as African American men and women have faced our own challenges of surviving and protecting our sense of self, in spite of racism and other hurdles put in our paths of lives—including those hurdles we ourselves created. . . . African American men and women must find complementary roles and tasks that allow each partner a sense of purpose and accomplishment. In other words, both parties in a relationship must find ways that our individual efforts achieve mutual goals. (p. 150)

Activities and interventions can focus on connecting one's gender role to one's family responsibilities, thus providing African American boys and young men important grounding in what it means to be a man.

REFERENCES

Alexander, M. (2010). *The new Jim Crow: Mass incarceration in the age of colorblindness*. New York, NY: New Press.

Boyd-Franklin, N., & Franklin, A. J. (2004). *Boys into men: Raising our African American teenage sons*. New York, NY: Dutton.

Franklin, A. J. (2004). *From brotherhood to manhood: How Black men rescue their relationships and dreams from the invisibility syndrome*. Hoboken, NJ: Wiley.

Gayles, T. A., Alston, R. J., & Staten, D. (2005). Understanding mental illness among African American males: Risk factors and treatment parameters. In D. A. Harley & J. M. Dillard (Eds.), *Contemporary mental health issues among African Americans* (pp. 49–59). Alexandria, VA: American Counseling Association.

Harper, S. R. (2012). *Black male student success in higher education: A report from the national Black male college achievement study*. Philadelphia, PA: University of Pennsylvania, Center for the Study of Race and Equity in Education.

Rice, D. W. (2008). *Balance: Advancing identity theory by engaging the Black male adolescent*. Lanham, MD: Lexington Books.

Thomas, A. J., Witherspoon, K. M., & Speight, S. L. (2008) Gendered racism, psychological distress, and coping styles of African American women. *Cultural Diversity and Ethnic Minority Psychology, 14*, 307–314.

Schwing, A. E., Wong, Y. J., & Fann, M. D. (May 2012). Development and validation of the African American Men's Gendered Racism Stress Inventory. *Psychology of Men & Masculinity*. doi:10.1037/a0028272

Speight, S. L. (2007). Internalized racism: One more piece of the puzzle. *Counseling Psychologist, 35*, 126–134.

Virella, K. (October 25, 2011). Census: 48% national increase in Black college graduates. *Dominion of New York*. Retrieved from http://www.dominionofnewyork.com/2011/10/25/census-48-increase-in-black-college-graduates/#.UGCJjEJBRT6

White, J. L., & Cones, J. H. (1999). *Black man emerging: Facing the past and seizing a future in America*. New York, NY: Freeman.

Willie, C. V., & Reddick, R. J. (2010). *A new look at Black families* (6th ed.). Lanham, MD: Rowman & Littlefield.

Chapter Three

GENDER ROLES AMONG AFRICAN AMERICAN WOMEN
Jorja A. K. Redway and Marie L. Miville

The experiences of Black/African American women in many ways reflect those of their male counterparts, given that their originating roles in U.S. society were to "work, produce, and to reproduce" (Almquist, 1995, in Bethea-Whitfield, 2005, p. 35). For centuries, Black women worked "alongside men and animals in what has been called a 'negative equality' . . . without the pretense of femininity afforded women of other ethnic groups" (Bethea-Whitfield, 2005, p. 36). As a consequence, generations of African American women were exploited physically, psychologically, sexually, and economically. At the same time, a number of negative images were perpetuated about Black women in the United States, including the asexual self-sacrificing "mammy," the immoral conniving "she-devil," and the emasculating matriarch (Bethea-Whitfield, 2005; Wyatt, 1997). Wyatt (1997) described a number of psychological survival strategies that African American women adopted as a result of these difficult conditions, including (a) learning to behave one way, while feeling another way, (b) not discussing the kinds of abuse being experienced, and, most importantly, (c) learning to live with a sense of dignity. African American girls and women today continue to adopt strategies of resistance to negative racist and sexist conditions, images, and expectations with research indicating, for example, that many have positive images about themselves and believe that career achievement as well as their families are important to their sense of self (Adams & LaFromboise, 2001; Petersen, 2000, in Bethea-Whitfield, 2005).

Mental health theories and research on gender typically have failed to adequately incorporate the unique historical and psychological experiences of African American women. In particular, research on gender roles has been inappropriately applied to all women without sufficient consideration of the racial-cultural values, norms, and behaviors of Black/African American women and other women of color (Nguyen et al., 2010). Two major gender-related instruments in use for decades, the Bem Sex Role Inventory and the Personal Attributes Questionnaire, assess gender roles by categorizing individuals according to the psychological traits they endorse (Nguyen et al.). However, these measures were developed based on unexamined White/Western perceptions of what is "masculine" and "feminine" (Bem, 1974; Spence, Helmreich, & Stapp, 1974) without consideration of the racial-ethnic contexts of these terms.

In the 1980s, women of color scholars began to call for a more intersectional approach to studying the experiences of Black women and other women of color. Unfortunately, much of the mental health literature regarding African American women still tends to separate the social categories of race and gender (E. R. Cole, 2009; Patterson, Cameron, & Lalonde, 1996), regarding them as distinct features of identity (Spelman, 1988). This either/or dichotomy rejects the possibility that constructions of race and gender can in fact be a "simultaneous intersection" of these categories (Patterson, Cameron, & Lalonde, 1996, p. 230). For example, using an intersectional framework to understand the racial and gender identities of 89 Black women, Settles (2006) found that the "intersected Black-woman identity was more important than the individual identities of woman and Black person" (p. 589); this kind of approach is only beginning to gain increased use across the literature (Babbitt, 2011).

Prevailing tensions based on the intersections of race and gender, as well as the conflicting roles therein, present unique and complex challenges for African American females, given the social, historical, and political context of the United States (Reid & Comas-Diaz, 1990), and can directly affect their psychological outcomes. Although much of the research on gender-related stress in African American women has placed emphasis on either gender discrimination or sexism (Woods-Giscombé & Lobel, 2008), studies such as that of King (2003) demonstrate that *ethgendered* prejudice (i.e., prejudiced attributions made about a person's race and gender) as well as perceived racism are significantly related to psychological stress and social self-esteem among African American women (Woods-Giscombé & Lobel, 2008). For many Black women, an expectation of femininity that is racially and culturally specific may center on "being strong," particularly in the face of overwhelming odds, and directly contrasts with Western definitions and images of this term. Moreover, the expectation to be strong paradoxically can encourage attitudes and behaviors leading to self-silencing and even depression among African American women (Beauboeuf-Lafontant, 2007, p. 29). At the same time, women in African American communities are expected to take a more subordinate role to men (J. B. Cole & Guy-Sheftall, 2003), thus setting up potential conflicts between how they believe they are expected to behave as Black women with what might be most adaptive to survive and succeed as individuals.

In this chapter, we explore the ways in which Black women construct their gender roles. Our aim is to gain a better understanding of the patterns, constraints, and conflicts among these women and to create a theoretical model of gender roles for racial-ethnically diverse populations (see Chapter 8). Using the grounded theory approach outlined in Chapter 1, we interviewed eight Black/African American women about how they construct their own meanings of gender and gender roles (see Table A.3 in the appendix for demographic information about our participants).

CONFLICT AND EVOLUTION OF GENDER ROLES

Although many themes emerged throughout participants' narratives, we believe five themes are key areas of concern for African American women; these fall under the main heading of *conflict and evolution of gender roles* (see also Table A.4):

1. *Gender socialization*, referring to the influence of past experiences on present attitudes
2. *Silent strength*, involving the notions of the strong versus weak woman
3. *Binary conceptualizations of masculinity and femininity* characterized by either/or parameters regarding what defines masculine and feminine
4. *Less than ideal*, or the misunderstood and misrepresented Black/African American female image
5. *"Bottom of the barrel,"* that is, the dilemma of being Black/African American and female

Contained within each of these categories are several important points that we discuss in the next sections using direct quotes from participant interviews.

Gender Socialization: Influence of Past Experiences on Present Attitudes

When asked to define the ideal man and woman, most participants identified similar personal attributes for both genders, for example: responsible, respectful, intelligent, honest, loyal, and hardworking. However, once our dialogue turned toward physical attributes, and participants were asked what being a man or woman meant to them personally, few similarities remained. That is, presumed physical/biological differences seemed to lay the foundation for participants' responses regarding learned societal expectations for men and women. According to Jennifer, a 30-year-old elementary school teacher, men are "physically strong" whereas "women are smarter." The male is therefore seen as:

> able to take care of a group of people, like as a leader. . . . A group of people will follow a Black man more than they'll follow a Black woman . . . but together, it's like they're a combination of complete strength.

Taylor, a 22-year-old graduate student, noted:

> Men are seen as being a little bit overbearing . . . because they want to be the leader . . . women are usually seen as the person that's supposed to be more submissive and passive, and men are supposed to be more aggressive.

Most participants viewed the home as having a primary influence on how gender roles were learned, stating that they gained much knowledge through observing others. In response to the interview question on learning messages about how men and women are supposed to be, Cindy, a 23-year-old psychology graduate student, stated:

> Well, by the things they do. I mean, their behaviors as far as, you know, everyday routines and, you know, how they interact with other people, it's how you see that's how a woman is supposed to act.

Thus, as Boyd-Franklin and Franklin (2000) note, children are always watching the adults in their lives, learning about roles not only by what they are told but also by what the adults actually do in front of them. Boyd-Franklin and Franklin urge parents and other adults to be aware and thoughtful about the values and expectations that are being taught to both girls and boys in the home.

Participants also discussed how they learned these roles from a racial-ethnic perspective. Simone, a 23-year-old undergraduate student, noted:

> Especially within the Black community, women are supposed to subordinate themselves to men . . . but when it comes like back to you, it's not there . . . just the idea that you have to be the everything and do all this stuff, but you have to like go to work, and you have to cook, and you have to take care of the kids, and like your men. Like your, even your husband has like "boys' night out" or whatever, and you're supposed to be like waiting up for him at home.

As Simone indicated, racial-ethnic expectations seem to promote a more subordinate role to men, even if this means staying at home with the children, while the husband can be out having fun. Simone also made specific references to her own life, identifying key differences in the expectations typically held for males and females in her family:

> Like I see the same thing within my family in terms of Black men and Black women. I think there's very different expectations, like with my brother, um, he struggles, and you know it's just looked at as like that's natural progression, and if he does the basic things like gets a job, then it's looked at as, um, you know a big deal, which I think it should be, but I just feel like there's this different like standard that I'm held accountable to. And I mean, I'm glad that I'm being held accountable to that high standard, but I also question why the expectation isn't there for my brother or other men in my family. . . . Or even in terms of raising a family . . . I'm just looking across to like my family in general and I don't know, just the expectation is that, yeah, they may have a child, but they may not be as involved in that child's life. . . . With the men sometimes it's like it's nice if they're there, they're commended if they are, but if they're not it's like well, life happens, oh well. And they're still part of the family,

but they're not like held to the standard of "Why are you not seeing your child?" "Why are you not spending time with your child in the same way?"

Boyd-Franklin and Franklin (2000) note that in the African American community, some families "raise our daughters and love our sons" (p. 19). This saying refers to how some parents "require little of their sons in terms of household responsibilities, good school performance, expected church attendance" (p. 19) and so on, whereas daughters may be expected from a very young age to cook, clean, take care of younger children—all while being a good student and faithful churchgoer. As we see with Simone's story, these mixed gender role expectations can sow the seeds of discontent, frustration, and even self-doubt about one's worth as a female child in the family. Moreover, Belgrave (2009) notes that gendered expectations of service-oriented activities may lead to lower life expectations and academic and career achievements for young African American girls.

Patrice, a 26-year-old psychology graduate student, also expressed the view that as a Black woman, self-sacrifice is a core value that strongly influences the role she plays in her relationships with others. She observed that Black women are:

> expected to put others first before us. We're also expected to sacrifice, um, to the point that it's not like, it's not about you, it's about your kids. Or it's not about your kids, it's about the person you're with. You know and you always have to prove yourself and like you're easy to put yourself last, and I think that's not, that's usually what happens, especially in expectations when it comes to family. And I think along with that, we're expected to have kids, we're expected to have a family. We're expected to get married.

As Belgrave (2009) points out, caring and sacrificing for others can be both beneficial and detrimental to Black girls and women. Having responsibility for others can promote responsibility and the development of important life skills. However, a primary emphasis on self-sacrifice also may suppress other important learning activities that young women like Patrice might benefit from, such as extracurricular activities (e.g., academic club memberships) that enhance other skills for future career and life aspirations.

As one grows older, Simone observed that these roles are reinforced "through television, movies . . . [and] music." For her, being female meant having to navigate her life amid media portrayals of the female as dependent on the male, with the achievement of self-actualization occurring only after forming a heterosexual relationship. She stated:

> I think the media much more than people realize and also just books in general have images specifically for girls of what they're supposed to be, that you're supposed to be waiting for your like Fairy Prince, and that's when you're happy, like when you find a man, that's when you're happy . . . and all the princesses are kind of considered helpless, and then they find a man, like a man comes and saves them, but they can't really do anything by themselves.

Cole and Guy-Sheftall (2003) argue that long-held negative images of Black women, described at the beginning of the chapter, continue to wreak havoc on the psychological and physical lives of African American women. In addition to reinforcing dependency and helplessness described by Simone, young women may internalize more recent "gangsta" notions of Black women ("bitches" and "ho's"), opening up the potential for them to hold negative views of themselves and be subject to violence from partners and others (Bethea-Whitfield, 2005).

Notwithstanding the strong impact of the media on gender role socialization, Brianna, a 28-year-old bisexual, added:

> It comes a lot from everything, from community, society, and our family, our peers. You know school . . . so it's like a mixture of everything . . . so it doesn't necessarily have to be one thing.

Thus, African American women are constantly learning from many people in many settings about the various roles they are expected to take up as a member of their families and communities.

For Andrea, a 39-year-old international (African) graduate student, gender role socialization is strongly linked to one's religious/spiritual beliefs. From her perspective, both the ideal man and woman are "God-fearing" and "faithful in terms of fidelity to one another in a marriage." Jasmine, a 23-year-old social work graduate student who identifies as bisexual, recalled her exposure to religious traditions within the context of her family's Christian-based church but found them to be in conflict with her sexual identity. She stated:

> My family is very religious and, um, they don't, a lot of them don't know about my sexuality and I think that has a lot to do with the way they act about two cousins in my family who are gay. They really talk about God and, you know, it's not accepted and it's not in the Bible and it's a sin, and you know, they're very, um, they expect everyone to be straight 'cause like if you're not straight, then you're, you have an illness, you need to fix it, and something needs to go, go down. . . . I kind of struggle a lot with that in my family still because I really feel that they never really question, you know, if your child's not straight, then they're gay. Like it's never an option, it's always, oh if you haven't been with a man in so long, it's because you haven't found a good man or it's because you're so into school that, you know, this is why you don't have a man.

Two participants also identified mode of dress, behavior, and leadership roles as strongly gender-based within the Black Christian church. Jasmine stated: "I remember it was expected that at church, you wore a dress and no pants whatsoever, for girls." In keeping with this point, Taylor also noted:

> My grandmother is from North Carolina, we would go visit her, and they have very strict rules at church of what you're supposed to do when you're a little girl. You have to sit down, sit up straight. You know, if you want to color, it's okay, but don't let anyone see you. You know, the little boys in the back would be running around. All the little girls would have the hats on with the dresses, and your bowties. If you had your bowtie out of place, you got smacked on the hand a little bit. You know, it's like "Sit up, stop doing that, don't chew your gum, don't chew gum, don't have candy." It was very rigid. You know, little girls, you had to behave a certain way. And my brother got away with murder in church! [*laughs*] You know, he could just play tic-tac-toe by himself and it would be fine! . . . but I definitely do remember pulling on one of my ribbons in my hair and just getting yelled at for it, because I'm supposed to look a certain way, and be pretty like a little girl and have your bows in place.

In Jasmine's experience, leadership roles were reserved only for the men in her childhood church, thus rendering the women second-class members:

I just like, I think it's ironic when I go to church at home in the South where my dad's side of the family is from, it's like the majority of the church is mostly women, but the leadership roles are held by the men. And like the pastor will be male, the deacons sitting in the front will be men. But then there'll be all these women, because, um, part of being single for a period of time, I would go to church and they'd be like "You know you should find a good guy in the church." And I'm like "Who, the deacon?" [*laughs*] And then I'm like, well why are the men in charge of so many women that are involved?

A number of scholars have identified the beneficial roles that religion, particularly Black churches and communities, play for African Americans in general. As Harley (2005) writes: "The Black church has always offered a sense of community, personal and psychological support, coping strategies, role models, and a sense of collective achievement" (p. 191). Indeed, Black churches provide essential spiritual nurturing on a variety of levels, including individuals, groups, communities, and networking. Moreover, given the relational orientation of many people of African descent, particularly women, close connection to a spiritual network provides a guide for how to construct their sense of self as well as "models of what to expect and how to behave" (Belgrave, 2009, p. 17).

However, as Jasmine noted, being different from church norms about how to conduct one's life, including choice of partner and construction of one's gender roles and expression, can lead to feelings of distress, even alienation and depression. Although Taylor and Jasmine were exposed to the oft-repeated presumption about women's subordinate roles, it also is important to remember that "in many Black churches, Black women have resisted words and actions that call for them to be subservient to men . . . .[Moreover] the cultural maxim, 'If it wasn't for the women, you wouldn't have a church,' challenges organized attempts to exclude, ignore, trivialize, or marginalize women in a number of capacities" in religious communities (Cole & Guy-Sheftall, 2003, p. 110). Thus, finding a spiritual community that supports one's emerging gender roles and gender expressions may be a positive way to resist automatic presumptions about gendered subordination present from childhood.

In line with this suggestion, participants also discussed settings in which messages about women's subordinate gender roles were contradicted, indicating evolving social attitudes or a shifting away from more traditional dominative/submissive relations between men and women. For example, Jennifer expressed the fact that for most of her childhood, her mother and grandmother enacted the traditional role of self-sacrificing caretaker, albeit with feelings of frustration:

> It was like this is mom and/or grandmother . . . and the only role that was played was like the caregiver . . . you know, it was sort of like mom will come home and be like disgusted from working all day, whatever, like that, but they'll still cook, they'll still take care of their three and a half kids or something like that and their two-bedroom apartment.

However, upon reaching college, she:

> started seeing more women just kind of like fending for themselves. Kind of like being individual, like I'm in my 20s, you know, "I don't need a man" hype. Like you know the 1990s, I don't need a man. So you started seeing like an empowerment of women, but then you still see this kind of pull-back effect.

Thus, it is possible, even likely, that Jennifer's more recent experiences reflect changing roles of African American women today, with Black women beginning to see, and even presume, that they are more empowered to live autonomous lives. We turn next to differing views of strength among Black women, including images of strong versus weak women.

Silent Strength

According to Jennifer, when compared to the physical characteristics of men:

> The woman is also strong, but she's strong in different ways . . . women have a different kind of strength which is more like cognitive. More cognitive and affect.

Taylor also noted that "some women are just as strong as men, but most people see women as being the weaker sex because of their emotions, not because of their intelligence." However, despite racial-cultural presumptions about sacrificing and subordinate roles for Black women, the idea of female strength holds a far more complex meaning, as it is often equated with the ability to maintain one's independence, should this become necessary. Patrice highlighted these complexities when she stated:

> For a woman to be independent, I know in my family, I was brought up to be "Oh it's good if you have a man, but if he doesn't last, you still have to make sure that you have a backup plan, you know you're doing school now to just better yourself so that if he doesn't come through as a father or husband or whatever, like you'll be good on your own two feet" . . . but I also see like this, just like conflict in messages that are put out there on one level. Like you're supposed to be independent, you're supposed to be strong, you're supposed to put your kids and everybody else first. But then on the same level you're supposed to put up with a lot with men and you're supposed to be in a relationship. . . . It's like you're always supposed to be, like you're supposed to have the attitude "Be Strong" but at the same time, you're supposed to be like this forgiving, always be able to take everything and just keep moving and never be, like you can't just break down as a Black woman.

She went on to explain that "a weak woman" is

> Someone who puts up with someone's, like puts up with her partner's crap, you know, and is like letting the person just abuse her. Like it doesn't have to be physically, it could be verbally or he could just be mistreating her, not respecting her at all. Walking all over her.

For Patrice, the main message being communicated is therefore:

> "We can be independent if needs be." . . . We're supposed to be prepared to be able to do it on our own, and if a situation is less than ideal and yet we're not able to do it on our own for whatever reason then that makes us the weaker . . . to not have the ability to be independent. [We] have the ability to be independent even if [we're] not independent in that moment.

When later discussing her own experiences of heterosexual relationships, Patrice stated:

> I think that I'm learning that it's okay to be dependent sometimes in my relationship now, and it goes back to what we were talking about earlier, it's this role of me wanting to be this

independent Black woman not needing my partner for anything. "I got it, I'm good, I am here, he is there," type of mentality that was causing friction for me. And it worked in my relationships in the past because when the person wasn't doing what they needed to do, I'm like see, that's why I have all of this to myself. But for me, I'm learning that, um, for me to be happy in my relationship and to be comfortable with the person that I'm with, I need to acknowledge his space and the benefits that I have in trusting him sometimes and not always having everything together on my own. But I think it's a hard thing to do because I feel in conflict sometimes with myself in doing that 'cause it's making myself, you know, it's making me feel vulnerable, making me question sometimes like what is weak and what is strong as a woman.

Participants' narratives thus portray the lives of many Black/African American females as a balancing act of sorts as they attempt to conform to societal as well as family/community expectations while constructing their own gender roles and working toward their life goals. *Invisible dignity* is a term coined by Black Episcopalian priest Katie Cannon to describe "a feistiness about life that nobody can wipe out despite the amount of suffering inflicted" (Hambrick, 1997, p. 74). As Patrice indicated, being "strong" and independent is an important aspect of African American women's gender role constructions, particularly if the woman finds herself in circumstances in which this is necessary for survival and success. However, treasuring autonomy may then lead a woman to hesitate in letting go and "counting" or depending on someone else, particularly a male partner, when times are difficult. As Black women pursue intimate partner relationships, build families, and seek an education and career, it will be important for them to learn to navigate through these choices, as well as their accompanying feelings.

Binary Concepts of Masculinity and Femininity

We asked participants to share what they thought it meant to be masculine or feminine. Most participants responded with descriptive words characterizing what they saw as the wider society's definitions of these terms, ascribing the former term only to men and the latter term specifically to women. Indeed, Jasmine described such an approach as "binary" in nature, pointing to the fact that these terms are used most often to refer to mutually exclusive categories. She went on to state that these terms are

> split in two, like there's only two ends and you're one or the other. Um, I don't know . . . you're put into one or the other by other people.

Across the interviews, participants used these words to describe what the term *feminine* meant to them: prissy, dainty, vulnerable, pretty, beautiful, soft, delicate, frail, afraid, petite, and perfect. With particular reference to Black females, Andrea argued that the word *feminine*

> carries both physical and nonphysical components. I think being feminine comes with looking like a female in the sense that females would normally dress up in a certain way, carry themselves in a certain way, and in terms of other qualities not physical, I think being feminine would mean one is kind of motherly, caring, and a good listener too. . . . Physical characteristics . . . well, maybe like growing hair long, that would be more distinctive. Yeah, and then there are natural features like growing breasts, growing hips.

Jennifer further expanded on the physical features characterizing femininity, stating "there are females that are kind of like feminine to me just because they maybe have longer nails or bigger hair, or, you know, wear tighter, thinner clothing." To Brianna, the term *feminine* described

> someone who's passive. Yeah, and I think the passivity goes along with the physique too. . . . So a feminine person is supposed to be petite and not speak too loudly and not impose. You can't be rough.

In light of the fact that femininity is associated with passivity, notions of the Black female as "strong" tend to promote a less feminine image. Black/African American women are often viewed, and even view themselves, as more self-reliant and independent than other women. As a result, the larger society masculinizes and views their presumed gender role as aggressive in nature. Although she appeared reluctant to do so at first, Patrice drew important connections between being a Black woman and White/Western notions around femininity, giving further support to this point:

> I think the reason why I'm pausing so long to answer is 'cause feminine to me is like White women . . . because it's like contrasted with what it means to be a Black woman. . . . It's like a lot of those images contrast with what is White feminine beautiful, or what a woman is supposed to be. So I think a lot of times, you know, as a Black woman, it's hard for me to say what I feel is a feminine Black woman.

When Jennifer considered the terms *masculine* and *feminine*, she said that she felt Black men and women "don't fit neatly into those categories." For her, social class played a significant role:

> Depending on like . . . I mean like more middle-class, high-class housewives of Atlanta you'll have the male and the female playing the more segregated like roles. . . . Then you'll have like a lower-class family income line of Black males and females that kind of play both because . . . them and their foreparents have had to play that, both roles. You have, you know, most people who have more money more than likely will have a mom and a dad in the family. . . . But most lower-class-family income people don't have that, so it's just like you kind of see the mom playing both *machismo* and femininity roles.

Belgrave (2009) writes that many African American girls and women enact gender roles that are reflective of both traditional masculine and feminine traits for a number of reasons. For example, because of the history of racism in the United States, Black women have had to take on enormous family responsibilities, often without a male partner, making sole decisions about food, housing, health care, and schooling of children. Moreover, family expectations about African American girls doing well with their education, combined with the lack of employment for many Black men, place Black women in roles and positions generally reserved for men in other racial-ethnic communities. Finally, observing female relatives enact more blended or androgynous roles also sends messages to young women that being independent and self-sufficient is necessary for survival and success. However, as Patrice shared, African American women may feel conflicted about taking on or at least expressing more masculine traits, particularly since, in the larger society, being autonomous still may be considered a more negative quality for women. At a minimum, many Black women may be concerned, perhaps rightfully, that taking on traditional masculine qualities may be confused with or detract from one's physical embodiment of femininity, womanhood, and beauty.

Several participants discussed how femininity is defined and embodied in the wider society. For example, Jasmine summed up the term as simply "ladylike:"

> You're supposed to close your legs. . . . You can't, you shouldn't throw yourself at a guy. You should talk to girls, not to the boys. There's just certain things that I remember growing up, my mother always told me "Okay, a lady is supposed to carry herself this way," and this way meaning, you know, you shouldn't wear baggy jeans, you should wear tight jeans. You should have your hair straight, you shouldn't wear cornrows 'cause you're getting to that age where it's like, you know you're not a lesbian so you can't be doing certain things.

Inherent in these descriptions was the expectation that the ideal female is heterosexual. Jasmine described her family's heteronormative presumptions:

> Again, what jumps out at me is that . . . before high school, it seemed your family didn't say anything to you but at a certain point . . . at a certain age . . . messages, all these things need to change now. . . . Just this expectation that not that it's different, just that it's assumed that you wouldn't be gay. Not like there's a conversation of "Oh, well, are you?" "Have you explored this?" Whatever, just like this assumption that, you know, gay is not something [*laughs*] that happens in the Black community.

For Brianna, the idea of being feminine seemed difficult to articulate and elicited feelings of discomfort and anxiety about her own constructions of gender roles:

> I think feminine, I guess maybe feminine to me has been, it's that, I'm a little biased to that too because I feel like feminine to me has been such a scary moment. Because I've always been identified as not feminine, and that's been my attractive nature, so me being feminine has always kinda given me the opposite. . . . So I'm a tomboy, right? As a kid or whatever, even as a young adult, you

say I'm not feminine . . . the opposite of feminine. . . . Like you wear like boys' clothes, play ball, you play sports, you hang with the boys, you roll with the boys, don't chill with the girls, you just don't. . . . That's a tomboy. Getting like hurt and not crying.

Importantly, one participant, Taylor, made the point that these stereotypical descriptors are changing as the word *feminine* may not necessarily be used to characterize a woman. She said:

You know, to be very feminine is just . . . just to do things that people classify as more of a thing that a woman would do, but that necessarily a man wouldn't do. But men now do! [*laughs*] Some men, especially metrosexuals! [*laughs*]

As Taylor and other participants noted, although rigid stereotypes and expectations may still be promoted and enforced for women in both the Black community and the larger society, lessening of gender role restrictions, at least for men, has begun to occur.

Exploration of the term *masculine* elicited these descriptive words: tough, strong, assertive, aggressive, *machismo*, dominant, overbearing, destructive, powerful, and having money. It also elicited physical characteristics, such as "tall" and "broad shoulders." With reference to Black males, the words *player*, *thug*, and *pimp* were used to highlight the fact that masculinity for this racial-cultural group is strongly tied to asserting one's sexual orientation as heterosexual in nature and is often demonstrated by having multiple female partners or sexual conquests. In elaborating on how masculinity is viewed within the Black community, Simone noted that, from her experience, the term typically refers to:

the local drug dealers on the corner or the block. That's masculinity to me because it's always going to be like which one's dick is bigger. You know, all of them is just like, I'm a man. You know, I'm this big boulder that can just plow you over and you won't even know.

Further dialogue with some participants highlighted the fact that they did not highly regard characteristics of men and women that seem to approach those commonly assigned to members of the opposite sex. For example, Simone observed:

I don't know, like if you see a woman or you see like, okay, on CNN, they're talking about a woman, like they have this woman that made, obviously made a lot of money, and she like couldn't find anyone like to date or whatever. She was like "I can't find anyone, they're scared of me and blah-blah-blah." But if there were a man in that position, like there'd be a different girl every night or whatever, so I think that that's something that's more masculine. I think being powerful is considered, and I think money is linked to people who feel that power, and that is considered very masculine.

Simone's sharp observation highlights a continuing dilemma for many African American women: Being independent and self-sufficient may be critical to their survival, even ultimate success. However, this may come at a price of being viewed as less feminine, and thus less attractive, by men. Belgrave (2009) suggests that parents—both mothers and fathers—as well as teachers and peers can play a critical role in negating these beliefs and at the same time affirming young Black women's beauty and independence. Wyatt (1997) encourages young Black women to "[w]alk with your head up. We have had to walk with our heads bowed for too long. Be proud of your Black beauty and demand respect" (p. 107).

Less than Ideal

In response to the question regarding what the ideal woman is, Patrice observed that in the context of American society, the ideal can be defined as being "wealthy, young, straight, and White." She went on to say:

Women are expected to have this specific image, and it feels even farther away when you're a Black woman. Like in terms of you meeting the expectation of what is beautiful. There's a White woman with White features, a certain size, and that's not what a Black woman is a lot of times. She doesn't fit into that box easily.

Gender role constructions for African Americans involve the transmission of racialized messages that focus specifically on physical appearance and compel Black women to conform to Eurocentric standards of beauty. These societal expectations tend to shift with age and accompanying biological changes, particularly as girls' bodies begin to mature into womanhood. Patrice stated:

I think physical appearance has a lot to do with it. Body image too, but in my culture, it's also hair has a lot to do with it. Your hair has to be straight because, you know, society views straight hair as a big thing and you are expected to accept it. . . . Like I just remember, even from my mom and other people in my life . . . when you hit a certain age like around 12 or 13, you were supposed to be starting to think about your body in a different way than you ever had before, and comments like "What are you eating?" or "Make sure you don't get too big." Like I just went from the big bom-bom [hair] thingies that were like little kid to I wanted to have braids and my mom wanted me to have my hair straight, and you know I felt like the rules began to change.

The inclusionary expression "Black Is Beautiful" is often used to indicate racial-ethnic pride while demonstrating preference for and identification with the Black race. Two participants, however, highlighted existing contradictions between societal portrayals of the ideal Black woman and commonly held images of the Black female. Taylor made reference to her own experience: Her most complimented physical feature, light-colored eyes, were those least congruent with the phenotypic markers commonly observed among African Americans and were more associated with Whites. She stated:

Like my schools that I went to and people in my neighborhoods, like remembering um the way that they complimented me and the way that they didn't . . . like for instance, I have light eyes and people always made a big deal about that when I was younger, to the point where I was like I wish I had brown eyes 'cause I felt weird about it. . . . And it's having that weird feeling of if that's not Black but that's the most beautiful part or the most noticeable part of me . . . like one of the things that is looked at as beautiful about you is something that's incongruent with how you see yourself as a whole. Like I see myself and from a young age have identified as being Black, and that's how my mom has always addressed [it], like be proud of being a beautiful Black woman. But feeling that this is something that betrays me, that's not representative of who I am as a Black woman.

A second participant, Cindy, drew a distinction between the idealized Black female image, often drawn from light-skinned and Eurocentric images, and existing Black female stereotypes. She observed that media portrayals of the ideal—that is, beautiful—Black woman are often different from commonly held societal assumptions or stereotypes about Black women in general:

> I think that an idealized image of Black women in the media is Halle Berry who's biracial, is Vanessa Williams who has green eyes, or those light-skinned people who are probably racially mixed people. But I think growing up in a household where that message was sent to me that you don't have to think that that's beautiful, and that you shouldn't think that that's the only thing that's beautiful is where the discrepancy for me was with them, feeling that that's always looked at as beautiful. . . . When I was thinking about what our community sees as the ideal Black woman, there were so many different images, I had a hard time narrowing something down . . . I think there's this idea that the Halle Berry's and whoever is this token; beautiful Black women are exceptions. Whereas what Black women look like is different. . . . Like I don't know if people are crazy as me and watch my soap *General Hospital*, but there's a Black woman on there, Epiphany, and she's like a heavyset Black woman, always giving attitude, like very demanding, strong, but like when I see that, that's what I think of as people's sometimes image of what Black women are. Like we're always angry, we always have this chip on our shoulder, we're always, you know, we're not taking care of ourselves or overweight. . . . Like yeah, Black people can be beautiful. Look at Halle Berry who is biracial. Whereas if I was to picture like what I suspect people think of when they think of a Black woman, it would be more like this character I mentioned named Epiphany.

Although the media do portray African American women in the larger society, these portrayals often reflect White standards of beauty, thus placing pressure on Black women to aspire to shape their appearance in this way. However, despite societal pressures on Black women to conform to conventional standards of beauty, other participants expressed Africentric standards in describing their idealized notions of Black women, as articulated by Simone:

> I think if you were to build like a woman that's the ideal or whatever, that she would have, she'd probably be like a little bit petite, and then she would be thin, but then she would be like thick at the same time. And so like your thighs would be like muscular and you'd have, I don't know, probably you'd have big breasts, but not necessarily, but you'd definitely have to have a big butt.

Although messages in the larger society, particularly those in the media, convey White or Eurocentric notions of femininity, womanhood, and beauty, these messages, and the potential negative psychological consequences, can be effectively countered via the communication of community values and standards by family, friends, and partners/spouses. The process of affirming and reaffirming oneself as an African American woman, as smart, capable, and beautiful, is a coping strategy that one is likely not to tire of. As Wyatt (1997) writes: "Each time I doubt that I can overcome my own negative experiences with the ways others perceive me as a sexual being, I try to remember my ancestors. I visualize them watching and showing me how to be free, to celebrate my womanhood, and to reach out to others" (p. 228).

"Bottom of the Barrel": Dilemma of Being Black and Female

Our final theme refers to the moving narrative that began our book's preface, seeing oneself as the "bottom of the barrel." As Cindy said, "Black women have two strikes against them because they're Black and because they're a woman." The interview question that invited participants to share how they felt Whites viewed persons of color elicited responses that described primarily negative traits. What was especially poignant among our participants' reactions was their discussion of the tremendous challenges associated with navigating the world not only as a woman but as a Black woman. In line with generations of racist and sexist images, Brianna stated that many Whites view Black women as

> nannies, they are the caregivers . . . they can braid hair, you know . . . they're mean, they're vicious, they don't know how to treat Black men. Sometimes how they think of Black women, as they're filthy, as they're jealous of White women.

Jasmine, who attended a predominantly White school, felt significant pressure to represent the Black race positively while also encountering negative stereotypes, particularly as the "angry Black woman:"

> I go to a predominantly White school and it's Jewish, so I'm actually a grad student and getting a master's in social work

and there's times that I'll be in class and I'm the only Black girl in the class and I feel like when I address situations about race and stuff like that—because my school, they really focus on the Western culture—and sometimes I feel like I have to talk about people of color. . . . And I notice at times when I talk about it, it's like I'm the bitter Black woman that's talking about it and this is how all Black people act, so I feel like I'm representing one race and I'm being looked upon. Whereas I'm not here to talk about every Black person, I'm here to talk about my experience, but I also—that's how I feel and I also feel like it's the stereotype. "Well, she's the only Black girl in this class, she probably, she's here because of affirmative action. She probably got a loan or a scholarship."

Stresses and pressures associated with having to represent the Black race in a favorable way also can be experienced at home. For example, Simone shared that her mother often encouraged her to speak and behave in a manner that was close to that of White women:

Like something my mom always said, she's like, we always had to like dress in a certain way or we always had to act in a certain way, and like . . . I don't really use slang and I talk like a White girl and know that because my mom was always, like, you have to do it a certain way because like people are going to look at you and they're going to see you as representative of Black people. And if there's like 100 Black people and one person's acting ignorant or acting crazy or whatever, they're going to be, like, "Oh, Black people," and they're going to ignore everyone else. Do you have to like go above and beyond to be thought of as just below?

Belgrave (2009) notes that it is common for African American parents to teach their daughters to look and act "American" as a means to ensure success, particularly in school and at work. However, as Simone poignantly portrayed, sometimes this can translate into nearly impossible behavioral standards to uphold, for, by doing so, Simone must mask her own Africentric values and ways of acting and act as a "representative" of her race. Simone also may feel alienated from peers and potential partners, particularly if she is viewed as a "sell-out" for acting White.

For two participants, there also seemed to be a sense of obligation and feelings of accountability associated with being a Black female. This issue is in keeping with our earlier discussion of gender socialization of Black women to be carriers of the race or culture. In the words of Brianna:

> It's like this expectation of Black women, we're going to be, we maintain the race so that we're going to be always about Black people. Whereas Black men are not tied in the same way to the family and what it means to be, I don't know if they're not tied to what it means to be Black.

Patrice stated:

> I feel like as a Black woman, we represent Black people, but there is definitely a different experience. And I think as Black women, we're expected to be supportive unconditionally to Black men. . . . But I don't feel like Black men have that same expectation that they're supposed to be supportive unconditionally to Black women. . . . I think we just, Black women, like we're just put in the bottom of the scale or ladder, whatever you want to call it. . . . I suddenly remembered another way that I, sort of both in terms of race and gender, learn[ed] sort of what my role was at the bottom of the barrel. There was a book that I was reading in fifth grade that was about this young Black girl who wanted to fight in the Civil War and in order to be able to do it she had to dress like a boy. And I think it was in the dialogue, she's talking about being a slave and being, being a child, so being under every adult; being a slave and so being under every White person; being a girl, and so being under every male. And that she was the very, very, very bottom of the ladder [*laughs*]. And I remember sitting there thinking that that was me, that I was, as a child, I had no power; as a woman, I had no power; and as a Black person, I had no power.

As Patrice noted, upholding the race is by no means viewed as an honored and valued tradition, but rather a burden that may pull one down the social strata toward poverty and disempowerment. Moreover, Jennifer contended that many Black women remain unaware of the unequal status that they hold in relation to Black men and may be manipulated into playing certain gender roles:

> But with our sex, I just, I just don't think women are seeing that there are problems and that they're not equal to men, like they're not seen as equal to Black men. . . . You know, it's just like we're given these roles.

This issue is closely linked to the notion that feminist views are held primarily by White women and are rarely seen among Black women. (Half our participants expressed this view.) For example, in response to the question of what feminism meant to her, Jasmine said:

> White woman is the first thing that crosses my mind. . . . My mom's voice just like comes to my head. Like "We don't got time for feminism!" [*laughs*].

In addition, if Black women attempt to assert themselves as equal in status, others typically view this as threatening in nature, according to Simone:

> I don't know, I guess I think it's a little bit crazy that thinking of a woman as being able to do everything a man can do, not necessarily in the same way, but in terms of like being just as smart as a man, being able to do like the same job as a man, is seen as so crazy and radical, almost scares me a little because why do people think that? Like why are people so almost afraid of women doing things that are outside the domestic realm that it's considered like, I think some people think of it as a concern and as a threat to their manhood. And I think especially in the Black community it's like that because women, in terms of education and professionalism, are outpacing men and I think that that's why it's such a big deal in the Black community and this community specifically because it's seen as like a threat. Like I'm not a man if this woman can do that or that or the other.

The experiences of Simone and other participants clearly indicate that hierarchical power relations between men and women remain a challenge within many African American families and communities and that Black women continue to face the risk of double jeopardy of multiple minority statuses. In response to these continuing racist and sexist stereotypes, Guy-Sheftall and Cole (2003), using bell hooks' terms, exhort Black women to "talk back" about being victimized, even within the Black community, because "the politics of sex and the politics of race are one and the same politics" (Hernton, in Guy-Sheftall & Cole, p. 72). Moreover, they cite Gary Lemons (1998, in Guy-Sheftall & Cole, 2003), who challenges many Black men's oppression of Black women in the larger fight for racial justice:

> Is our attainment of patriarchal power through the oppression of women any less insidious than white people's perpetuation

of a system of racial oppression to dehumanize us? Many of us have become so obsessed with fighting racism as a battle for the right to be patriarchal men that we have been willing to deploy the same strategies to disempower black women as white supremacists have employed to institutionalize racism. (pp. 72–73)

Interestingly, one participant, Simone, also said that educated Black males are perceived as threatening in the larger society, particularly among Whites:

> And I think there is kind of like two main stereotypes of Black men. That they're like the crazy, Black guy that does like thug-slash-robber-slash like whatever. And then there's the angry Black man that's like very educated but is like also really scary because [*pause*] I think a lot of people are afraid of educated Black people and afraid of [*pause*] really I think that they're afraid that [*pause*] that I think that there's still the idea that White people are smarter, and whether people want to admit it or not, I still think that the idea is very prevalent. And I think that the fact that it's been shown now that it's not real, like people can get ahead, that it's making those people even scarier than maybe the people that are considered like criminals or whatever because it's like something that's closer and something that like that's in your, maybe your daily life, working environment.

Thus, perhaps one area of mutuality between Black men and women is working together to understand that stereotypes can prevent any and all individuals from achieving their greatest potential. Seeing the impact that stereotypes one individual might have toward another person may go a long way in diminishing their presence and impact.

APPLICATIONS FOR MENTAL HEALTH PROFESSIONALS AND EDUCATORS

Our findings highlight several important considerations for mental health professionals and educators. Many of the narratives emphasized emotionally charged, deeply felt, and often quite painful issues for the participants as they discussed navigating their individual lives in a double-jeopardy status and facing stereotypes that were simultaneously sexist and racist.

For the young women in our study, the core narrative of evolution and change of gender roles recognizes not only the central socialization processes that have so strongly affected their current constructions and experiences of race and gender, but also takes into account the many inherent contradictions, negotiations, and shifts that occur among Black/African American racial-ethnic norms, the larger society, and within each woman as she makes sense of these multiple values, expectations, and norms in constructing her gender roles.

Conflicting Definitions of Femininity and Female Gender Roles

Several participants poignantly described contrasting notions and expectations of femininity learned from the larger society as well as within their families and communities. Norms about women taking on a caretaking, nurturing role were commonly communicated through many important people in participants' lives as well as through the media. Participants were told by their mothers and extended family members, church leaders, and others that their role was in support of, even subordinate to, those of men, who were viewed as leaders. At the same time, given the oppressive circumstances facing most participants and their families, African American women also were expected to be ready to care for themselves and their families, should the circumstances arise. Taking on major responsibilities associated with maintaining a family, particularly as a single parent, was a potential concern for several participants, along with the need to have traits and abilities necessary to carry out those tasks. Some of these responsibilities were generally linked with masculine traits, such as independence and autonomy, which usually were associated with men in other racial-ethnic groups.

This mixture of gender role expectations was not always consistently communicated to participants, nor were there clear indications that more masculine traits might be considered acceptable or even desirable to others within the community as well as in the larger society, particularly potential male partners. Thus, some Black women felt pressure to present themselves in more traditional feminine (i.e., "ladylike"), even Eurocentric, ways, even though this might not match how they actually led their lives or saw themselves. Others were able to see and value themselves and other Black women through

Afrocentric lenses, celebrating Black women's unique qualities and features. Belgrave (2009) encourages parents, teachers, and mental health practitioners to affirm the expression of both masculine and feminine traits and roles in African American girls, given girls' potential to take on both "independent" and "nurturing" roles. Doing so, she notes, also might facilitate higher self-esteem and more positive identity constructions and even lessen the risk of sexual acting out and substance abuse. Wyatt (1997) describes the experiences of Black women in the United States as being "stolen" due to their long histories of racial and gender-based exploitation and abuse, particularly in the form of negative images and expectations, which can undermine confidence and self-belief. She identifies several principles by which Black women can heal themselves and be role models for the next generation, including having the courage to obtain adequate knowledge, connecting family values to socialization and behaviors, and valuing one's ability to control one's decision making.

Both personal and sociohistorical contexts seemed to be quite influential on participants' understandings of gender roles and their racial underpinnings. Thus, it may prove beneficial for mental health professionals and educators to provide opportunities for Black girls and women to reexamine the ways in which such norms and values help and/or hinder their psychological functioning, particularly within modern society. Class activities and clinical interventions might therefore be developed to help Black girls and women become more aware of what norms they may be operating under in order to better understand how these might be linked to their current behaviors and gender role expectations and expressions. For example, courses in gender and women's issues that are offered at the high school, community college, or university level can encourage critical thinking with regard to gender and gender inequality while also providing information on historical contexts as well as cross-cultural approaches. For adolescent girls, Belgrave (2009) suggests a number of activities to increase awareness about gender role expectations, including opportunities for girls to do community service projects that boys might normally do, such as clearing a field, as well as tasks involved in caring, such as visiting an elders' center. Another option might be for girls to think of women and men they are close to and describe their careers/jobs, then compare these choices and experiences.

Belgrave also suggests having girls carefully review a film clip or magazine images of African American females; in short, she encourages "girls to become media critics" (p. 29).

Self-Silencing and Strength

Participants also pointed out that concomitant with racial-ethnic gender role expectations that blended masculine and feminine traits was the norm that Black women maintain a strong, never-break-down facade to the world. Benefits that might accrue from these expectations are a positive sense of self-efficacy about oneself and one's abilities to carry on in the face of extreme challenges to self and family. Black women also commonly were expected to be sacrificing of their individual lives and desires, viewing themselves as carriers of the race—a role that was not necessarily granted privilege and honor but rather service and great responsibility to others. Participants further felt they were held to higher standards than their male relatives for major caretaking responsibilities in the family; such behavior was not necessarily rewarded or recognized, and was presumed of them.

Thus, in addition to some psychological benefits, the normalization of self-sacrifice, struggle, and tendencies toward internalization and silencing also may have important psychological costs. Such values may leave many African American girls and women unable to effectively manage emotional distress or unwilling to seek professional help/support. As Bethea-Whitfield (2005) notes, "[W]omen driven by the idea that they are supposed to be able to master any situation may too often choose to go it alone for too long trapped by their isolation" (p. 41). She notes, however, that "a part of the solution may be giving up the notion that one can do it all." In order to further manage the emotional impact of these burdens, activities and interventions can be developed that help girls and women find important support networks with others in similar situations and help them negotiate constructively with their partners about how to share accountability and roles in the family. For example, given many Black women's emphases on interpersonal relationships, Adams and LaFromboise (2000) developed a relational group therapy program for mothers and daughters that each week focused on different themes, including relational masks and the hidden self, exploring the ways the women silenced themselves in relationships. The sessions provided a safe place for girls and women to take off their "strong" masks and authentically share their emotions of anger, fear, and sadness with others.

Another innovative project, Project Naja, developed by Belgrave and colleagues (2009), concerns the multiple caretaking roles often required of older girls and women. The program, developed for adolescent females, focuses on self-esteem, positive values, racial identity, and peer relations. Belgrave and associates also partnered with a local Head Start agency to run programming simultaneously for younger siblings, so that all children could benefit from this project.

Redefining Gender Roles

Although most participants were aware of their presumed social locations within their racial-ethnic community and the larger society, many were not willing to accept this as the ultimate fate of their own or their children's lives. To be sure, participants were aware that others might view as threatening breaking away or changing these strong expectations and negative stereotypes, particularly as these changes might challenge the racial and gender status quo. Others also struggled with internalizing these perspectives themselves, leading to continued patterns of self-silencing.

Perhaps a more socially acceptable path toward constructing more flexible gender roles lies in the pursuit of educational and therapeutic activities, particularly if these can be viewed as an effort to promoting family and community success. Helping Black girls and women to acknowledge and critique their social locations might be achieved through class activities or clinical interventions designed to open dialogue about role expectations and images of women and men within their own racial-ethnic community and in the larger society. Daphna Oyserman and colleagues (2002, in Belgrave, 2009) developed a possible selves intervention for adolescents, conducted in a small-group setting, in which students imagine their future selves as adults and, over several sessions, map their way to that image, including identifying educational goals, learning how to solve everyday problems, and engaging with their parents about how to move forward. Providing these kinds of exploratory opportunities for young African American girls and women to envision their future selves may be one way to help them construct multiple complex roles and traits that are part of being a Black female.

A number of organizations can facilitate more flexible and positive gender role constructions for Black girls and women. For example, the National Coalition of 100 Black Women, Inc. (NCBW 100) is an advocacy organization for "the health, education, and economic empowerment of Black women." The organization consists of thousands of women of African descent who represent 60 chapters in 25 states and the District of Columbia. Its mission is "to advocate on behalf of women of color through national and local actions and strategic alliances that promote the NCBW agenda on leadership development and gender equity in the areas of health, education and economic empowerment." In order to meet the diverse needs of its members, NCBW implements programs that "provide an effective network among Black women, establish links between NCBW and the corporate and political sectors, enable Black women to be a visible force in the socioeconomic arena, meet the career needs of these women and facilitate their access to mainstream America, use the tools of role modeling and mentoring to provide meaningful guidance to young women, and recognize the historic and current achievements of Black women." (For more information, see http://www.ncbw.org.)

Another organization is Black Girls Rock! Inc., a nonprofit mentoring outreach program that targets teenage women of color who are "at risk." The charity was established to promote the arts, stimulate discussion regarding the images of women portrayed in hip-hop music and culture, and encourage analysis of the ways in which the media portray women of color. The organization seeks to build self-esteem and self-worth among young women by "raising awareness and offering support through discussion, education, counseling, internships, mentoring, and advocacy." (For more information, see http://blackgirlsrockinc.com.)

Finally, as a way of building self-efficacy and motivation for Black girls and women in pursuit of leadership opportunities, the Executive Leadership Council (ELC) is designed "to build an inclusive business leadership pipeline, and to develop African-American corporate leaders—one student and one executive at a time." The ELC consists of more than 500 members, one-third of whom are women, and boasts of involving the most senior African American corporate executives from Fortune

500 companies in their activities. The organization has hosted an annual women's leadership forum for the past nine years. The 2012 program emphasized increasing the number of Black women holding senior leadership positions across the corporate United States. The ELC also plans to work with companies to promote at least one African American female to the position of chief executive or senior-level executive at every Fortune 500 company over the next five years. (For more information, see http://www.elcinfo.com.)

REFERENCES

Adams, V. L. L., & LaFromboise, T. D. (2001). Self-in-relation theory and African American female development. In D. E. Pope-Davis & H.L.K. Coleman (Eds.), *The intersection of race, class, and gender in multicultural counseling* (pp. 25–48). Thousand Oaks, CA: Sage.

Babbitt, L.G. (2011). An intersectional approach to Black/White interracial interactions: The roles of gender and sexual orientation. *Sex Roles*. No pagination available. Advance online publication. doi:10.1007/s11199-011-0104-4

Beauboeuf-Lafontant, T. (2007). "You have to show strength:" An exploration of gender, race, and depression. *Gender and Society, 21*(1), 28–51.

Belgrave, F. Z. (2009). *African American girls: Reframing perceptions and changing experiences.* New York, NY: Springer.

Bem, S. L. (1974). The measurement of psychological androgyny. *Journal of Consulting and Clinical Psychology, 42*(2), 155–162.

Bethea-Whitfield, P. (2005). African American women and mental health. In D. A. Harley & J. M. Dillard (Eds.), *Contemporary mental health issues among African Americans* (pp. 35–47). Alexandria, VA: American Counseling Association.

Boyd-Franklin, N., & Franklin, A. J. (2000). *Boys into men: Raising our African American teenage sons.* New York: Dutton.

Cole, E. R. (2009). Intersectionality and research in psychology. *American Psychologist, 64*, 170–180.

Cole, J. B., & Guy-Sheftall, B. (2003). *Gender talk: The struggle for women's equality in African American communities.* New York, NY: Ballantine Books.

Hambrick, A. (1997). You haven't seen anything until you make a Black woman mad. In K. M. Vaz (Ed.), *Oral narrative research with Black women* (pp. 64–82). Thousand Oaks, CA: Sage.

Harley, D. A. (2005). The Black church: A strength-based approach in mental health. In D. A. Harley & J. M. Dillard (Eds.), *Contemporary mental health issues among African Americans* (pp. 191–203). Alexandria, VA: American Counseling Association.

Guy-Sheftall, B., & Cole, J. B. (2003). Collisions: Black liberation versus women's liberation. In J. B. Cole & B. Guy-Sheftall, *Gender talk: The struggle for women's equality in African American communities* (pp. 71–101). New York, NY: Ballantine Books.

King, K. R. (2003). Racism or sexism? Attributional ambiguity and simultaneous membership in multiple oppressed groups. *Journal of Applied Social Psychology, 33*(2), 223–247.

Nguyen, A. B., Clark, T. T., Hood, K. B., Corneille, M. A., Fitzgerald, A. Y., & Belgrave, F. Z. (2010). Beyond traditional gender roles and identity: Does reconceptualization better predict condom-related outcomes for African-American women? *Culture, Health and Sexuality, 12*(6), 603–617.

Patterson, L. A., Cameron, E., & Lalonde, R. N. (1996). The intersection of race and gender: Examining the politics of identity in women's studies. *Canadian Journal of Behavioural Science, 28*(3), 229–239.

Reid, P. T., & Comas-Diaz, L. (1990). Gender and ethnicity: Perspectives on dual status. *Sex Roles, 22,* 397–408.

Settles, I. H. (2006). Use of an intersectional framework to understand Black women's racial and gender identities. *Sex Roles, 54*(9/10), 589–601.

Spelman, E. V. (1988). *Inessential woman: Problems of exclusion in feminist thought.* Boston, MA: Beacon Press.

Spence, J. T., Helmreich, R., & Stapp, J. (1974). The Personal Attributes Questionnaire: A measure of sex-role stereotypes and masculinity-femininity. *JSAS Catalog of Selected Documents in Psychology, 4,* 43–44.

Woods-Giscombé, C. L., & Lobel, M. (2008). Race and gender matter: A multidimensional approach to conceptualizing and measuring stress in African American women. *Cultural Diversity & Ethnic Minority Psychology, 14*(3), 173–182.

Wyatt, G. E. (1997). *Stolen women: Reclaiming our sexuality, taking back our lives.* New York, NY: Wiley.

Chapter Four

LATINO MALE GENDER ROLES
Manuel A. Diaz, Marie L. Miville, and Natalia Gil

Latinas/os are a very diverse racial-ethnic group whose ancestry is from Latin American countries, including Mexico, Puerto Rico, Cuba, the Dominican Republic, and South and Central American countries, such as Colombia, Nicaragua, and Costa Rica (Miville, 2006, 2010). Today Latinas/os represent the largest racial-ethnic minority group in the United States, numbering more than 52 million in 2010 and representing approximately 17% of the population (U.S. Census Bureau, 2012). Although Latinas/os reside throughout the United States, most live in certain regions and states, including the Southwest and Northeast regions, Texas, Florida, and Illinois.

The 500-year history of Latinas/os in the Americas reflects complex events affecting multiple racial-ethnic groups, including European, primarily Spanish and Portuguese, indigenous, and African people (Santiago-Rivera, Arredondo, & Gallardo-Cooper, 2002). Oppressive forces of enslavement, persecution, enforced religious conversion, and the disempowerment of both indigenous and African-descent people were present for many centuries throughout Latin America (Gonzalez, 2000). In the 1800s, the United States began the infamous "Manifest Destiny" policy, expanding its borders into existing Latin American countries, primarily Mexico and Puerto Rico, forcibly reclassifying many Latinas/os as "aliens" (Mexican Americans) or "noncitizens" (Puerto Ricans, although they were made citizens in 1917). Since that time, migration issues have been central to the lives of Latinas/os in the United States, who, for many reasons, still tend to be overrepresented in the areas of poverty and unemployment and underrepresented in the areas of education and high income (Miville, 2010). Recent impressive gains at all points of the academic pipeline, however, paint a more complex picture of the increasing success of this heterogenous racial-ethnic group in the United States (Fry & Lopez, 2012).

Despite the heterogeneity among Latinas/os, most Latina/o cultures place great importance and value on gender roles among men and women, often drawing on common religious beliefs and values. When considering the notion of masculinity from a Latino cultural framework, the concept of *machismo* most frequently comes to mind (Santiago-Rivera et al., 2002). For most Latino men, *machismo* describes the essence of manhood, although it is important to note that no single definition of *machismo* exists (Mirande, 1997). The word *machismo* is derived from the word *macho* and is often defined by excessive masculinity and chauvinistic behavior. Some definitions include "a term that describes a Latino man as controlling, possessive, sexist and dominant, and often is associated with violence against women" (Santiago-Rivera, 2003, p. 7) as well as a "man's responsibility is to provide for, protect, and defend his family" (Morales, 1996, in Santiago-Rivera et al., p. 50). *Machismo* also has been described as "a complex interaction of learned and reinforced social, cultural, and behavioral components constituting the content of male gender role identities in the sociopolitical context of the Latino society" (Torres, Solberg, & Carlstrom, 2002, p. 167). In sum, "machismo shapes how Latin societies have been perceived by outsiders and how many Latin Americans describe their own society in relation to others" (Beattie, 2002, p. 303).

To date, much of the psychological literature on Latino masculinity has focused primarily on negative connotations of *machismo*, and research has portrayed it as a set of maladaptive characteristics in Latino men. As a result, alternative views have been neglected as Latino scholars have yet to fully examine multidimensional concepts of *machismo*. Bacigalupe (2000) states that, in the United States, the concept of *machismo* as an ideology has perpetuated negative stereotypes of Latino men. Similarly, Latino scholars have called for research to examine and reevaluate these presumed negative characteristics in order to expand beyond these one-dimensional views (Casas, Wagenheim, Banchero, & Mendoza-Romero, 1994; Mirande, 1997; Torres, 1998). Negative stereotypical characteristics of *machismo* include male dominance and chauvinism, bravado, womanizing, aggression, violence, alcoholism, emotional restrictiveness, antisocial behaviors, hypermasculinity and excessive masculinity, focus on individual power, sexual promiscuity, extreme rudeness, lower education, and less affiliation with ethnic identity (Arciniega, Anderson, Tovar-Blank, & Tracey, 2008; Casas et al., 1994; Hurtado & Sinha, 2008). Additionally, dominative and manipulative relations with women are commonly associated with both negative stereotypes and enactments of *machismo* among Latinos. For many Latino men, adhering to these characteristics and practices validates their masculinity and is central to their sense of manhood. However, Latino men who adhere to these characteristics are often placed at great psychological risk. For example, according to Pleck (1981), the term *gender role strain* refers to negative psychological consequences of attempting to live up to the demands of masculinity. Moreover, societal and cultural expectations of what it means to be a man contradict one another, often leaving men feeling ambiguous about their masculinity. Questions about one's masculinity often result in conflict-related dissonance (Pleck, 1981). For example, how should Latino men act according to the larger society? What are some Latino cultural influences on masculinity? Constructions of *machismo*, therefore, may have negative implications for the psychological well-being of Latino men.

Besides investigating negative connotations and consequences, Latino scholars have begun to explore more positive dimensions of *machismo*. For example, Mirande (1997) argued that Latino male gender roles represent dynamic and multidimensional elements that encompass a multitude of qualities that include functional and nondestructive qualities. Positive depictions of *machismo* refer to men who abide by a code of ethics and male chivalry that signifies a Spanish gentleman (Arciniega et al., 2008). According to this view, the counterpart to *machismo* is *caballerismo,* in which Latino men follow a code of ethics that emphasizes strong interpersonal and intrapersonal relations. Positive characteristics of *machismo* include protecting and providing for the family and less fortunate members of society; being family oriented; having dignity, wisdom, honor, and responsibility; showing bravery; being emotionally connected to others; being affiliated; giving and showing respect to others; having a strong connection to ethnic identity; focusing on intrapersonal interpersonal relationships; and having a higher satisfaction with life (Arciniega et al., 2008; Casas et al., 1994; Falicov, 1998; Hurtado & Sinha, 2008). Villereal and Cavazos (2005) also note that *caballerismo* can be portrayed positively through having pride in raising one's children. Wester (2008) suggests that these men are likely to consider and define their masculinity through inner qualities (i.e., integrity, honor) rather than outward qualities (i.e., physical strength) that are more associated with *machismo*. Although traditional *machismo* and *caballerismo* represent both negative and positive depictions of machismo, Latino scholars continue to expand their research in order to include more positive aspects while not rejecting negative conceptions that explain the concept of *machismo*. Additionally, Falicov (1998) argues that researchers need to explore Latino masculinities beyond traditional narrow, biased negative perspectives that currently exist.

In this chapter, we explore the experiences of masculinity and gender roles among Latino males to examine ways these men construct meanings of these important constructs and experiences. We interviewed 12 Latino men for the project, using the data analyses procedures described in Chapter 1. Eleven participants were recruited within the greater Los Angeles, California, area and one from New York City (see Table A.5 in the appendix for more information about our participants).

DEFINING MALE GENDER ROLES WITHIN A LATINO CULTURAL/FAMILY CONTEXT

Our analyses of participants' narratives reflected a core narrative of *defining male gender roles within a Latino cultural/family context* involving several themes: (a) masculinity influences, such as physical definitions, traditional gender roles, *machismo* and *caballerismo*, and stereotypes; (b) parental influences, including egalitarian relations, ethnic pride, emotional expression versus emotional restriction, and strengthening and building Latino masculinity; (c) social-cultural influences, including family and religion; and (d) developing one's own definition of being a Latino man (see also Table A.6). These themes are described in detail in the following sections.

Masculinity Influences

From the data, multiple themes of masculinity emerged as being important to what defined masculine characteristics of men and, in particular, Latino men. Although participants often identified general characteristics of masculinity separately from those of Latino masculinity, there was considerable overlap between these characteristics.

Physical Definitions and Characteristics of Latino Men

Participants often described masculinity as embodied in the physicality of Latino men. Many of these physical characteristics reflected strength, muscularity, athleticism, toughness, aggression, and dominance. For example, according to Pablo:

> A man comes out in a masculine way, they analyze, they think, and they come out with a firm way of going about stuff. A macho man to me [is] someone's got some muscles, runs around like a big, tough, like a, like a pitbull, like when you think of a pitbull, you think of something mean, tough, rough, a fighting machine. That's what I think of [as] something more masculine.

According to Carlos:

> physically speaking, [you] have to look athletic, you know, you gotta look like you take care of yourself. . . . I think the thing is, ideally, mentally speaking or educationally speaking, you also want to be the ideal of your physical appearance as well. I think it's important to take care of your body and work out and you know, be as athletic as you can be.

As Pablo and Carlos described, being a Latino man means playing the part of a "big tough guy," always ready to take on a counterpart or foe, if needed. Moreover, being ready also means staying in shape, mentally and physically, since one cannot predict when one will be called to act. In addition to general qualities, some participants, such as Gabriel, utilized very specific physical characteristics in their descriptions of a Latino man:

> I would say that a Latino man is probably at least six foot tall, black hair, slight tan, blue-collar man, hardworking man, family man, curses a lot, drinks beer, you know? Keeps his tradition, always going, teaches his kids about their own culture. . . . With a truck—El Dorado, Chevy Dorado, four doors so the family could fit in there. That's a Latino man.

Thus, some men may have a very specific image in mind that personifies a Latino man that they idealize or wish to enact. Interestingly, in addition to traditional machismo images (e.g., cursing and drinking), Gabriel also referred to teaching children about their culture, keeping them physically close by. Other characteristics identified by participants described Latino men as being "handymen" who should be knowledgeable when it comes to household maintenance and as evidenced by their fathers. In addition, industrial, technical, and mechanical knowledge were commonly identified. Diego reported:

> Growing up, my dad was very handy.... Every time he had to fix something, whether it was something in the bathroom, something with the plumbing, something with the car or something with the flooring, he would always bring me to check up also.... So that was kind of like my first real experience where I'm just like, Okay, this is a boy's thing, like I need to know this stuff.... As you hang out with your dad more or just the male figure in your life, you kind of—you start to pick up on a lot of those things.

Gabriel explained:

> The ideal man should stay in the household, get into doing things like keeping up with the yard, taking stuff that, you know, working on the wall that women may find hard to do or too dangerous for them to do. Making oil changes or mechanics where they can get hurt, something that could be too tough for [women] to do. My dad, you know, he was very handy with a lot of stuff. Okay, so this is what you do, you know, to be a man, or this is what you're supposed to do, you know? . . . like you know, there's electrical wires and, you know, fixing stuff and learning how to use big tools.

These narratives again portray images of Latino men in terms of their skills and abilities as well as their purposes for doing so—that is, teaching their sons not only how to do or fix something but also the importance of these skills in maintaining or protecting the family. In addition to physical aspects, Gabriel noted how struggle and hope were central aspects of being a Latino man:

> It starts with a struggle, so if you're Latino, you just [have] to struggle, [be] hardworking, and hope for everything you're going to have because, you know, we might make it seem like everything is handed to everybody else but not us, so in a way, we gotta pay our dues to get where we're at.

Gabriel's inspiring words reflect that, in addition to physical strength, emotional strength via realism and hope also can help keep Latino men ready to handle the many difficulties they face in life.

Traditional Gender Roles

Participants reported that ideal men are those who can provide, be responsible, and are successful. The previous category reflecting the physical nature of Latino men was linked with their need to be mentally strong and the protector of others. Hector and Jorge shared their beliefs about ideal men being providers and protectors, whereas women are nurturers and supporters. According to Hector:

> An ideal man, then, would be somebody that could provide for himself, could provide for whoever he cares for or takes care of. . . . When I think of a woman, I think of a nurturer, somebody that loves unconditionally. I think nurturer is a big one. . . . I don't think there's really a way to define an ideal woman other than one that loves because I think a woman has that capability of nurturing, of giving without expecting anything back.

Jorge said:

> The ideal man and woman . . . for me, the man, to me, is supposed to be the man's household. That means the head of the— of the house, providing with money. To pay bills. To pay, um, for clothing for his children. To help his wife, with the household . . . The man role is more muscular. That means the man should protect the family, not just for bills and so on. But the man should be there to protect his family in case of any—of anything that could happen around his family. To protect the family. The man should be the head, the foundation. Not just, um, mentally, but sometimes physically. He should protect his children and his wife . . . I believe that that is an ideal man . . . A woman is more peaceful. A woman is more gentle. A woman is there to comfort the children when they fell—when they fall, they cry. Uh, when they're hungry . . . She's the one that comes with an icepack, rub with alcohol. You know. The woman is more there to comfort the family. To support the family. To keep it together.

As both men state, the traditional roles of men and women are clear and complementary, with men presumed to be head of the household, provider, and protector, whereas women are more in a supportive role, albeit one that keeps the family together. Other participants discussed how men ought to be mentally strong, willing to act as well as to be successful. For example, Eduardo stated:

> If you want to say for me, a man that I want to be, it would be, responsible, headstrong, you know, confident, loving, caring. That's who I want to be . . . and successful in anything he puts his mind into.

He further noted:

> Pretty much a straightforward guy, you know. Like straightforward, like, you know, quick with an answer. Quick with action. You know. Very strong, you know. Appearance, being strong in appearance. Verbally. And action.

Jorge added:

> Masculine, to me, is someone with an attitude, with a strong personality, that nothing will break 'em down. That could be strong, powerful and don't give a hell about it. . . . That's masculine. . . . Um, other areas of masculine could be doing, teaching others. Other persons how to be, um, strong-minded, more, I would say more stronger than others.

Participants thus saw the physical and mental elements of manhood as being intertwined, with a common image of strength reflected in all aspects of being a man: quick and confident in thought and action. However, in addition to traditional protective functions, thought and action also incorporated love and care for others.

Machismo and Caballerismo

As we noted earlier, attitudes, beliefs, and feelings about masculinity among Latinos in particular have led to the well-known, albeit often misunderstood, construct of *machismo* and its more positive alternative, *caballerismo* (Arciniega et al., 2008). Most participants were aware of the term *machismo,* which almost all participants mentioned spontaneously, though often in fairly negative terms, sometimes as modeled by fathers and significant others. Hector told us:

> My male role model, which was my father, was a really difficult one to, to swallow only because of the whole *machismo* part

of my growing up—um—so when I think of, of those types of roles of what my father taught, a lot of times I, I end up turning away from those types of unintentional messages because it's not really something that I wanted to, to embrace per se.

Javier explained:

Within my own dad, my own father. He kind of carried the *machismo* attitude where he knew he made the rules in the house. Whatever he said went, and whenever my mom tried to overturn that, things got horrible, things, you know, he started yelling and, you know, arguments would break out, and so that's, that's kind of it, just one aspect of like the Latino lifestyle that I just never liked, I never agreed with.

And Roberto explained:

And even my dad was like that, he was a *machista*, like he had to be better than my mom. . . . He did not let my mom learn English because he thought that if she did, that she would leave him.

As these men described, as they grew up, their fathers and other important role models often enacted nearly stereotyped images of *machismo*, resulting in a negative impression regarding the impact of this role on others, particularly women, such as their mothers, whom they cared for. Ricardo related a very poignant incident with a well-regarded mentor who attempted to teach him about *machismo* by encouraging him to become sexually active:

He's like, "What you need to do is you got to get—you got to practice first. And that way—you know—with these other women, then you'll know what to do once you finally get married." And I was like "Nah, it's not worth it to me. I don't want to—I want to give my wife this gift. Be like, 'Look, I saved myself for you.' That, to me, means more than be—knowing what to do in the sack, right?" And he's like, "Listen, let me tell you something." He's like, "Every man has his cathedral and his chapel." I said, "What do you mean by that?" He's like, "You know what I mean. The cathedral is your wife. Your chapel is the girl you got on the side. Right?" In other words, trying to say that, you know, every man has a wife and a girlfriend on the side or a lover on the side, or an affair on the side, right? That that's just the way it is.

Like other participants, Ricardo simply rejected this advice and ultimately felt less respect for his mentor: "Because I didn't agree with him and I didn't like that this man that I really respected—I just kind of lost respect for him at that point." As befits the mantle of *machismo*, Ricardo's mentor was acting in what he felt were the young man's best interests, attempting to share his perspective of what it means to be a man, which included being more knowledgeable, skillful, and active than his wife in sexual relations. However, Ricardo disagreed with this lesson and had developed his own sense of what a man can best "give" his wife, his loyalty and trust, rather than the effects of a presumed skill set.

Roberto and Gabriel described the term *machismo* as they felt it was generally viewed and passed on among Latinos. Roberto said:

> They want to start fights. If the girl is looking at some other guy who's better looking than them, they always want to act tough and try to beat that guy up. They always pick on, they're always looking to start fights with someone. They think that the guys are better than the girls and the girls can't do shit and the girls' responsibility is to the household and take care of the kids, that girls are just there to have kids and to cook, clean, those types of things, and that the man should be the one being the breadwinner. That's what I think *machistas* are.

Gabriel explained:

> You know, I think *machismo* is passed on to men. I can say that a lot of friends that I know that I've visited their home when I was younger, I think their fathers were a perfect example of *machismo, machismo* was just to yell out, Hey, you know, bring me my—bring me my beer. Oh, I want my clothes done now, or go take care of the kids and don't ask me questions. Or you know, I think jealousy, jealous and insecurity could be a part of *machismo* 'cause you get to use that as a power to control your relationship.

As Roberto and Gabriel acknowledged, Latinos share expectations among themselves about what a man looks and acts like, leading some to posture to others, both men and women, that they are the ones in charge. Some participants, such as Jorge, acknowledged they were not immune to these dominative behaviors, acting in the more traditional *machismo* ways, at least for a time, though ultimately seeing the negative impact of doing so on themselves and their families:

> I have many fights in my life. When I was a gang member, um, I used—um—that, what my father taught me. To not be afraid. Uh. To fight. Um. To stab. To bumperjack somebody. To crowbar somebody. To hurt 'em. To use that much strength and power to hurt somebody. Send 'em to the hospital. Um—um. To go in front of anybody and just hit 'em. Right in the face. Um. I never jumped anybody. I had thought that fighting 101 was the best thing to do. But I think it hurt people.

Moreover, some participants noted that *machismo*, both its prevalence as a term and actual practice, was slowly disappearing in the United States among Latinos. Ricardo said:

> My definition would be like a *machista* is kind of stuck in older gender roles. I think in the United States it's dying out. . . . I still meet fellow Latino males who ascribe to this idea that men, you know, are somehow higher above the women. In Latin America, I haven't really had enough contact, but I think it could be more prevalent—more acceptable, if you will, in Latin America still. . . . I think it's dying out in the United States.

According to Gabriel:

> I think that's in the past, that's old. I don't think that nowadays the Hispanic family in today's society, it can't be like that anymore. It just wouldn't work, you know. I don't have relationships but others kind of challenge that nowadays. So I think it's slowly disappearing from the Hispanic culture, and I hope that, you know, society how people, you know, guys are wearing pink shirts and pink polos and sandals and all that, and in a way it kind of challenges the whole machismo, the whole ideal man idea that's tough. So I think those are practices that are trying to change the whole machismo thing . . . put it all in the past.

As these participants suggest, one reason for *machismo* being phased out is the current U.S. context in which men are less likely to be punished socially for violating more traditional male gender role behaviors. Another reason may be the impact of immigration to the United States on Latino family structure, with more women working outside the household in order to provide important financial support and more men helping out with household tasks as a result.

In place of traditional notions of *machismo*, many participants personally identified more with positive notions of Latino masculinity, described next. This *caballerismo* (Arciniega et al., 2008) also was learned from fathers, uncles, and other relatives. For Pablo:

> Being a Latino man personally, for me it's love, honor, and most of all respect. Not just for the familia, but friends and people and all living things, the planet. God.

For Gabriel:

> Going back to that whole side of being *macho* and all that, my dad was very patient, you know? He's a very smart man and he likes to talk things through and he never likes to argue, you know? He teaches you how to get along with people and, since we were little, he always thought that we should be very patient with everything.

Thus, as Gabriel observed, fathers and other important role models play an important role in teaching their sons a more balanced approach about being male, injecting patience and wisdom in interactions with others. Gabriel further describes other sources of *caballerismo*:

> Like when you're small, you watch cartoons and you see like Tarzan and, you know, stepping in front of the woman and trying to kill a lion and stuff like that, so you kind of see things like that, and oh okay, so that's, that's how you become a man, you know? Personal experience, you know, pretty much, I don't know how but one of my early experiences was to be like a gentleman. I would also hold the door for people and, you know, for—not just for women but for men and the older and my peers. So little things like that kind of, you know, those are the first thoughts I remember how do you, how do you learn how to become a man, you know? Just being a gentleman.

As Gabriel noted, in addition to important role models, he also learned on his own the positive impact of being kind and respectful with others. Similarly, Ricardo spoke of *caballerismo*, or gentlemanly behaviors, emanating from a reverence of others, particularly women, usually a maternal figure. He quoted song lyrics to illustrate his point:

> So, in Spanish the lyrics—one of the lyrics are "a esa mujer la venero." So, like—"That woman, I revere her." And it's a song about his mother. And the whole song is about how—how much I revere and respect this—this mother. . . . There is definitely that influence of the mother and it influencing gender roles, right? So, I do—since I revere my mother and my grandmothers. . . . The second song also refers to that and it says, "porque fue una mujer la que me dió el ser por eso te bendigo." So, "Because it was a woman that gave me life, that's why I revere you, sublime woman" or, you know, "wonderful" or "divine woman." Right? So that's what that song was about. He's talking about how much he loves and reveres women, right?

However, rather than using these beliefs to further objectify women—a common result of more traditional notions of *machismo*—Ricardo instead recognized

> the importance and the value and the role of the mother and then applying that to everyone. So this woman is somebody else's mother . . . or somebody else's sister or whatever. And that we're all related.

Thus, he expressed the more nuanced understanding of *machismo* that Latino scholars have recently called for, emphasizing interpersonal relations that are characterized by respect and love rather than dominance.

Pablo shared a story growing up in which his mother taught him the importance of one aspect of *caballerismo*, respecting others, particularly women:

> When I was like maybe three, four years old, I used to love girls. I don't know what it was about girls, but if they didn't kiss me, I'd end up biting [her] [*laughs*]. I bit this one family friend one time. . . . A horrible bite on her cheek because she wouldn't kiss me. And I was taught. I got spanked and, you know, I was taught a major lesson. My mom bit me back. And she showed me, you know, that's not right, so it's like a personal life experience that I had to be taught like, hey, you don't treat women like that, you don't touch a lady. And this is just a written rule, as well as a woman. Even if they hit you, which they're not supposed to, but if they are to hit you, you let it go. You be the bigger man.

Pablo recognized that although one can "love" girls, one must treat females with respect and gentleness. He also learned that such lessons may come from important female role models, such as his mother, in addition to significant male figures. Mirande (1997) describes his own critical encounter with the multiple dimensions of *machismo* as personified in his family, when, in full view of the family, his intoxicated uncle was physically abusing his wife. His father rushed to his aunt's help, after which the uncle grabbed a knife to use as a weapon against Mirande's father. Mirande's mother then entered the fray, coming physically between her brother and husband, saying to her brother, "How can you call yourself a man if you go around beating up defenseless women? What kind of a man needs a knife to fight an unarmed man? Put down the knife and let's see what kind of man you really are" (p. 5). Mirande learned a number of lessons about *machismo* that day, including that "one of the worst or lowest things that a man could do is to hit a woman" (p. 5). He also learned from his father that part of manhood is to stick up for those who are abused or otherwise treated unjustly. Finally, he learned that "strength of character and valor are not gendered qualities" since he could not imagine his own father hitting his mother, not only because he knew his father would not do such a thing but also because his mother would never tolerate such behavior.

Other participants described their evolution toward more nurturing, patient, or understanding ways of relating to others and accessing what they viewed as more feminine aspects of themselves. Jorge explained:

> You don't need a *machismo* man in your home. What you need is a person that does care for his family. Not a *machismo* man.

According to Diego:

> There's a balance too because, you know, even though they're taught to be masculine, they're also taught to not necessarily be sensitive, but be like sympathetic to other people because you can't be too masculine or else you're too aggressive. I think there's like a balance that you've got to find in between.

Thus, although most participants were aware of negative traits associated with Latino masculinity (usually characterized as dominative, sometimes abusive, power over others), for the most part, they identified with more positive notions of Latino masculinity, such as thinking of and putting the needs of others first. Interestingly, despite a more accepting social world, some participants acknowledged being embarrassed at showing more feminine or nurturing aspects of themselves in public, due to their concerns of how this might be viewed socially. Eduardo commented:

> You do it at home. The passive and the—you know—the caring and the loving, you do it at home. Once in a while you—But the passionate part [such as masculinity] actually is in public. Because you show "This is mine." You know? But at home you're more caring and more giving, you know. And if you sh-show that kind of stuff outside in public [*audible intake of breath*], it makes you seem a weaker person.

As Eduardo noted, the larger social world remains a tricky landscape to navigate, since others, particularly other men, may not be as willing or accepting of a more caring or attentive stance as being a part of manhood or machismo.

Perceiving Stereotypes

Cultural stereotypes of Latinas/os, particularly Latino men, also were apparent to most participants as they discussed influences on masculinity. One main stereotype was of Latinas/os as being uneducated, reflected by speaking with a Spanish accent, as Carlos stated:

> But they get upset because they had to deal with somebody with a Spanish accent, and I think that as soon as they hear the accent—and when I say "they," I'm talking about your average White American—they automatically relate that with being, they think it means uneducated, and they think it means beneath them.

Thus Latina/o people are often assailed with images of their not being educated or even having the abilities to learn in school. Another common stereotype was of Latinas/os as second-class citizens who are in U.S. society to be "the help." As Carlos said: "I don't think they see us in real definitive roles of power or decision making in government or—let's not even say government, because . . . none of them are." Jorge also commented:

> We're not—we're not in—in the tenth floor yet. From one to—to ten floors, we're probably at number four.

Immigration status was a related category of stereotypes that participants were aware of, with Latinas/os being viewed, as Javier suggested, as "invading their [Whites'] turf" and "taking the positions and jobs once held by Caucasians." Carlos parroted the comments he often heard in the media: "all those damned illegals . . . who tax our welfare system . . . our school system . . . our medical system." But as he sharply perceived: "They're not observing what's good of that cheap quote-unquote labor that comes over from Mexico . . . they're [Mexican immigrants] doing jobs that nobody else wants to do at a much lower rate of pay." Thus, in addition to being viewed as less educated, many Latinas/os are often bombarded with messages, in the media as well as through public policy and legislation, that communicate a second-class social location in the larger society. Although many participants outwardly rejected these notions, at the same time, these messages also convey a kind of vulnerability that Latinas/os continue to experience in the United States regarding their legitimacy and abilities.

Many of the participants consistently expressed two stereotypes regarding Latino men in particular. The first related to the notion of the "Latin lover." Ricardo in particular discussed this concept in terms of what he learned from the media about who Latino men were. He noted:

> You also hear that stereotype of the "Latin lover," right? So, this idea that a Latin is passionate. A Latin man you know is good at romance, whether it be physical, sexual romance or just, um, traditional, you know, romance in the more like a heartfelt sense or mind—a mind and heart and not so much body. The Latin lover is good at that. You sometimes see the Latin lover also synonymous with, uh, a womanizer, right? Someone who is promiscuous, right? Also, uh, you see the Latin male like a passionate person. You also see the stereotype of the Latin male who is passionate—also is so passionate that he's uncontrollably passionate. In other words, a hot and spicy temper. Hot-blooded. You hear that a lot. The hot-blooded Latin.

As is common with other men of color (Wyatt, 1997), Latino men have been objectified and exoticized in the larger society in a way that some Latinos themselves may attempt to enact: promiscuous, emotional, and uncontrollable. A second stereotype depicted the epitome of a traditional Latino father, as described by Roberto:

> From a cultural perspective, probably a man who has a bunch of kids, has a wife, has parties on the weekends, listens to Spanish music, drinks, but I guess that all of these are stereotypes of what a Latino man is. . . . He drives a truck.

Other stereotypes of Latino men mirrored common stereotypes of men of color in general regarding alcoholism or drug abuse, violent behaviors, and laziness. Most participants expressed strong reactions about these stereotypes as well as individuals whom they perceived as believing them, such as Whites, and typically involved intense feelings of anger, frustration, and even disgust. However, internalization of some of the stereotypes was evident in some of the participants, as was expressed in Carlos's narrative:

> Look at any Mexican and most of them—a lot of them are fat and have diabetes! [*laughs*] You know, I think it does boil down to, you know, how comfortable we are. If we're not hurting, if we're not, you know—nothing's going to try to, nothing's really going to move us out of it, that, that real [*pause*], that comfort zone. And so maybe sometimes we don't want to move beyond that. . . . I think Latinos have kind of fallen behind, and you know, it's just kind of the quote, I guess, you know the quote, It takes a village. I mean, we all do what we can in our own little, you know, in our own little village, and so I think that's . . . where it goes as far as, you know, personally what it means for me to be a Latino man.

As Carlos indicated, internalizing generations of oppression sometimes leads to blaming the victim or, in this case, one's own cultural group. What may be hard for Carlos and others to see is that living a life with minimal resources and multiple responsibilities can be linked with physical outcomes and diminished motivation. Carlos also might be confusing the effects of poverty and prejudice with what may be cultural values of focusing on the present and one's family. However, he did indicate his own willingness to somehow help other Latinos get ahead, as he used the now-common quote "It takes a village."

Parental Influences

Nearly all participants pointed to the significant impact of parents in shaping their ideas of what it means to be a Latino man. Several themes, including emphasizing egalitarian relations, instilling ethnic pride, facilitating emotional expression versus emotional restriction, and building and strengthening Latino masculinity, reflected this impact.

Egalitarian Relations between Men and Women

Despite the awareness and prevalence of *machismo* attitudes and behaviors as modeled by family members, beliefs about egalitarianism, at least in terms of the complementarity of roles, were evident across all interviews. All participants felt that men and women need to work together, whether it was in the home to pay bills or perform household chores, raise children, or keep a marriage or relationship alive, in order to create a sense of equality. These perceptions sometimes were the result of observing parents engaging in such behaviors, or their failure to do so, sometimes leading to divorce. As Pablo responded:

> But the man's role is to go to work, go make money, work hard, don't be lazy, don't be a lowlife, don't be a nobody, don't sit around waiting for something to come. You gotta go and get it. Hunt, you're like the hunting, the hunter and gatherer, that's the role of man. And for the lady, if they choose to go to work, then they can go to work. The main role is, though, if they got kids, take care of your kids, your husband, and your family. The woman's supposed to be there and play that family role. . . . Now, if the woman's working, I feel that, or what I've seen, there's gotta be some type of equality too, you know? Not just all the responsibilities being dumped on somebody just because you're male or female, there's equality.

Pablo recognized that although women's primary role is to care for children, this does not necessarily stop them from seeking work outside the home. However, as Roberto noted, not all men are accepting of women's pursuit of work beyond the household, sometimes resulting in the end of the marriage:

> Equal, I mean, you know, be able to bring the same to the table as far as money, taking care of the kids, school, education. It should be, it should be the same. A man shouldn't have to

take care of her and she shouldn't have to take care of him. It should be equal. . . . I think because my parents weren't equal or my dad didn't let my mom be equal and she wanted to be able to bring this, bring her own individuality, I guess, into the relationship, and so I think maybe that's where that started from for me, that my mom wanted to do that for herself. And now that they aren't together, that she has done that for herself, now her own individual, bought her own house without him. . . . I think on the surface, most of these things have changed. I think it's in the more healthier, more productive way now, instead of it was the girls stay at home and did all these things to the guys. It's more like now they're a team and they work together doing team goals.

Interestingly, Roberto revealed his own perspectives on gender roles, which are different from those of his father, especially for women. He described his mother's disaffection with her traditional role as wanting to "bring her own individuality" into the marriage, which he himself viewed as ultimately healthier and more productive to the family as a whole. Both Jorge and Eduardo similarly observed the increased number of women working beyond the household, acknowledging that economic realities also play a role. As Jorge explained, referring to women's roles:

Especially in this country. This country is very hard to support. Especially families of four or five. The woman needs to work, beside the men. To also help with bills, buying clothes and everything else for his family. Like, I saw my mother work hard and struggle. I learned that it's better to have the father and mother working together than just one, uh, individual.

According to Eduardo:

Women and men should actually work together, you know, in a relationship or even at where I work, it should be 50–50. You know? You both have to bust your ass. To make something work. You know. And me being in a country where—where males actually were so dominant [when I was serving in the military in the Middle East]. You know, women had to sit in the back and, you know, and I've never saw [sic] that, you know? And it was surprising to me.

As both Jorge and Eduardo observed, women working outside the home promotes the economic survival of families, particularly in the United States. Thus, both felt it was more adaptive for men to accept and work within this reality than to belittle or undermine their female partners for doing so.

Embedded within notions of egalitarianism was the notion of respect, particularly men respecting women, as Eduardo stated:

> My wife is gonna sit in the front because she is my wife. And she needs to be respected. She needs to sit in the front. You open her door. You let her go in. You know. And let her sit down. Let her get comfortable while the male puts the kids in the car and everything.

Eduardo mentioned his military experiences around the world in which he saw women often being relegated to the backseat, both in reality and metaphorically. He rejected what he saw as a second-class status for women, instead promoting the notion that women should share the front seat, if not the driving. Moreover, he viewed the previously described notions of respectfulness of men toward women as part of these equal relations.

Although most participants believed that men and women should have equal roles, many participants rejected the notion that men and women should have the *same* roles or that women should take on masculine traits or roles. Diego explained:

> Not everything is equal. Not everything—it isn't—we don't function the same way. We don't think the same way. You know, when it comes to kindergarten teachers, most of them are women. Women have a better nurture mentality, they have a better—they're softer, they're—I don't know, like I think everybody who's ever been in kindergarten comes back and say that they were women. You know, they're good with kids. It's part of the biological process, like they have kids, they have that connection with kids, and that's something that is, I think, to their advantage when it comes to like that type of situation.

Carlos stated:

> I still understand the need for a woman to, to be strong and to I guess climb out of that particular, those particular gender roles that they feel maybe sometimes imprisoned in. I don't think necessarily that it's always a bad thing. I think that maybe more

respect needs to be just given to a woman from a mass perspective, as opposed to a woman necessarily having to like change her, change herself to be more like a man.

As both Diego and Carlos observed, although equal does not mean same, women's roles are equally important and necessary for the survival of the family as men's roles. However, some participants reacted strongly to the idea of women "acting" like men or trying to subvert their unique position and responsibilities in the family and community. As Carlos noted, perhaps if women are given the recognition and respect for the work they do, they would be more accepting of and feel less vulnerable in expressing themselves in traditional feminine ways.

Instilling a Sense of Ethnic Pride

Some participants shared that while they were growing up, their parents frequently taught them about their cultural background. This sense of cultural knowledge sometimes led to more positive images of themselves as Latino adult males. Hector reported:

> Well, I'm very proud to be a Latino man, first of all. I feel that I—well, especially a Latino man in this country, because I feel that I have the best of two worlds.

Carlos told us:

> Number one, for myself as a Latino man, it's important—I have a very strong sense of, of my heritage. I'm very proud to be a Mexican or Mexican American. I think I've educated myself enough about my heritage and about my people and the society that I come from to have a lot of, you know, you know, once again just I have a lot of pride in being Mexican. . . . Getting back to being a Latino man, it's being proud of my heritage, and in a way, if I'm going to be able to kind of like, I guess, make my mark within my society or within my community of friends and family.

Latina/o scholars have long emphasized the psychological and educational importance of a sense of pride about one's racial-ethnic background. Although Latinas/os represent a great diversity of ethnicities and related cultural values, the notion of constructing a shared identity remains critical, particularly for those living in the United States. As Hector noted, having the "best of two worlds" may be an increasingly adaptive approach to negotiating one's identity. Bicultural identification does have its benefits, including positive psychological outcomes, healthy relations with one's family, and even academic achievement (Santiago et al., 2002).

Emotional Expression versus Emotional Restriction

Participants noted the differing, sometimes conflicting, influences of their mothers and fathers regarding their emotional development as men. For example, some participants discussed their abilities to be emotionally expressive as being learned primarily from their mothers. Jorge described his mother's influence:

> She taught me that being a man doesn't mean just being a hoodlum. But she taught me to understand, to help, and to bring money also, of course. . . . For the household uh—bills. And food. She taught me that the woman is the right hand of the man. She taught me that without a woman a man can't really run a household. She taught me that—she taught me to express my feelings. She taught me to understand her.

Hector similarly noted:

> I think that my mother's role gave me my, my sensitive side or what, what I sometimes refer to as my feminine side. The emotional part, the showing my feelings, and not being afraid to say what I feel or what I'm feeling about another person in my life, or, or to be able to talk to my siblings on the phone and tell them that I love them before hanging up. Those are the types of things that I feel I learned from mom, versus the total opposite with dad.

Thus, as we highlighted with Mirande's (1997) story earlier, mothers and other female relatives can play a significant role in the constructions of gender roles for Latino men. As both Jorge and Hector observed, these influences can facilitate a more nuanced understanding of the importance of feelings, particularly their open expression. Jorge and Hector learned that embracing, rather than being tacitly afraid of, one's emotions as well as their expression are major components in their ability and willingness to embrace their roles as fathers and spouses.

In contrast, many (though not all) fathers of participants taught the opposite, that displaying most emotions, except in the context of fighting, was not useful or manly. Diego said:

> I remember being raised and rolling down a hill and starting to cry. [*laughs*] And my dad told me, "Crying doesn't solve anything, stop crying, you're just making noise, it doesn't make any sense." So that was kind of, I think, one of, one of the [messages] when it came up to be, what is it to be masculine. Not because, not because it wasn't that crying didn't solve anything, because it obviously made sense because you're just making random noises. But my sister was never given that same explanation. It was okay for her to cry. It was okay for her to be emotional and, you know, cry and be sad.

Thus, both fathers and mothers can play critical, though different, roles in their sons' emotional development. Mothers may facilitate the open expression of emotions that, at times—for example, when establishing and building intimate relationships—is critical. Fathers, however, may promote the restriction of feelings, particularly in contexts involving challenge or fear. However, if young boys or men do not recognize the different contexts in which these different messages are offered, they may feel some confusion or conflict. For example, as Diego noted, he did not necessarily view the message of restricting emotion as negative, since he agreed that crying as a response to the situation did not resolve much. However, as a boy, he was confused as to why he, and not his sister, received this message.

Strengthening and Building Latino Masculinity

Besides their differing roles, mothers and fathers also can play a similar role in teaching their sons about what it means to be a man. Participants described critical incidences wherein standing up for oneself in the face of an adversary, whether it was with family members or others, became a vital point of learning, particularly in their resulting interactions with their parents. For example, Jorge shared his experiences of masculinity learned from his father through physical punishment:

> My father taught me to be masculine. And he taught me to be a fighter, don't give up. When somebody comes at you, push you, don't take it. Hit 'em back. He taught me to don't care who it is, where he's coming from, how big it is. You hit. And you hit. And

you hit. My father taught me to don't be afraid. Being afraid, in my father's vocabulary, was never there. My father wanted me to fight a giant if I have to. And if I didn't fight him he was gonna fight me. An example. One guy in New York came and took my ice cream out of my hand. And my father was looking out the window. And I saw that kid took the ice cream out of my hand. I looked up and my father was looking at me. And he was looking at me and glancing at me that I'd better get it back. If I would have never got that ice cream back, my father would have whipped me so bad upstairs that I don't know how I would have been left. And he would. Because my father was the kind of guy to go get a stick, a two-by-four, a wire, a pipe. And he'll make sure that he was getting his message through. So masculinity to me is don't be afraid of anything. And don't take anything from anyone. As to this day, I'm in some kind of way like that.

For Jorge's father, standing up to a bully became a training situation of teaching his son to react quickly, strongly, even violently, to a perceived adversary. Similarly, Hector told of the incident in which he stood up to his father as his father was about to become physically abusive with his mother:

And I stood right in front of him and I said, "This is the last day that you ever attempt to hit my mom." Um, I said, "So if you want to hit somebody, you hit me. [*pause*] And, and live the consequences, whatever they might be when you do that." I said, "Because if my mother doesn't hit back, I will." So I remember my dad telling me, "So you think you're a man now?" [*pause*] And I said, "Well, if that's what you consider being a man, being able to hit you back, then yes, I am a man now because I'm not going to allow you to do it anymore" . . . at that certain point in my life, it was really interesting to see how my dad saw me as a man with the simple fact that I was standing up to something that I believed in.

Unlike Jorge, Hector's adversary was his own father who was about to beat up his mother. His father reacted with a mixture of condescension and pride, and the incident was a memorable one for Hector in his own construction of seeing himself as a man. A third participant, Carlos, shared his experience with a neighborhood bully and the important role his mother had in shaping a presumably more masculine response to the bully:

I was walking home from school one day, elementary, and as I'm walking down the hill, halfway down the sidewalk on the hill, you could see the front porch of my house and my mom was on the front porch. And she had seen me walking down the hill, and there was some, you know, local neighborhood bully that came up to me on the sidewalk while I was walking down the street, and he just started laying into me. . . . He got into a fight with me. He started to, you know, he started to beat on me and wail on me, and he kind of had me in a chokehold, and I finally got away and I was screaming. And I saw my mom was on the front porch and I was calling for her, and she didn't—she did nothing. She didn't come and help me. But my mom walked up to me as I was walking home and the first thing that she said was like "How come you didn't fight him? How come you didn't stand up for yourself?" And I didn't know what to say. I was like I guess I've got to, you know, as a man, I gotta stand up for myself. I guess in the end, my mom was right. She couldn't always be there for me, either. And I think that was my earliest experiences where I realized that, you know, to be a man means that, you know, I need to defend myself. That's important to being a man. How to take care of yourself, how to not let people walk all over you.

Thus, both mothers and fathers can play similar roles in teaching their sons to take on a traditional role as a man. However, rather than physically demonstrating how to fight another person, Carlos's mother simply asked, "How come you didn't stand up for yourself?" staying within her more feminine role while challenging him to enact his masculine one.

Social/Cultural Influences

Participants identified two other sources of social/cultural influences in defining their gender roles: family and religion.

Role of the Family

Many participants discussed how a major aspect of being a man, particularly a Latino man, was being a family man, and that one's family should be a primary responsibility. As Diego stated:

> When it comes to the ideal man, it's definitely being family oriented and just not only being there for the income, but being there for all the other aspects of having a family, the strength at home, the discipline, you know, the life lessons. . . . But ideally, for being a Latino male, it's definitely the family orientation.

Gabriel said:

> A family man, you know? Very family oriented. Being with my family the whole time. People in traditional cultures, in my case, you know. As far as me being an ideal Latino man.

Antonovsky and Sourani (1988, in Falicov, 2009) write of the importance of a "family sense of coherence" as a way of making life "comprehensible, manageable, and meaningful" (p. 278). Falicov builds on this notion by describing the primary importance of family among Latinas/os as a way of building *"relational resilience,* those processes by which families cope and attempt to surmount persistent stress" (p. 278), as might be found among many Latina/o families, including our participants, who are struggling in the face of poverty, lack of resources, and undocumented immigration status. Moreover, as Abalos (2002) asserts, "The family is the context within which Latinas and Latinos struggle against the destructive aspects of their cultural past and an often hostile society" (p. 155). He mirrors several comments made by our participants about the intersecting roles that Latinas and Latinos can play in building their families: "Together they can create and put into practice fundamentally more loving and compassionate alternatives . . . Only relationships enacted with a creative drama of loving mutuality . . . will be able to create the kind of family necessary to meet the challenges of the twenty-first century" (p. 155). As Diego and Gabriel stated, being a family man can promote strength and discipline as well as adherence to one's cultural traditions, qualities that are all important to survival and success.

Role of Religion

Participants also discussed how the principles and beliefs of religion influenced how they defined their roles as men. Pablo shared how staying close to his religious faith helped him to follow the social prescriptions linked with being a man:

> I myself am a Roman Catholic, and we were just always taught to basically follow God and a simple request, you know, the Ten Commandments being a major thing to follow, and most of all, having self-respect because your body is your temple. . . . Basically just following God and what he asks and the teachings of the Roman Catholic church. . . . So I guess that's the main thing for men and women to follow is God.

Diego shared how the gender roles of men in the Bible are similar to those of today:

Well, I'm Christian and, you know, in Christian, you know, in church, you learned about Adam and Eve, you learned about Abraham and his wives, you learned about Cain and Abel, Noah, you know, you learned about all these men that have these roles. They are the dominating personalities, they are in charge, they are leading the way for new revolutions and everything. They never talk about the wives, but the wives' role when mentioned is to cater to them. We're taught that the husband is in charge, you know, they work for the family, you know, they work for the decision making. So, yeah, you know, religion has a lot to do with it because it's one thing that's instilled in you ever since you're little.

As Pablo and Diego noted, religious and spiritual beliefs can provide an important anchor and script for how to construct male gender roles, albeit in different ways. For Pablo, religious beliefs emphasized the importance of respecting himself and treating his body as a temple. Diego instead emphasized the traditional male role of being dominative and decision makers. Interestingly, Ricardo noted that he learned of egalitarian gender roles from the Bible:

The New Testament of the Bible, uh, really outlines what I—what I believe to be the ideal person. Not necessarily the ideal man or the ideal woman. Because really the New Testament doesn't really make a difference between the two. On occasion sometimes it'll say this is what the man is supposed to do, this is what the woman is supposed to do. But, for the most part, it's just this is what the ideal person is supposed to do. So, that—a lot of that comes from the New Testament as well.

Santiago-Rivera et al. (2002) note that religious/spiritual beliefs play a central role in the lives of most Latinas/os. However, as Pablo, Diego, and Ricardo together demonstrated, the specific impact of these beliefs can differ, depending on the messenger, the message, and the recipient. Although Diego felt he learned of more dominative expectations in his role as a man from biblical teachings, both Pablo and Ricardo felt the religious/spiritual beliefs provided important guidance about general values regarding how a person, man or woman, should act—for example, with respect.

Developing One's Own Definition of Being a Latino Man

In sifting through multiple influences and messages about Latino masculinity, many participants stated that they also had begun to construct their own ways of being a man. For example, Jorge, a survivor of childhood abuse and gang membership, stated:

> A good quality of—of being a Latino man, myself, is I have changed my life. One more time. Um—I got out of prison. I went back to school. Um—I have learned that to respect other people, that we all live in the same world. That by me being here and doing bad things is not gonna help life. It's just gonna destroy it. But by me doing good, it will help.

As Jorge noted, he survived many difficult experiences as a child and a man that initially led him down a path of destruction, both of himself and others, and he recalled many violent encounters with others. However, when reflecting on messages from his father and well as his own experiences in prison, he learned:

> A *macho* man is not the answer. But being humble and understanding the people you're having conflict with and give the hand is better than hurting them. See how can you make your enemy the best friend in your life. Because you never threw that punch. But because you understood him. And because you gave him that hand. To pick him up when he fell. And that's what I learned . . . sometimes it's best to understand than act. And walk away.

Surviving these experiences gave Jorge a chance to change his views of what being a man meant. Similarly, Eduardo, a military veteran, also spoke of lessons he had learned on his own. For example, he observed the negative impact of his father on himself and his relationships with others, such as his daughter:

> My father said never marry another race. And it was constantly pounded into me. [*Audible intake of breath*.] And it came down to the point where—where am I gonna listen to my dad or am I gonna see my [own] point of view?

Eduardo stated that, even though he had married a non-Latina woman, he ended up with similar views as his father about interracial marriage. However, he believes he will simply express his views to his daughter as a means to protect her rather than attempt to force them on her:

> Now if she decides to actually, you know, marry outside her—of her culture or race or whatever, then that's fine with her. As long as she's happy. You know? But I'm gonna tell her . . . some of the consequences that you have to look forward in the future. I'm not gonna tell her not to. But I'm gonna tell her, "These are the consequences."

Finally, Javier expressed his own evolved views on *machismo* and what it means to be a Latino man:

> If you know you're a man and, and you can prove it to others, there's no need for you to use force or there's no need for you to use fear or just any kind of method to kind of show yourself to other people that you have the power . . . a man knows what he has and knows what he is and doesn't have to prove it to anybody. . . . I really don't associate being masculine with like, Oh, well, what kind of hobbies do you have? You like to fix cars, you like to watch football games. No, because there are men out there who have other interests, but it doesn't mean that makes him less of a man, they're still masculine.

Abalos (2002) has written extensively about transforming traditional definitions of masculinity among Latino men as a way of opening up new ways of viewing themselves and others and exploring possible varieties of expression, both masculine and feminine, in order to live fuller lives. Abalos strongly believes that "Latino men have it within their capacity to go beyond the inherited traditional stories of patriarchy and uncritical loyalty that leave them partial selves. They need their own selfhood, the ground from which they can bring forth the fundamentally new and better" (p. 3). As Jorge, Javier, and Eduardo all have shown, renegotiations and reconstructions of male gender roles that both incorporate and transcend the traditional are not only possible; they are necessary.

APPLICATIONS FOR MENTAL HEALTH PROFESSIONALS AND EDUCATORS

Our participants' poignant stories as well as their personal transformations as they learned many lessons in life yield important applications for both mental health professionals and educators. These center on developing positive body images, constructing gender roles that are positive and in balance, and negotiating healthier relationships.

Developing Positive Body Images

It was clear from our interviews that many if not most participants were comfortable with, even proud of, their physical sense of being male. Participants felt that, in particular, their strength and athleticism provided an important and unique contribution to the family structure and the larger society and helped prepare them for their roles as provider and protector. As a result, it would be important for educators to provide learning opportunities to increase the potential for Latino boys and young men to begin to articulate and develop a positive body image, particularly in enhancing their sense of strength, quickness, and agility. For example, Mora (2012) explored body image and masculinity among a group of 11-year-old Latino boys and found that tough strong bodies were highly valued among these children. He also found that these boys were very concerned about not being fat (what they called "flubber"), since muscularity is considered a sign of bodily control, an important aspect of urban minority neighborhoods in which the male body is viewed as a type of weapon. In sum, Mora found "how the boys, as U.S.-born Dominicans and Puerto Ricans residing in low-income neighborhoods, constructed their masculine identities while seeking to abide by the dominant gender expectations in localized social worlds and the norms from their countries of origin" (p. 455).

Moreover, such a focus might prove an effective framework for health promotion activities, not only for students but for Latino men of all ages. Opportunities for Latinos with disabilities to develop positive body images, including those disabilities that arise as a result of bodily traumas, illness, or aging, also will be critical for educators and health professionals to provide, perhaps focusing on how physical traits might be enhanced for men with disabilities (i.e., help develop personal definitions of strength, speed, and agility). For example, in their study of the link between health behaviors and masculinity, Munoz-Laboy et al. (2012) found that moving from a "knucklehead" to "street smart" cognitive framework was helpful for their sample of formerly incarcerated Latino males to begin to engage in fewer high risk behaviors. Mental health professionals similarly might focus their clinical work on how boys and men perceive their bodies, with an emphasis on developing positive images, and identifying important individuals in their lives that either support or deflect from this evolution.

Constructing Positive Balanced Gender Roles

Nearly all participants spoke of what they had learned about masculinity within the context of *machismo*, reflecting on its negative impact (i.e., dominative, even coercive, power over others). An important correlate of this construct was aggression and toughness, particularly in the stance of protector and fighters. Many participants viewed this latter aspect as something to continue to promote and maintain in themselves and others, given its vital role to the overall family.

However, although participants felt that toughness was critical to their sense of manhood, so was their ability to relate to others, be responsible, and be caring and respectful, particularly with women. Fathers played significant roles in constructing gender role attitudes, as did mothers, but in different ways. Fathers provided a basis for becoming an effective protector (i.e., how to fight) but also unfortunately sometimes demonstrated the negative, even abusive, aspect of this stance. Moreover, mixed messages about the importance of expressing feelings (expression versus restriction) were common for many of the young men, with mothers often encouraging freer expression of emotions, though within the traditional roles of their sons as providers.

Thus, both educators and mental health professionals must be aware of the sometimes confusing and conflicting expectations that may be at play for young boys and men. Providing classroom and clinical activities that allow for the articulation of these messages, as well as important incidents that highlight the impact of the messages, will help identify potential areas in need of further clarification and resolution. Such activities will allow boys and young men to see the complexities and nuances of what it means to be a Latino man in today's world. Mora's (2012) study of Latino boys during puberty demonstrates how multiple messages in the social world (e.g., the male physique as a weapon) shaped these youths' gender role attitudes as their bodies began to transition into manhood.

Many participants shared the harsh realities of witnessing their fathers being abusive with both their wives and their children. As a result, participants reported that they internalized what was happening by attempting *not* to follow in their fathers' footsteps, leading sometimes to greater confusion and self-doubt as well as the construction of their own definition of manhood. These early experiences played a role with how many participants came to define themselves within the context of *machismo*, instead taking on more positive alternatives to manhood that emphasized respect, responsibility, and caring for others. In Serrano's (2012) study of a group therapy intervention for Latino men who had been mandated to seek counseling as a result of intimate partner violence, he found that gender role stress arising from attempting to enact traditional expectations of Latino masculinity played a role in risks for such violence, even though participants were unwilling to let go of these expectations. As with our participants, Serrano found that his participants used multiple definitions and images of Latino masculinity, including "*de respeto* (of respect), *recto* (straight), *firme* (firm), and *don* (sir)" (p. 63). He interpreted these findings as indicating that Latino masculinity represented "not a single characteristic but a spectrum of behaviors that males demonstrate which are assigned meaning by the social and familial structure (p. 63)."

Serrano (2012) recommends using structured psychoeducational approaches with Latino men that incorporate discussions of masculinity as well as the roles of husband and father. Exploring Latino men's definitions of manhood and masculinity also may play a role in their potential for academic achievement. For example, in her study of Latino males and their involvement in academic bridge programs (or lack thereof), Glenn (2012) found themes that reflect "how the participants' scholar identity is connected to their masculine identity, how they balance their 'coolness' quotient with their desires to achieve academic success, how they depend on personal relationships and collaboration, and how their families and communities have influenced them" (p. i). Thus, normalizing alternative definitions of *machismo*, even helping boys and young men redefine their gender roles as Latino men within these alternative frameworks, will be critical for young people to continue on a constructive life path.

Developing Healthy Relationships with Others

In keeping with more positive alternatives to Latino manhood, redefining relationships within the family, especially with spouses and children, will be an important area of emphasis for educators and mental health professionals. Most of our Latino participants were supportive of women having a more equal role or say within the family and recognized the unique context Latino families were in, as a result of immigrating to the United States. However, traditional enactments of Latino masculinity involving restriction of emotions sometimes may keep men from being able to communicate effectively with their partners, even as they attempt to work together for the family. For example, Serrano (2012) found that in his sample of Latino men who had engaged in intimate partner violence, many were interested in communicating better with their spouses but had not yet learned the skills to do so. Instead, prior to coming to group therapy, escalation into confrontation and a battle of wills was a more common scenario. Serrano found that what he called Collaborative Couple Communication involving the monitoring of emotions during dialogue helped men and their partners become better able to deescalate rising tensions during a confrontation.

Despite more flexible notions of masculinity and gender roles in general, most of our participants did not necessarily view equality of roles as meaning *similarity* of roles. Thus, it is critical for both educators and mental health professionals to be aware of this distinction and develop activities and interventions that affirm and promote equality between boys and girls and between men and women. Such activities and interventions also may need to affirm multiple roles and role expressions between and among women and men. That is, given more modern developments of the family structure within the past decades, it is critical to normalize the fact that traditional as well as nontraditional family structures exist and that children can grow up well in a variety of structures.

Abalos (2002) takes this suggestion a step further and calls for a radical transformation of gender roles among Latinas/os in the context of relationships, contending that rather than being at odds with each other, men and women need to "create mutually more loving relationships that heal the wounds and release the repressed energies within" (p. 167). By doing so, men and women both can finally "become whole—not perfect or finished but whole (p. 167)." Abalos further asserts that "men and women can create marriages and families in which Latino men nurture the feminine and masculine in themselves and Latina women nurture their masculinity and femininity as coequal dimensions of their humanity" (p. 169). Thus, Abalos calls for relations between men and women that are both conscious of the multiple oppressive forces from without that can put great pressure on effectively co-creating a family structure characterized by mutuality rather than dominance/submission and transformative in that they can help each other and their children find meaning in their lives and become strong enough to complete the necessary tasks for doing so, particularly within *la comunidad Latina* (the Latina/o community).

REFERENCES

Abalos, D. T. (2002). *The Latino male: A radical redefinition.* Boulder, CO: Lynne Rienner.

Arciniega, G. M., Anderson, T. C., Tovar-Blank, Z. G., & Tracey, T.J.G. (2008). Towards a fuller conception of machismo: Development of a traditional machismo and caballerismo scale. *Journal of Counseling Psychology, 55*(1), 19–33.

Bacigalupe, G. (2000). El Latino: Transgressing the macho. In M. T. Flores & G. Carey (Eds.), *Family therapy with Hispanics: Toward appreciating diversity* (pp. 29–57). Needham Heights, MA: Allyn & Bacon.

Beattie, P. M. (2002). Beyond machismos: Recent examinations of masculinities in Latin America. *Men and Masculinities, 4*, 303–308.

Casas, J. M., Wagenheim, B. R., Banchero, R., & Mendoza-Romero, J. (1994). Hispanic masculinity: Myth of psychological schema meriting clinical consideration. *Hispanic Journal of Behavioral Sciences, 16*, 315–331.

Falicov, C. J. (1998). *Latino families in therapy: A guide to multicultural practice.* New York, NY: Guilford Press.

Falicov, C. J. (2009). Ambiguous loss: Risk and resilience in Latino immigrant families. In M. M. Suarez-Orozco & M. M. Paez (Eds.), *Latinos: Remaking America* (pp. 274–288). Berkley: University of California Press.

Fry, R., & Lopez, M. H. (2012, August 20). Hispanic student enrollments reach new highs in 2011. *Pew Hispanic Center.* Retrieved from http://www.pewhispanic.org/2012/08/20/hispanic-student-enrollments-reach-new-highs-in-2011/

Glenn, K. (2012). *Hispanic males and AVID: Who are they?* (Unpublished doctoral dissertation). Tempe: Arizona State University.

Gonzalez, J. (2000). *A history of Latinos in America: Harvest of empire.* New York, NY: Viking Press.

Hurtado, A., & Sinha, M. (2008). More than men: Latino masculinities and intersectionality. *Sex Roles, 59,* 337–349.

Mirande, A. (1997). *Hombres y machos: Masculinity and Latino culture.* Boulder, CO: Westview Press.

Miville, M. L. (2006). Hispanic Americans. In Y. Jackson (Ed.), *Encyclopedia of multicultural psychology* (pp. 224–230). Thousand Oaks, CA: Sage.

Miville, M. L. (2010). Latina/o identity development: Updates on theory, measurement, and counseling implications. In J. G. Ponterotto, J. M. Casas, L. A. Suzuki, & C. M. Alexander (Eds.), *Handbook of multicultural counseling,* 3rd ed. (pp. 241–251). Thousand Oaks, CA: Sage.

Mora, R. (2012). "Do it for all your pubic hairs!": Latino boys, masculinity, and puberty. *Gender & Society, 26,* 2012, 433–460.

Munoz-Laboy, M., Perry, A., Bobet, I., Bobet, S., Ramos, H., Quinones, F., & Lloyd, K. (2012). The "knucklehead" approach and what matters in terms of health for formerly incarcerated Latino men. *Social Science and Medicine, 74,* 1765–1773.

Pleck, J. (1981). *The myth of masculinity.* Cambridge, MA: MIT Press.

Santiago-Rivera, Azara. (2003). Latino values and family transitions: Practical considerations for counseling. *Counseling and Human Development, 35,* 1–12.

Santiago-Rivera, A., Arredondo, P., & Gallardo-Cooper, M. (2002). *Counseling Latinos and la familia: A practical guide.* Thousand Oaks, CA: Sage.

Serrano, R. (2012). *Intimate partner violence and group therapy: The voices of Latino men* (Unpublished doctoral dissertation). Los Angeles, CA: Pepperdine University.

Torres, J. B. (1998). Masculinity and gender roles among Puerto Rican men: A dilemma for Puerto Rican men's personal identity. *American Journal of Orthopsychiatry, 68,* 16–26.

Torres, J. B., Solberg, V. S. H., & Carlstrom, A. H. (2002). The myth of sameness among Latino men and their machismo. *American Journal of Orthopsychiatry, 72,* 163–181.

U.S. Census Bureau. (2012, August 6). Hispanic Heritage Month 2012: Sept. 15–Oct. 15. *U.S. Census Bureau News.* Retrieved from http://www.census.gov/newsroom/releases/pdf/cb12ff-19_hispanic.pdf

Villereal, G. L., & Cavazos, A. (2005). Shifting identity: Process of change in identity of aging Mexican-American males. *Journal of Sociology and Social Welfare, 32*, 33–41.

Wester, S. R. (2008). Male gender role conflict and multiculturalism: Implications for counseling psychology. *Counseling Psychologist, 36*(2), 294–324.

Wyatt, G. E. (1997). *Stolen women: Reclaiming our sexuality, taking back our lives.* New York, NY: Wiley.

Chapter Five

LATINA GENDER ROLES
Lucinda Bratini, Marilyn C. Ampuero, and
Marie L. Miville

In addition to experiencing the history of Latinas/os described in Chapter 4, Latinas also share similar cultural expectations regarding the values and importance of gender roles in maintaining families and *la comunidad Latina* (the Latina/o community). As with Latino men, women's gender roles are heavily drawn from religious/spiritual influences, including Judeo-Christian, indigenous, and African traditions. For example, many Latinas/os revere the Catholic figure of *la Virgen María* (the Virgin Mary), or Mother of God, who is believed to have made miraculous appearances throughout the world, especially in areas ravaged by poverty, war, and disease (Santiago-Rivera, Arredondo, & Gallardo-Cooper, 2002). Many Latinas/os daily practice devotional rituals to *la Virgen* and other religious figures and patrons, even building small altars in their homes to call on the spirit of these figures for protection, strength, and support. It is thus not surprising that many, if not most, Latinas aspire to enact through their gender roles the very qualities that are the hallmark of *la Virgen*, including purity, self-sacrifice, endurance, and maternity/nurturance.

The term *marianismo* describes female gender role expectations of Latinas who generally are perceived by most Latinas/os as "virtuous and humble, yet spiritually stronger than men" (Santiago-Rivera et al., 2002, p. 49). *Marianismo* also is considered to be the counterpart to Latino male gender roles as signified by both the negative and positive qualities of *machismo*. Together, both *marianismo* and *machismo* prescribe socially acceptable behaviors for women and men to enact what may be summed as "a man's place is *en el mundo*, in the world, and a woman's place is *en la casa*, in the home" (Gil & Vazquez, 1996, p. 6). More plainly, men (especially fathers, brothers, and husbands) traditionally give the orders, and women are expected to obey them.

In the now-classic book *The Maria Paradox*, Gil and Vazquez (1996) outlined 10 commandments associated with *marianismo*. These commandments are framed in the language of unacceptable behaviors, which, if they are actually followed, paradoxically may lead to a number of negative psychological and educational consequences. Gil and Vazquez contend that Latinas are often exhorted by their parents, spouses, extended family members, and religious leaders *not* to do the following: forget a woman's place; forsake tradition; be single, self-supporting, or independent-minded; put their own needs first; wish to be more than a housewife; have sex for pleasure; be unhappy with their husband, no matter what he does; ask for help; discuss personal problems outside the home; and, most important, change. For example, not discussing personal problems outside the home is considered an important component of respecting the family's privacy. However, this also can lead to Latinas struggling alone in a dysfunctional web of family relations instead of seeking much-needed solace or support. Although many Latinas have mothers, aunts, sisters, cousins, or lifelong friends they might count on in times of trouble, the cultural prescription to protect family privacy may dissuade them from seeking help beyond their inner circle, potentially shutting out new and different ways of conceptualizing and solving a problem. Following these so-called commandments ensures that a Latina will be perceived by others as *una buena mujer* (a good woman); not doing so can lead to sharp negative criticism, leading one to be viewed as *una mala mujer* (a bad woman) or, worse, a *malinche* (traitor) and even a *lesbiana* (Latina lesbian) (Gloria & Castellanos, 2013).

Gloria and Castellanos (2013) suggest that, despite continuing expectations for Latinas to follow old traditions about how they should behave, today Latinas are transforming many archaic images and expectations into new ones. For example, they assert that Latinas have converted the image of *la malinche* to *la mujer radical,* a radical woman and a spiritual survivor, "through personal stories and intuitive abilities to understand . . . invisible and parallel spiritual processes" (p. 175). The processes of transforming old images into new empowered ones, both individually and collectively, is important for promoting mental well-being, since like other women of color in the United States, Latinas have been marginalized and exoticized in the larger society. As Arrizon (2009, in Gloria & Castellanos, 2013) contends,

"Latina sexuality and its representative 'brown' body [have become] the product of objectifying stereotypical processes" (p. 176). At the same time, many Latinas are now working outside the home, both for economic reasons as well as their own career interests. Thus, learning to negotiate the traditional roles of promoting family functioning and cultural survival without losing the self in the process may be a key aspect of constructing gender roles for Latinas in today's complex society.

This chapter seeks to understand the meanings that Latinas today construct about gender and gender roles. We interviewed 10 Latinas living in the United States, using the data analytic procedures outlined in Chapter 1. Participants were residents of either New York City or California, where the authors reside (see Table A.7 in the appendix for more demographic information about our participants).

LATINAS IN PROCESS OF TRANSFORMATION AND NEGOTIATION

A core narrative of how Latinas experience and understand gender and gender roles emerged from our analyses, *Latinas in the process of transformation and negotiating roles*, and encompassed three key themes: (a) Latina socialization, (b) identity constructs, and (c) from internalized ideals to one's own values (see also Table A.8). First, *Latina socialization* refers to some of the contextual factors implicated in Latinas' experiences, including many socializing institutions and agents that play a major role in learning gender roles and gendered expectations: the American or mainstream U.S. culture, Latino/a cultures and communities, religion, media and pop culture, as well as work and school settings. Latina socialization also incorporates some of the direct and indirect messages participants heard about what it means to be Latina. Participants described messages related to cultural expectations as essential to being socialized about Latina roles. Cultural expectations included notions of *respeto* (respect) toward men or male figures, ideas around submissiveness, "ladylike" physical and behavioral attributes, and notions around Latina endurance, which we termed "superwoman." Moreover, many participants wrestled to distinguish cultural values and expectations from Latina/o stereotypes. Participants seemed to point to various intersections of social categories of race, social class, and sexual orientation as they described some expectations and/or stereotypical views of Latina roles.

A second major theme was the intersections of *identity constructs* that included gender identity and racial-cultural identity in their relation to gender roles and gendered politics. The third theme, *from internalized ideals to my own values*, involved an engaged process of change or shifts from internalized received societal ideals to the construction of their own views and perspectives. Part of this process involved changes in values, critical questioning of gendered expectations, and transformations to definitions of gender roles. The next sections describe the three themes involved in the core narrative of Latinas in the process of negotiation illustrated by direct quotations of participants. Although we present categories as distinct aspects of the narrative of Latina gender roles, there is great overlap among these themes; they are presented separately for the purposes of description and simplification.

Latina Socialization

Socializing Agents

Participants identified several elements related to their gender role socialization, including a number of institutions through which they learned powerful lessons about gender and gender roles. Latina participants openly pointed to the social-relational contexts in which they were taught about the meaning of being girl/woman or boy/man. The majority spoke in detail of "society's views" as well as family lessons about gendered behaviors and expectations. Primary socializing agents included U.S. or mainstream society; families of origin, especially parents; religious institutions; academic and work settings; the media and popular culture; and peer relationships. Many participants emphasized the traditional or conventional lessons received about gender roles through their interactions with these socializing institutions.

Julie, a biracial (Puerto Rican and African American) 19-year-old lesbian, described some of her experiences and interpretations of societal views about gender and gender roles. At the time of our interview, she was a social work intern at a public hospital clinic working with older Latina/o clients and spoke very passionately about her cross-cultural experiences. As she defined her understanding of ideal notions of gender, she made differentiations between "society's views" versus "my ideal." Julie's distinctions between these messages convey her understanding that she was aware of socially prescribed gender roles that differed from her own evolving views.

Mercedes, a 46-year-old Peruvian psychologist, also shared her perspective about socialization. She stated, "I mean you learn, but at least you heard from society that that's supposed to be" a certain way, even as she provided her own definition of ideal notions of gender. Carolina, a Mexican American 30-year-old, relayed a very thoughtful perspective as she critiqued society's impact on gendered expectations. She discussed institutional rules and restrictions impacting women's experiences:

> One of the things that I feel is very frustrating is the method of birth control. I think that it's really frustrating that, you know, women have to pay out of their pockets . . . for birth control. I think that it's a shame that scientists are trying to find a way to prevent pregnancy for women, but there really isn't anything out there for men, and then whatever is out there for men, you know, the percentage is low and it's cheap, and it's easy to access. If a woman wants to get some type of birth control, she has to go to her physician and she has to be examined and then, you know, insurance?

Carolina critiqued the gender differences in the means, availability, and costs of birth control, noting that these are unfair toward women in their efforts to control how and when pregnancy may occur. She noted that women must consult with and be examined by a doctor, whereas men can simply buy something cheaply at a local convenience store. This specific example highlights for Carolina the different impact and ultimate message about gender roles between men and women in the larger society: Women have less access to convenient methods of birth control and more restrictions regarding their basic bodily functions.

Along these lines, some participants pointed to the role of *popular culture* as they discussed societal views. Glenis, a 30-year-old Dominican American working at a Latina/o-serving nonprofit organization, suggested that the media played a major role in her socialization:

> The first place is home and the second place is television. I mean . . . whatever you learn at home and whatever you learn from the television is what's imprinted in your mind.

She spoke very openly about some of the messages that she realized she had internalized from television sitcoms and films. For instance, when asked about ideas related to the embodiment of masculinity and femininity, she described images learned from Latina/o soap operas:

> I immediately got two Hispanic soap opera guys in my mind.... I think they're both Mexican and ... macho or whatever. He has like greaser hair, which is like his hair is probably oiled back in a ponytail, big muscular, like he's been working out, just big and muscular, and um [*pause*] and ... like the native Mexican skin tone.

Later on in her interview, Glenis identified some of the differences between Latina/o media images and U.S. media images. Throughout the course of the interview, she often laughed in amusement or disbelief as she recognized the impact of such socialization. Glenis was very transparent about her experience and related very comfortably to the interviewer. She demonstrated great insight about her socialization process, as she labeled herself a "conformist" and questioned her interpretation of her experiences.

Johanna spoke on the impact of U.S. popular culture and the *media* when it comes to American socialization. She explained:

> I'm a huge fan of *Sex and the City*. I love that show because that was me for quite some time. You know, I related so much to that when I was growing up. I mean, I was like ten years younger than they were when they were doing what they were doing, but [*laughs*] you know, I thought there was, you know, the one girl who really wanted to get married and that was partly me. Then there was the one girl who was very career-oriented and that was partly me too. So I identified with—you know, there were four separate women but I identified with each and every one of them [in] at least one aspect of their lives.

As Johanna suggested, she was able to identify with each of the Anglo-American characters in the TV show *Sex and the City*, absorbing the messages that it was acceptable to pursue a career as well as enjoy personal relationships of one's own making rather than to having relations to meet familial expectations. However, the role of the U.S. media in reinforcing traditional gender roles of women *en la casa* (in the home) and men (*en el mundo*) also was evident, as Eliza, a 30-year-old Mexican American woman, noted:

> I think growing up watching like *The Brady Bunch*, *The Partridge Family*, *Growing Pains*, like those kind of things, uh—even like, uh—*The Wonder Years*— you see that. The mom is always in the kitchen, always cooking or always cleaning or picking up after her kids. And then, the husband was always coming home from work. So I think it did kind of show you—or teach you, in a sense, that the woman should be home and the husband should be working type of thing.

These images further drove home the message regarding gendered restrictions about what is socially acceptable for women and men to do. Still other participants, like Eliza, added that other media sources reinforced these traditional roles, including "the Internet . . . the magazine[s]. They show you a cover with this ideal family: mother, father, child." Xiomara, a 19-year-old Mexican American college student, added "music videos" to the list.

However, Julie did not relate to these traditional images, saying

> I'm not really into like—not that all girls are into pop culture. But like, I don't really care for fashion.

Instead, she spent most of the interview discussing some of the cultural lessons within her *family* about gendered expectations. For instance, she shared:

> I think growing up, I spent a lot of time with my mother's side of the family. She's Puerto Rican and just the whole like women serving men.

Julie highlighted the significant role that family of origin plays socializing girls and boys regarding their presumed roles. As she spoke about the dominant images of men and women, she said:

> That image definitely came from my family as well, mostly my family. As well as observation. Just like uh, you know, you grow up and they teach you gender related, um, you know, well, it starts with the whole like girls have to play with dolls, guys have to play with GI Joes.

Julie identified her mother as someone who played a strong role in her gender role socialization. She stated: "My parents are, my mom is . . . she's very big on fashion and dressing like a girl." She also identified her aunts and uncles as models of men and women.

Glenis interpreted the role of her family experiences very differently:

> I'm still seeing it as males being more dominant than the females, which is interesting because I don't know where I get that from, living in a like female-dominated home. Or maybe because I live in a female-dominated home.

Nonetheless, the majority of participants agreed that, as Lorena, a 43-year-old Domincan woman who immigrated to the United States, stated, *"la crianza que le dieron a uno"* (the rearing one received) played a dominant role in the learning of gendered expectations. She also said that religion and religious teachings remained significant as well: *"Para mi, primeramente el hombre ideal es el hombre que tiene conocimientos Cristianos."* (For me, first and foremost the ideal man is a man that knows the ways of Christianity.)

As both Julie and Glenis suggested, family was a primary socializing influence in how they learned about gender roles, even in family structures where women dominated. Glenis also noted the major impact of religion as communicating what she saw was a major characteristic of men, knowing spiritual beliefs and ways.

Finally, a few participants also highlighted the role of *educational and work settings* on their gender role socialization. Mercedes captured this theme very vividly, sharing a touching childhood story:

> When I was a child, I was kind of like very outspoken. . . . And because of that, I always had troubles, I always end[ed] up in the principal's office . . . the teacher was kind of worried that I would end up kind of being—I don't know, masculine or something. So they called my parents and they had a meeting, with good intentions . . . I always end up getting in trouble. I don't know if it's because the fear was that I end up being a boy or that I end up being aggressive, like a troublemaker . . . so they kind of decided that I should go to more feminine activities.

As Mercedes shared this anecdote and its impact on her gender socialization, she seemed to find humor and understanding in it as well as make sense of her current gender identity. Mercedes recognized that she was silenced as a girl by school officials who were fearful that her outspoken nature would be seen as too masculine or male-like in the larger society. Consequently, her teacher had her engage in activities that were deemed more feminine and thus more socially acceptable. Mercedes learned to use her assertiveness in different ways as she grew up. For example, at the time of this interview, she worked as a mental health professional within an alternative-to-prison program for men in a very poor urban neighborhood.

Carolina expressed a similar understanding of gender role socialization. She related that individuals learn important lessons in the social milieu: "The people that they're surrounded by every day, the people that they work with, whether it's a coworker, whether it's a client." She added:

> I think there's teachers and there's mentors, and it could be someone in your local church. It could be your neighbor. It could be your friends or the parents of your friends.

Like Glenis, Eliza agreed that

> depending on the kind of friends that you have growing up, you might get . . . ideas to see from others how they are treated at home or the things that maybe their dad does that maybe your dad doesn't do or stuff like that.

Messages about Gender

Participants also discussed the ways in which they learned about gender roles and expectations. Although they mainly highlighted indirect messages, they also mentioned direct as well as mixed or conflicting messages. These messages were received from both U.S culture relayed through media portrayals as well as through opportunities for play (e.g., toys) and work within their own ethnic communities, especially family members and parents. Modeling seemed to play an immense role in participants' gender socialization, as did the overt differences in the actual rearing practices of boys and girls. For example, Julie described learning about gender roles:

> It wasn't really so direct. It was modeled. . . . Yeah. It didn't really become direct. I think just watching my aunts growing up—my aunts and my mother.

Thus, for Julie, observing other female relatives provided important lessons about how she was expected to behave. Xiomara also illustrated the importance of modeling and observation as she shared childhood stories. She suggested:

> I feel like secretly she's telling me [*laughs*] you're the woman so don't forget that. You have certain limitations to you. . . . Or like I see at home how, when I was 14, 15, I couldn't go out with my friends because, oh no, something might happen. I mean, I see my brother now, he's 15, and he's out at the movies, he's always at the park, he's going everywhere. . . . So it's like, What are you saying? Because I'm female, I can't do certain things because I'm not as smart as my brother or what?

To Xiomara, learning about her female gender role emphasized what she was not allowed to do or be, with fear used as a means to ensure these limitations. She saw differential treatment of her brother, who was granted greater access to the world by her parents. Glenis, who was raised by a single mother, shared how she learned about gender roles by observing the behaviors and interactions of others, mainly other families. She explained:

> Seeing it from just friends, like there's the male figure and he's the one that's in charge, he's the one that's taking care of the house, even though the mom is out there doing her own thing at the end of the day.

As Glenis noted, she observed both what female relatives did not do as well as what male relatives did, particularly in identifying leadership and decision-making responsibilities.

In addition to observation, Julie also talked about receiving very direct messages about appropriate behaviors and expectations. She suggested that throughout the course of her development, her mother's messages about gender role expectations changed. She stated:

> Actually, as I got older it became more direct. Um—and I would be all right with just modeling. . . . When I started to kind of like rebel. . . . Especially even now, to this day, it's like I, a few years ago I cut my hair really short and my fam—my family is very honest and it's just like "No." And it wasn't even boy short, like how I wanted it. But it was too short. My mom was like the biggest deal in the world. My uncle called me radical . . . and that I was getting

a little out of control. . . . I wear sneakers a lot, like all the time. Um. You know, I was at my cousin's house and his girlfriend was over. And she dresses nice. Nicely. My uncle was like "You know, you should try to wear some nice shoes like she has."

As Julie poignantly noted, messages about gender role expectations, particularly restrictions for girls and women, became stronger and more direct as she grew older, with even the length of her hair and choice of clothing becoming a focus of control by her family. Besides her mother, her extended family, such as her uncle, became involved, contrasting Julie's gender role expression with her cousin's girlfriend, which was deemed as acceptable and "nice."

Mercedes and Xiomara recalled receiving mixed and conflicting messages from their parents. Mercedes shared some of the endearing conversations she enjoyed having with her father as a young girl. She described him as the parent who most influenced her educational and career aspirations:

> My father told me . . . that, or he thought that girls usually don't like to be professionals because probably they have some troubles learning, especially mathematics. Women don't go to engineering careers or for to be a doctor because it's kind of harder to understand things, so he made sure that we got some tutors, so when we were in the age when we could make a decision of what we want to be, we wouldn't only choose what traditional female uh choices. . . . And he wanted to make sure that also when we are adults, um, we were able to support ourselves, be economically independent. And if we had an abusive partner, we wouldn't need him to support us to do our lives. So that's what he told us. I want you to have your career.

Mercedes's father played an influential role in how she viewed both her academic abilities and her career aspirations. On one hand, he told her that women might not have the same abilities for science and engineering professions, but on the other hand, by hiring tutors, he communicated that it was still important for girls and women to pursue an education and career as a means of self-protection and survival. Mercedes also spoke of learning from her mother's modeling:

> from my mom was, yes, it was maybe a more passive way to do. You have to, to do your good things that you have to do.

She described her mother as a stay-at-home wife and caretaker.

Racial-Cultural Expectations

Many participants discussed some of the specific cultural expectations around gender and gender roles learned through socializing experiences within Latino/a communities as well as U.S culture. Xiomara discussed the differences between the expectations Latinas/os must live up to in comparison to those of White Americans. She pointed to some of the intersections between race-culture and gender role expectations:

> Like oh, I feel pressure. And my friends are all Black and Hispanic, so I don't. . . . I feel like because they've [Whites] always been the dominant race . . . they've never been too pressured as to what they should be.

Respeto to the Provider

A few of the women in this sample of Latinas discussed notions of *respeto* (respect) as an essential value within Latino cultures. According to Julie, within Latino cultural patterns, masculinity, strength, and "respect" are strongly linked. She described the man's role:

> Just being able to control, you know, your family and have the upper hand and everything. And—um—that's a huge thing, I think. Having—being able to have your family members respect you is a really big [thing]. Not even just the fam—but just having—getting respect, being respected. A huge thing. In my culture.

Julie expressed strong feelings of anger as she discussed the meaning of women's roles as being viewed as "less than" when compared to men. This mixture of cultural messages and accompanying feelings is a major source of conflict for many Latinas. That is, Latinas may work hard to promote and maintain cultural expressions of respect for the provider, and at the same time, feel frustrated and unvalued for the roles women play in the family.

Not all participants felt angry that husbands and fathers had different roles from women. For example, Lorena stated,

> *Yo estoy de acuerdo de que al hombre se le de un lugar especial en la casa. Porque claro, em—e—es la figura masculina y se le debe un respeto. Un respeto. No como enseñan en nuestros países a tenerle miedo. "Ah! Llegó fulano! Ay!"* (I agree that the man should have a

special place in the house. Because, um, he is the masculine figure and he has to be given respect. A respect. Not like they teach you in our countries to have fear. "Oh! He's here! Ah!")

Although Lorena agreed with the notion of men being respected for their unique role, she differentiated the male role of authority, deserving of respect and status, from an authoritarian figure that ought to be feared. Along this same line, Glenis explained that "guys are the ones that should be like the dominant ones, quote-unquote, and—[*laughs*] and they should, you know, step up and take care of a woman."

Regarding the notion of dominant male roles, it is important to highlight that participants' responses ranged from endorsing this perspective to labeling such notions "stereotypes." Although all participants had conflicting views regarding their perspectives on roles, those who acknowledged stereotypes also described and seemed to embrace more egalitarian gender roles among both Latinos and Latinas. Eliza, for example, attributed respect and similar roles to both men and women. She explained:

My dad was a ver—very involved in everything we did. Whether it was cooking, cleaning, folding clothes.

As we can see, Latinas have very mixed views regarding the unique roles of men and women in the family and larger society as well as how these roles might be differentially valued. For example, Lorena was comfortable providing respect to a male figure in the home, although she viewed respect from an authoritative rather than an authoritarian viewpoint. In contrast, Eliza experienced blending of gender role behaviors within her family and felt men's and women's roles were of equal value.

Subject to Men

Most participants discussed the Latina/o cultural value regarding women's subservience to men. A number of participants questioned these ideals, discussing them as "stereotypes." For example, Candida, a 31-year-old Puerto Rican American woman who shared that she struggled in relationships with Latino men, said:

I know in a lot of Hispanic communities, it's like women are supposed to be subject to men. Like they have to be obedient, they have to be the housewife.

Later on in her interview she spoke of the impact of this submissive role on career expectations.

> If you go to school, that's fine, but you're going to be a teacher, you're going to be something quote-unquote easy, like a secretary . . . you can't be a police. . . . You're not going to be a doctor.

Mercedes described women as expected to be "submissive, passive, receptive, tolerant, uh beautiful, and has to be her . . . main concern, raising the children." Julie shared that she had been socialized to understand femininity as "being subservient. Being kind of delicate." Later she added, "Being treated like inferior."

Thus, many participants were aware of cultural expectations regarding subservience of women to men, recognizing how these expectations could diminish their self-efficacy and sense of self-worth. Gil and Vazquez (1996) encourage Latinas to find *la fuerza potente*, the powerful force, that is within each Latina. They emphasize Latina empowerment by figuring out how to maintain aspects of cultural tradition that are important, such as honoring the family, while affirming one's own skills, abilities, and interests. They suggest that it is important for Latinas to distinguish what might be a clash of cultural expectations about gender with *una ofensa personal*, a personal offense, with the former being something that is changeable and negotiable. Gil and Vazquez refer to Chilean novelist Isabel Allende, who stated "it took me forty of my fifty years to build my self-esteem and confidence after growing up in a strict patriarchal household" (p. 17).

Ladylike/Girly Girl

Another theme among most participants' discussion of cultural expectations of women, particularly Latinas, captured socialization around a code of "proper" behavioral and physical expectations and expressions. As they reflected on ideas about femininity, they often used words like "girly-girl" and "ladylike." Eliza described femininity as

> very girly, frilly—um—I guess, in a way—um—you know, not like a—I think the opposite of a tomboy. So very like girly. Makeup.

Julie shared a number of childhood anecdotes, highlighting the ways in which she felt pressured to live up to such expectations around physical gender expression. She spoke of not fitting in and being labeled a "tomboy." She also spoke in detail about expectations around dress:

> My mom is like "You need to [wear] . . . some nice heels, some nice shoes—some nice, you know, boots."

Glenis described the stereotypical feminine image as "a girl wearing a pencil skirt with her white top and like shoulder-length brown hair, straight hair." As Eliza, Julie, and Glenis also noted, women are subjected to fairly specific and rigid expectations about how to express themselves as girls and women, particularly in feminized ways. For Julie and others, these expectations formed another area of potential self-silencing in expressing oneself in socially conforming, rather than self-congruent, ways.

Participants not only discussed expectations around physical appearance and presentation but also presumably "ladylike" behaviors, along the lines of Julie's description of "delicate, polite, proper." Eliza pointed to the influence of the socialization provided by children's toys very early on:

> Girls play with these things and boys play with these things. . . .
> Girls play with Barbies and bows. And boys play with trucks.

Finally, Carolina captured this theme as she shared lessons taught to her by her mother:

> One of the things that my mom taught me that was really important was, you know, being ladylike, and to her, being ladylike was someone who wasn't, someone who wasn't loud, you know, and someone who wasn't abrasive, that you can still be, you can still verbalize yourself and you can still stand up for yourself, but in a certain manner, you know, where you don't become aggressive and you don't become physical. You know, you can still be a strong person but you can do it with mannerisms and with self-control, you know, and you can even do it with a soft voice, you know? If it's the physical aspect of being a lady, I remember that when you're a young girl, they teach you that, you know, you keep your legs crossed when you're wearing a dress, and that, I think when it came to the physical part, you

know, of growing up and being a girl, you know, during picture day, you were supposed to wear a dress.

Thus, from childhood on, Latina participants were aware of the many ways they were expected to embody femininity, with an emphasis on softness, not being loud or aggressive, and wearing clothes that match this behavior.

Superwoman

A few of the women in this study gave voice to the multiple roles that Latinas are expected to play. Johanna, a 30-year-old Ecuadorian American woman just months away from getting married, shared many of her experiences and observations:

> You're supposed to be a superwoman. . . . [W]hen I do get married, then I'm supposed to be everything. That's the key, the magic door that unlocks my whole universe to be superwoman. I can't be superwoman if I don't have a husband.

Johanna, Candida, and Lorena each outlined the struggles they faced when pressured to play countless roles. Candida wondered how much her childhood socialization around gender was a result of her being raised by a single mother: "She was supposed to be bring home the bread, take care of us, and look good while doing it . . . that's a Latina." Similarly, Lorena stated:

> *Nosotros—principalmente yo . . .—me crié en un país, um Latino, donde la mujer ideal e consiste en muchas cosas.* (We, especially me, —I was raised in a Latino country where the ideal woman consisted of many things.)

Lorena spoke of her own personal experiences as a mother, wife, and worker. She added,

> *Es aquella que puede tener lo doble- e- rol en la vida. . . . Ya la mujer puede hacer el rol de un trabajo afuera. . . . Y puede también mantener su casa. Y sus hijos.* (She is the one that can have a double role in life. . . . Now a woman can play the role of the one that works outside. . . . And can maintain her house. And her kids.)

Throughout the course of her interview, Lorena expressed feelings of great distress as she considered the multiple roles she played: *"Es dura, porque yo digo, a veces es injusto porque a mi me trabaja triple."* (It's hard, because I say, sometimes it's unfair because my work triples.)

Gil and Vazquez (1996) affirm that one of the Ten Commandments of the Maria Paradox is exactly what Johanna, Candida, and Lorena all experienced: the expectation of Latinas to play the superwoman, often at the cost of their physical and emotional health. Many Latinas operate from the framework of doing everything for everyone: parents, husbands/spouses, children, grandparents, and others. The cultural expectation to endure all the suffering of one's family is many generations old; if unmet, it can lead to depression, overwhelming feelings of inadequacy, guilt, even self-contempt. Gil and Vazquez suggest that Latinas engage in prioritizing their tasks and asking their spouses and children for help in making changes. Asking oneself if one desires to complete a task out of necessity or guilt is one step toward changing from doing everything to doing something for others: "The message is simple but deep: Don't try to be good at everything you do, and don't try to do everything in order to be good" (p. 198).

Gender Expectations or Latina Stereotypes?

Most participants expressed some confusion when outlining their learned gender role expectations as Latinas. A few questioned whether these were truly fair and reasonable expectations, or simply stereotypes of Latinas, or some mixture of both. Separating expectations from stereotypes of what men and women are supposed to be was challenging for many. Carolina captured these issues as she shared the images that came to mind when she reflected on the role of Latino men:

> When I hear the word *machismo*, I think of someone who is not sensitive and is not emotional, someone who is more interested in controlling. And when I think about controlling, I don't think about them as controlling those that are around him but controlling women more.

Xiomara added:

> It's like men are supposed to be this tough macho guy who have no feelings, don't cry. Very like dominant. And then the females are supposed to be weak and obedient.

Thus, participants struggled to articulate as well as to enact what they perceived as genuine cultural expectations or simply stereotyped versions of them. Additionally, in terms of questioning Latina stereotypes, Mercedes openly spoke of the impact of U.S. cultural stereotypes about Latinas/os. She shared:

> At the beginning, when I came here, I didn't want to go with those stereotypes, I didn't want to know what is the difference between how to identify a Puerto Rican and a Dominican. . . . I just wanted to ask you this straight, Where are you from? And what do you think. . . . But I think that eventually . . . with the time and the culture, you learn, oh, this group is supposed to be like that, and this group is supposed to be like that. And in general, Latinos are supposed to be this way or lazy or always taking money from the government or having too many children, and not being able to graduate from high school. But those are the statistics, not only perceptions or stereotypes, they are also statistics.

She added that upon migration to the United States, she learned about the expectations and/or stereotypes of Latinas. Thus, as with other people of color, Latina participants were aware of the variety of negative stereotypes that many Americans held about Latinas/os. At the same time, she recognized some of the harsh realities about economic survival and educational attainment of Latinas/os in the larger society, as reflected by their overrepresentation in poverty and lower educational outcomes. Moreover, as she described Latinas, she said, "We're more caring, we're more loving, we're more expressing [of] our emotions. We're hotter, sexier," struggling to distinguish her perceptions from a larger U.S.-based societal message. Like many other Latinas, Mercedes may have internalized some of these stereotypes while attempting to transform them to have a more positive tone. Learning to critique the social locations as well as the history of Latinas/os in the United States may empower her and other Latinas to develop more genuine images of themselves as Latinas rather than images based on negative images that dominate U.S. media and policies.

Identity Constructs

The impact of group identities also played a role in how Latinas learned about and negotiated their own gender roles. Key identities centered on gender and race-culture.

Gender Identity

Most participants in this study expressed strong identifications with their gender group membership. Several shared very complex definitions of what being a woman had grown to mean to them, especially in terms of the choices, roles, and challenges linked to this identity. However, others expressed fewer feelings of connection to their gender identity or to women's movements. Not surprisingly, a number of Latinas in the sample pointed to the intersection between their definitions of gender and gender roles, expressing contradictory or conflicting views and feelings. For example, Carolina talked about her gender identification in terms of universal personality traits, such as "humble," "compassionate," and "accepting," rather than gender stereotypes. She expressed some conflict in her experience and understanding around gender roles:

> Even though in the home, I wasn't brought up to think that cooking and cleaning was supposed to be my job, when I became a mom and a wife, it just became instilled in me, not because—not because it was expected from my husband or is expected from my daughter, but because of what society says. That this is what the perfect wife and perfect mother does: She works, she comes home, she takes care of the child, she cleans the home, you know, she cooks, she takes care of the husband. So no matter how much you try to convince yourself that you're equal, a lot of the work and the responsibility is on the woman, and it's not—I have a husband that's very supportive and I have a husband that's very open-minded, and I myself, I myself like to think of myself as his equal. I like to think of myself as his partner. But I think it's me. You know, I try to tell myself that there's a lot of—that, you know, there's a lot of equality in the home, but at the same time, I'm telling myself . . . to do more because it's my responsibility.

Despite having a supportive and accepting spouse who sees himself as an equal partner, Carolina has difficulty letting go of her own *marianismo* expectations to do everything for everyone. The power of these expectations, as she noted, can be fairly covert, particularly through multiple images and messages given within one's community and the larger society. However, as Gil and Vazquez (1996) suggest, owning these expectations and changing priorities is one way to lessen the conflicts about these gender roles.

The majority of participants expressed awareness of gendered politics and issues of women's oppression. Xiomara described her understanding of women's oppression or sexism in the following way: "Because I am female, I can't earn the same pay as a man, so I mean I do have freedom to some extent, but I have my limitations." Johanna, a corporate professional, compared her experiences to those of the men she has encountered in work setting. She described her understanding of women's sociopolitical experiences: "For so long, women were entirely dependent on the men in their life to do whatever, and even in the relative modern age, that was still the case." She spoke of women continuing to face various challenges "and overcome many hurdles," adding:

> I think that's what we've grown up with, at least my generation. We've seen it firsthand what goes on and there's sexism that's not going to leave us anytime soon.

Later on in her interview, she reflected on her mother's experiences and choices and expressed admiration of her mother's selflessness. She suggested that she too would make difficult choices for her own family:

> I like my career, I've had a good run [*laughs*], and if I continue with it, great. But my fiancé and I recently had this discussion that if his career takes him somewhere—you know, his office has a partnership in London. If they decide to send him over there, will we go? And without thinking of it, I said yes. I mean, that's what I've gotten. You know, the greater good of our family and possibly the greater good for my husband.

Johanna clearly was proud of her accomplishments as a professional woman, seeing herself part as of a generation that has overcome much in fighting sexism and discrimination of women as a whole. At the same time, she also felt that promoting her family well-being was important and was willing to leave her career to accompany her husband in a new job if that was best for the family. Learning to negotiate these decisions is key to balancing the importance of preserving one's family and culture with pursuing professional aspirations. Gloria and Castellanos (2012) urge redrawing and expanding the cultural image of *la buena mujer* to incorporate these multiple dimensions of womanhood in nurturing wellness of self and others, as Johanna has done in her own life.

Although most of the Latinas in this sample embraced more complex understandings of gender roles and gender politics, an important distinction emerged between participants in terms of their negotiation of gender roles. Women with higher levels of education, who expressed greater levels of exposure to diverse gender expressions, spoke of encountering much more conflict. Moreover, women who reported being married or engaged also expressed greater conflicting ideas and emotions. For example, Carolina, expressed this internal conflict in this way:

> I think there's a lot of mixed messages and I think there's a lot of mixed messages with ourselves. No matter how much we try to convince ourselves and everyone else that we don't see it that way.

Learning to listen not only to the multitude of messages but also to one's own voice and responses to these messages may be an effective way to resolving conflicts that may arise. Gil and Vazquez (1996) suggest Latinas ask themselves a number of questions to clarify the nature and potential resolutions that may arise, including feelings about competing with others, qualities for which one feels pride versus guilt, feelings about ending a relationship in order to keep a job, as well as feelings about working late hours and seeing one's children for only brief periods. Different Latinas will have different responses to these kinds of questions, each of which is correct for that individual.

The younger women in this study, both college students, Julie and Xiomara, attempted to actively challenge social expectations around gender through their physical presentation as well as their values and beliefs. However, all participants seemed to endorse the idea of "choices." Julie, for instance, was very vocal about her stated belief that despite the challenges women face, they still should be able to embrace their power by making their own choices:

> The ideal woman to me is one who wouldn't have to be scared to come out of her circle of trusts. . . . She should have power over her life because it's her body. If she wants children, that's up to her. . . . So the ideal women would do what she wants and what is best for herself without pressures of living up to certain expectations and limitations.

hooks (1990, in Espin, 1997) has urged women of color to engage in just this kind of critical consciousness as a way of enabling "creative, expansive self-actualization" and the invention of "new habits of being" (p. 73). Espin further supports not only the necessity, but the inherent difficulty, of doing so, because Latinas, along with women of color in general, are only just coming to know that they are the unknown.

Interestingly, although most Latinas in this study expressed feeling connected to their gender identity and to experiences shared by women, particularly women of color, feminism/womanism and feminist identification were not salient identities. The majority linked feminism to the women's movement and the struggle for women's rights. However, only one participant positively identified with this term. Julie, for instance, spoke in detail about her involvement in women's and well as lesbian/gay/bisexual/transgendered activism. She, like other participants, associated attributes such as "angry," "aggressive," "die-hard feminists . . . hate men" to participants of a movement she defined as "supportive of women's rights." She was the only participant knowledgeable of the term *womanist*. Like the rest of the participants, she did not connect to either movement, stating: "I would use the word *humanist*." In contrast, Xiomara, a first-generation college student from an immigrant family, spoke very passionately about the relevance of feminist politics among Latinas: "All Latinas should know that they live in a male-dominated world and feminism should be something that we're upholding and we should know of and we should be proud to be females and . . . fight for what women should get."

Espin (1997) has criticized the feminist movement in the United States as being limited to and by the experiences of White women. As our participants clearly point out, some Latinas agree. Although most participants were quite supportive of egalitarian roles and beliefs, many felt disenfranchised or disaffected by the feminist movement that characterized the mid- to late-twentieth century in the United States. While recent trends in feminist psychology have become more inclusive (Enns & Williams, 2013), Espin argues that as long as feminists view Latinas and other women of color as "the different one," as "objects" rather than "subjects," this movement will be "as partial as all other" movements have been (p. 72). Hurtado (2003), in her study of young Chicana women, similarly found ambivalent reactions to the term *feminist*, with a common response being "it depends what you mean by feminist" (p. 202). As with our participants, key beliefs centered on their right to decide and have control in their lives: "At issue was not so much the assignment of gendered tasks, like cooking or cleaning, but the right to decide whether they wanted such assignments, rejecting the *expectations* that the tasks were their responsibility because they were women" (Hurtado, 2003, p. 203; emphasis in original).

Racial-Cultural Identity

Participants expressed a strong identification with various racial-cultural groups. Even when not explicitly discussed, they highlighted multiple dimensions of their identities (e.g., race, ethnicity, gender, social class, religion, sexual orientation) as being influential to the meanings they constructed about gender roles. For example, Glenis talked about encountering racism in the context of her interactions with White Americans. She shared her experiences of gendered racism, as she wondered whether White men sexualized her because she was Latina: "I do feel like as if there is some racism, like . . . they're the men, that they should have some kind of control." Throughout her narrative, Glenis discussed her own internalized notions of gender from her Latina/Dominican upbringing as well as her exposure to White American notions of patriarchy. She also emphasized learning from literature and films, such as *Pride and Prejudice,* about the "proper" code of conduct for men and women.

A few participants also expressed a strong connection to other people of color. Johanna observed:

> I think there's probably more of a camaraderie. . . . There's so much kind of oppression that we share.

As she reflected on the gendered and racialized experiences of Latinas in general, she described this intersection of oppression as an additional hurdle to overcome. Johanna reframed these oppressions as symbolic of Latina strength and resilience:

> Unfortunately, she has another hurdle there. But I happen to think that it doesn't have to be a hurdle. She can turn it into an asset. I've turned being a Latina into an asset for me. I've made sure that I never obscure this fact or that I never—I'm very proud of it, and I took kind of a mainstream path for me. I went to col—I went to like a big-time university where I was definitely in the minority in that, but it was a big school, so I went there. But I never tried to obscure [the fact of my being a minority]. In fact, my parents always told me, even though

where I grew up was 90 percent Hispanic, that we're special because of that. We have this second language that's beautiful and just the fact that we're bilingual means our brains work a little differently, so we can be helpful and we can see another point of view, whereas some people might just see one.

Johanna also highlights how this positive view about her cultural background continues to help her today, and she encourages other women to view themselves similarly:

So this has carried me and has taken me—I've turned it into an advantage and into an asset where in the jobs I've had, the fact that I'm bilingual has come in very handy and there's never been an occasion for me to—I mean, I've been discriminated against a handful of times in my life . . . but I've never let it be a burden. I've turned it into an asset. And I would hope that even in this society, that women who haven't had the opportunities that I've had to go to a mainstream school or to even work after getting an education, that there's nothing to be ashamed of there. That for somehow, some way, you can turn it into something that is an advantage to yourself and maybe somebody you're working for or working with. Somehow it's got to be a good thing.

In Johanna's interview, elements of her working-class and immigrant socialization seemed to interact with her understanding of Latina strengths and resilience. As several Latina scholars have suggested (e.g., Espin, 1997; Gil & Vazquez, 1996), being able to deconstruct oppressive images to allow recentering of oneself and one's culture is critical to responding to constant multiple messages aimed at devaluing Latinas as women and as racial-cultural beings. Johanna's view of her bilingualism reflects her accurate perception that this indeed means greater cognitive complexity and ability to comprehend multiple points of view.

Finally, along the lines of intersections, a few participants also pointed to the connections among the racial-cultural socialization, gendered expectations, and sexual orientations. These intersections seemed to suggest, for instance, that "men and women will be together, like there's no other option," as Xiomara reported. Julie described these binary heteronormative presumptions in the Latino community,

There's really very little acceptance of having that middle ground. Like either you're a man or you're a woman. If you're a woman that identifies as lesbian and you're a little bit on like the butchier side, then you go into the "man" category. There's no in between and that's a problem, because—that's exactly where I am. Exactly where a whole lot of other people I know are.

Julie's experience as existing in between categories defies and even transforms her understandings of what these categories are. Anzaldúa (1987) described these in-between experiences as part of negotiating the borderlands of contradicting and oppressive experiences in which Latinas often find themselves. Even though Julie finds little acceptance for her transgressive self-definitions, she has found community with others with similar identities.

Latinas in Process: From Internalized Ideals to My Own Views

Throughout the interviews, participants described a process of change or evolution as they attempted to understand the vast array of messages regarding their gendered socialization and accept the roles that felt most congruent with their individual experiences and constructions of those experiences. Our participants passionately highlighted the differences among societal notions, cultural and familial views, and their own. For example, Julie captured this theme vividly. She very clearly worked to differentiate her own ideals from societal notions of the ideal man or woman. Johanna also described the various transformations she had undergone in the process of understanding and identifying with gender roles. She discussed her changes in her definitions of the ideal men and women.

> I'm pretty sure it's changed. If you would have asked me this question 10 or 15 years ago, I would have started listing tall, dark, handsome for the man, and kind of curvy and long hair for a woman. I think since I've actually found a partner and that I've, you know, dated around here and there, kind of being exposed to different people in different settings, that at this point in my life, I'm much more concerned and more aware of who people are on the inside and what they exhibit versus—like has nothing to do with how they look. There's just—I mean, I could think somebody is really good looking and all that, whereas before when I was younger, I would have approached them solely because of that. Now I hang back and I see what

kind of person they are first before I even engage or encounter them into my world for everything, because it's just—I think it's something that as you get older, you're just, there's no need for some people in your life [*laughs*]. And it's difficult to extricate yourself from the people that you no longer want to associate with, you know, the friends that you had when you were younger that are maybe not doing much, or something like that has happened in their lives that you can't relate to anymore, they can't relate to what's happened in your life. There's—if their presence or your presence in their life isn't a factor and not something they really need anymore, you kind of drift away and it's not because of their physical appearance at all. These kinds of things happen because of who a person is.

Johanna described a process of change in her definition and understanding of gender roles. When she was younger, she used the cultural prescriptions of men and women to identify qualities she sought in a partner as well as in herself. However, she found as she grew older, external qualities did not equate with desirable inner aspects that were more important in defining herself and someone with whom she wanted to be in a relationship, intimate or otherwise. Furthermore, her gendered encounters in diverse work settings also helped her begin to question previously held notions about presumably desirable qualities in herself and others.

Similarly, Mercedes spoke of learning to integrate various aspects of her socialization and her social encounters over time. She described herself as not yet "discovered" and discussed a process of integrating societal notions with her own personal definitions of gender and gender roles:

> I think it's something integrated. I mean, I [have] not discovered the idea of the ideal. But I think it's something that you learn from society, but at a certain point, you also are able to determine what things, what the society is trying to impose on you or things you value as something personal. And something that it has to do with the society, but it's not necessarily in how we use.

As Mercedes observed, she is well aware of societal and cultural expectations that have been imposed on her. However, at some point in her life, she began to see herself as determining what sociocultural values she adopts as her own, alongside her own personal values.

Renegotiating Gendered Values

A number of participants made explicit the distinctions between the cultural values embedded through their socialization and the gendered expectations they now held as important. Lorena, now involved in her second marriage, often compared the values of home to those learned in the United States. She observed:

> *La mujer que viene de los países Latinos, criada allá, viene con una idea de que la mujer es de la casa.* (The woman that comes from Latino countries, raised there, comes with the idea that the woman is of the home). . . .
> *Eso fue lo que yo vi en casa. Mi papá era quien traía el pan a la casa y mi mamá era la que atendía al hogar.* (That was what I saw at home. My father was the one who bought home the bread and my mother tended to the home.)

For Lorena, her Dominican roots provided the road map of gendered expectations of the unique and complementary roles men and women played in the family. However, she expressed some conflict when she spoke of the changes in gendered roles as a result of her immigration to the United States. She said:

> *Aquí es distinto. Porque una persona sola. Por ejemplo, el hombre solo no puede con todo. . . . Entonces, al alguna ve que también hay que ir afuera, hay que venir y recoger los niños y venir a cocinar y muchas veces a limpiar, a lavar. Es un choque fuerte.* (Here it's different. Because one person alone. For example, the man alone can't do everything. . . . So, at times you see that also one must go outside, one has to come and pick up the kids and come to cook and many times clean, to do the laundry. It's a bit hard.)

Thus, her experiences in the United States contrasted with her gender socialization as a child in the Dominican Republic. Instead of clear and complementary roles, Lorena saw both Latinas and Latinos struggling alone to do the many tasks of raising a family. Although she expressed some positive feelings as she spoke of adjusting to the work world, she still struggled to adjust to the multiple roles she was forced to play in the United States.

Other participants also spoke of changes and renegotiations of expectations and what they valued as important in men and women as well as their renegotiations of masculine and feminine roles. Carolina captured this theme vividly:

> I don't really view, you know, a woman on how feminine she is or a man on how masculine he is. To me, personally, I just, I just see a person as they are, and I know sometimes that that's hard to believe because we do have certain criticisms or certain expectations, and I guess depending on a person, I can have a certain expectation of someone.

Carolina struggled with conflicting feelings as she spoke of challenging gendered values and expectations, attempting to see each individual as a person rather than a gendered being with prescribed roles, abilities, and responsibilities. Yet at the same time she continued to struggle with internalized stereotypes of Latino men and women. Both Johanna and Mercedes pointed to changes in their values—from external and somewhat superficial values related to gendered expectations to values about gender roles that linked to personality and relational traits. Johanna, for example, spoke of valuing a sense of "responsibility" in a man, where she previously valued physical attributes. Mercedes shared coming to value the importance of being "hardworking, good sense of humor, sincere, faithful, caring for family" when thinking of both men and women. As Carolina, Johanna, and Mercedes all portray, redefining gender roles as these better fit personal experiences and values helped them make better sense of their social world and facilitate their successful negotiations with intimate others.

Questioning Gendered Expectations

A few Latinas in this sample pointed to the important role of critically questioning their socialization. Julie, a young outspoken student, passionately shared her internal questioning of gender roles she sought to challenge. She described gendered behaviors and physical attributes modeled by members of her Puerto Rican family that caused her distress and a sense of dissonance from a very young age:

> I remember I was at my godfather's house one day and he called and my aunt and I were cooking. We'd finished cooking. And he was like, "Okay, um, I'll be there in ten minutes. I'd like my plate heated up and on the. . . . I was like, Are you kidding me? I'm

like, that's crazy. What is that about? . . . it made me angry, but it's like, that's how it's kind of always been.

Julie's godfather's presumptions that he would be served in ten minutes appalled her. She was angry yet recognized that these expectations were nothing new to her aunt or other women in her family. As a young woman, Julie continues to consciously challenge gendered expectations and to experiment with different gendered expressions through clothing and appearance.

In contrast, Glenis, a second-generation Dominican woman who also spoke very openly throughout the course of her interview, described "still seeing it as males being more dominant than the females, which is interesting because I don't know where I get that from, living in a like female-dominated home." She expressed great conflict because she identified as a "conformist" who did not question gendered expectations yet, at the same time, sought to value women having

> choices. . . . If the woman wants to stay home, she should go ahead and stay home . . . at the end of the day, it just depends on the person and what they want or what they need.

The experiences of both Julie and Glenis highlight the feelings and beliefs that occur for Latinas as they make sense and critique traditional patriarchal expectations of their culture and family. Anzaldúa's (1987) borderlands metaphor is again relevant to help Julie and Glenis navigate the multiple contradicting realities. Moreover, as Arredondo (2002) suggests, "The 'wild zone' . . . is another metaphor of contextualization or space that applies to the mental, physical, and spiritual chaos that has enveloped many Latinas" (p. 308). As Arredondo views it, "space for women in patriarchal and hierarchical societies is limited by gender identity expectations and behaviors, which are deemed necessary but not powerful or prestigious and are, quite often, the focus of derision" (p. 309). Julie and Glenis bravely challenged these notions and questioned gendered expectations, despite few social rewards, primarily because they have found their own inner rewards for doing so.

Transforming Definitions

All participants described gender role images and perspectives that may be considered unconventional when compared to what they described as traditional Latina/o gender roles. The definitions expressed in the narratives of this group of Latinas ranged in perspective from ideals reflective of patriarchal notions of gender and gender roles to more self-defined, flexible, and liberated perspectives and experiences. Eliza defined an ideal man in this transformed way:

> An all-around man typically shares equal values with the woman as far as, you know, how to raise the kids. Equal work ethic, um. Coming home, having dinner, sharing the household things . . . you know, be flexible and understanding and compassionate. . . . I would say provider as well. Caretaker. Shares an equal amount of duties as far as you know.

Along these same lines, Xiomara discussed the idea of individual power to redefine and reconceptualize these constructs. She stated:

> Well, you know, you can be whatever you want to be and really mean it, because I know parents do say that, but they really don't mean it . . . that's just like telling your child that gender roles are, this is what is expected of a woman. You can break out of that. You don't have to follow what society says or what history teaches. You know, you really have the power . . . to be whatever you want to be and not be limited to what everything around you tells you. And even if somebody tells you, "This is what we want from you," it's up to you basically. It's always up to you because it's your life.

Gloria and Castellanos (2012) contend: "As Latinas broaden the notion of *la condición de mujeres Latinas* (Latina womanhood), or what it means to be *mujeres Latinas* at the individual, group, community and societal levels, their diversities become evident" (p. 174). As our participants demonstrate, breaking beyond the prescriptions of being a woman is not only possible, it is an important way to empowering Latinas and redefining their oppressive experiences of patriarchy and racism.

APPLICATIONS FOR MENTAL HEALTH PROFESSIONALS AND EDUCATORS

Our participant narratives suggest a number of applications regarding how Latinas construct their sense of self as gendered beings through an analysis of their experience of gender roles. The core narrative that emerged here suggests the main theme of Latinas is the continuous transformation and negotiation throughout the process of learning who they are as gendered beings, which includes negotiating among a variety of roles along the way. Participants described progressively learning and constructing gender roles. Thus, Latinas' views about themselves and their roles are constantly changing, in some cases from traditional views on gender roles (given their socialization) to more unconventional views on the roles of women in general and of Latinas in particular. Our analyses indicate that the process of change in perspectives can be quite challenging and socially risky, given the various stereotypes and expectations of Latinas (e.g., submissiveness). Moreover, depending on their education and career aspirations, women may be both willing and able to challenge their traditional gender roles. The process of transformation and change begins with questioning internalized ideas that Latinas learn or are expected to learn in order to develop their own ideas and perspectives. Specific incidents that participants had while growing up regarding how men and women are supposed to behave stood out as significant experiences that provided them with multiple contradictory messages about gender roles.

We now turn to specific applications of our findings for mental health professionals and educators, focusing on navigating family expectations and responsibilities, establishing safe spaces to facilitate dialogues on gender and culture, and facilitating gender role transformations.

Navigating Family Expectations and Responsibilities

One of the major sources of information about cultural prescriptions of gender roles were family messages that came from many individuals, such as mothers, fathers, uncles, aunts, and godparents. Most of these messages centered on the various roles women were expected to take, particularly in being dedicated mothers, wives, and daughters. Most Latinas held *la familia* as one of their most cherished values and sources of strength. As women, they knew they were expected to be primary caregivers of their children, responsible for maintaining relationships as well as imparting religious beliefs to their families. However, Latinas also shared that they struggled to maintain the multiple roles that are expected of them in order to keep from disrupting the family life. Thus, activities and interventions might help Latinas articulate what messages they have learned about what these multiple roles might be, the stress that may arise from conflicting values and potential outcomes that are difficult or unhealthy to achieve (i.e., superwoman), and how they may begin to reevaluate and renegotiate these roles. As we have noted, Gil and Vazquez (1996) provide one of the few guides for mental health professionals that help to facilitate Latinas bridging Old World cultural traditions and New World opportunities. They ask a key question: "Can a [Latina] woman learn to skillfully steer a course through North American society without sacrificing the Latin traditions she treasures? Our answer is a resounding yes" (p. 18). Gil and Vazquez also provide many useful suggestions for helping Latinas transform gender roles beyond the rigid standards enacted in *marianismo* to more flexible and psychologically manageable expectations.

Similarly, Gloria and Castellanos (2012) recognize the centrality of *familismo* (familism) for most Latinas: "It is from the context of *familismo* that Latinas negotiate their interactions. Regardless of whether they themselves have children or are married, they are frequently defined by being part of *la familia*, as a woman, daughter, or co(mother) simultaneously" (p. 174). They further believe that the family, through mothers and grandmothers, can provide a *patron* (blueprint) for surviving, managing challenges, and building strength. As our participants found, sometimes strength and survival skills can come from the most unexpected sources, such as Mercedes's father, who encouraged her to seek an education to help ensure her survival. Rather than presume one family member's values or role, Gloria and Castellanos suggest that mental health professionals ask clients how different family members self-identify and the values they have imparted regarding their family *patron*.

Espin (1997) provides suggestions regarding how traditional feminist therapy might be incorporated in mental health work with Latinas in difficult family conflicts. For example, she highlights her own disclosure to a Latina client who was in a domestic violence situation that she was intolerant of such abuse of women, despite cultural expectations regarding the dominance of men. For the Latina client, hearing such a disclosure from another Latina liberated her to consider "the possibility of rebelling" against her abusive husband (p. 63). Espin further asserts that "a therapist who does not have an analysis of the social world could not be a good therapist," explaining that the analysis must include "the impact of oppression due to gender, race, ethnicity, class, sexual orientation, disability, and age . . . indeed to espouse a theory [such as feminist theory] or use a skill without understanding its embeddedness in the social context in which it was developed can, in fact, be dangerous and unethical" (p. 68).

Given the high importance placed on family, Latinas who are in the process of renegotiating their gender roles to better fit their own needs and desires may face conflicts between expressing their evolving beliefs while not disrupting family functioning, particularly because these new beliefs might not always be welcomed within the family. Expressing one's own ideas about gender roles and deviating from the norm may be perceived as going against one's culture and exercising values that belong to the American culture (i.e., becoming "Americanized"). Furthermore, in addition to family, *respeto* (respect) to the provider is an essential value within Latina/o cultures; however, some participants expressed concern that endorsing this value created conflict for Latinas trying to renegotiate their role within the home by endorsing more egalitarian views on gender roles. Some felt that the value or expectation of subservience of Latinas within the Latino community impacted women's career choices; some even recalled being encouraged by family members to pursue stereotypical careers (i.e., secretary, teacher). Counselors and educators can help Latinas find different ways to empower themselves within these cultural boundaries and always must be aware of the spoken or unspoken expectations that Latinas might face.

Establishing Safe Spaces for Dialogue and Exploration

Another important application concerns the need for information about gender socialization and gender role constructions to be included in K–12 school settings as well as higher education. When participants were asked where they learned what it means to be a man or a woman, the majority stated that family and the media were the primary sources of direct and indirect messages regarding roles. None of the participants mentioned school, or even a class, where they learned about gender issues and the construction of gender roles. Thus, it appears that this topic is not generally discussed in the classroom setting, perhaps adding further to the role confusion and distress that emerges from gender role construction.

Given that negotiating gender roles is already a stress-filled process, it might be helpful to disseminate accurate information and normalize the process of gender role construction as a means of better supporting Latinas and perhaps helping improve their potential academic success. For example, Savitt (1984) suggests lesson plans to encourage young Latinas to identify female heroes in literature and history. She emphasizes three famous Latin American women—Mexican poet Sor Juana Inés de la Cruz, political leader Eva Perón, and Puerto Rican poet Julia de Burgos—as possible heroes for young Latinas to learn about. Similarly, Arredondo (2002) celebrates a number of Latina icons, leaders, and writers who have challenged traditional gender role restrictions of Latinas and who provide "new lenses for understanding the complexity of the Latina" (p. 316). Arredondo contends these individuals provide important contrasts to the presumptions inherent in adopting *marianismo* as a life role. Teachers might personalize this classroom lesson by developing activities in which young girls identify and discuss heroes from their own lives.

Ginorio and Huston (2001) urge educators to be aware of stereotypes and biases about Latina girls that may be communicated through lowered academic expectations and tracking into nonprofessional careers more in line with what is be considered "women's work." They suggest adopting the framework of "possible selves" to help Latina students focus on their potential and plan for their future by reconfiguring traditional gender role images they may have been exposed to:

> A multitude of possible selves—from school girl to family member—may be fraught with confusion and conflict. Conversely, this multitude may provide a fluidity and flexibility that allow a young woman to maintain comfortable relationships in a variety of settings that would otherwise seem contradictory—what Chicana feminist scholar and activist Gloria Anzaldúa characterizes as a dual, *mestiza* consciousness (Anzaldúa, 1987). (p. xi)

Facilitating Gender Role Transformations

Mental health professionals and educators can provide important support for Latinas as they transform their gender roles from cultural prescriptions and racialized stereotypes to ones that genuinely reflect their emerging values and beliefs. Affirming the chaotic and confusing "wild zone" this entails is key to helping

Latinas negotiate roles in a complex social world (Arredondo, 2002). As mentioned, gender role transformation can be particularly stressful for Latinas, as they are often pulled in different directions due to mixed messages from family members as well as the larger society regarding who they are or who they should be as gendered beings. Asking Latinas to explore what these different roles mean to them and how these roles may be impacting their lives is an important step to articulating the thoughts and feelings associated with these transformations.

In addition to culturally transcribed roles, such as those based on *marianismo*, Gloria and Castellanos (2012) suggest that "Latinas have created a *mujer*-grounded culturally centered skill set in which they translate and transform everyday processes while preserving and nurturing healthy elements of tradition to reinforce their evolving identities and values" (p. 176). They further acknowledge that, like our participants, Latinas in general "learn to be present in one world, consistently working toward an internal seamless continuity in the midst of change" (p. 176). Learning to move across worlds, though, is not conducted to serve others or lose one's personhood but rather "to grow and persist despite challenges" (p. 176).

Gloria and Castellanos (2012) suggest several questions that can guide therapy with Latinas as they negotiate multiple roles, including being aware of gender role scripts, cultural values, and current realities. They suggest directly assessing the various roles a Latina client may be juggling to identify ways in which the roles can be integrated. Gloria and Castellanos also urge therapists to be aware and reinforce the "inner strengths that Latinas bring to their challenges or concerns. Empower them to find their own voice and cultural processes that are congruent to their worldview and sociocultural *patron* as they find wellness and balance" (p. 178). These authors caution, however, that mental health professionals must first explore their own biases, values, and assumptions before engaging with their Latina clients.

REFERENCES

Anzaldúa, G. (1987). *Borderlands/La frontera*. San Francisco, CA: Spinsters/Aunt Lute Book.

Arredondo, P. (2002). Mujeres Latinas: Santas y marquesas. *Cultural Diversity and Ethnic Minority Psychology, 8*, 308–319.

Enns, C. Z., & Williams, E. N. (Eds.). (2013). *The Oxford handbook of feminist multicultural counseling psychology.* Oxford, England: Oxford University Press.

Espin, O. M. (1997). *Latina realities: Essays on healing, migration, and sexuality.* Boulder, CO: Westview Press.

Gil, R. M., & Vazquez, C. I. (1996). *The Maria paradox: How Latinas can merge Old World traditions with New World self-esteem.* New York, NY: Perigee Books.

Ginorio, A., & Huston, M. (2001). *Sí, se puede! Yes, we can: Latinas in school.* Washington, DC: American Association of University Women Educational Foundation.

Gloria, A. M., & Castellanos, J. (2013). *Realidades culturales y identidades dimensionadas*: The complexities of Latinas' diversities. In C. Z. Enns & E. N. Williams (Eds.), *The Oxford handbook of feminist multicultural counseling psychology* (pp. 169–182). Oxford, England: Oxford University Press.

Hurtado, A. (2003). *Voicing Chicana feminisms: Young women speak out on sexuality and identity.* New York: New York University Press.

Santiago-Rivera, A., Arredondo, P. & Gallardo-Cooper, M. (2002). *Counseling Latinos and la familia: A practical guide.* Thousand Oaks, CA: Sage.

Savitt, D. J. (1984). Latin American women: Finding new heroes. *Yale-New Haven Teachers Institute.* Retrieved from http://www.yale.edu/ynhti/curriculum/units/1984/3/84.03.07.x.html

Chapter Six

GENDER ROLES AMONG ASIAN / ASIAN AMERICAN MEN

Michael Y. Lau, Yu-Kang Chen, Jill Huang, and Marie L. Miville

Individuals of Asian descent have a long and complex history of settling in the United States as immigrants (Liu, Murakami, Eap, & Hall, 2009; Takaki, 1993). According to the 2010 U.S. Census, some 17.3 million people, or 5.6% of the U.S. population, identify as Asian or some multiracial combination with other races (U.S. Census Bureau, 2010). Furthermore, this racial group has seen a dramatic growth in size in recent decades, with the population increasing 46% between 2000 and 2010 alone (U.S. Census Bureau, 2011).

Historically, the first major wave of Asian immigration to the United States began in the1800s and was made up primarily of male laborers from China, Japan, the Philippines, Korea, and India, who were recruited to work in settings such as plantations, canneries, mines, agricultural fields, and railroads. Although these Asian Americans presented as a resource for cheap labor, some White workers saw them as a threat to their jobs and to White women. Consequently, Asian Americans frequently experienced hostile and anti-Asian sentiments in their daily lives (Chua & Fujino, 1999; Shek, 2006; Takaki, 1993). Racial-hatred attitudes were manifested institutionally through the passage of several race-based immigration federal laws and policies. Furthermore, the greatly skewed gender ratios among Asian Americans produced by the immigration policies led politicians to worry that the rates of interracial marriage between Asian males and White females might increase. Consequently, antimiscegenation laws were written and implemented to revoke citizenship of any White woman who married outside of her racial group (Chua & Fujino, 1999; Shek, 2006).

Not surprisingly, one consequence of early low-wage labor practices and discriminatory immigration policies was the promotion of negative racially stereotyped images of Asian American men as both effeminate and hypermasculine. For instance, after the bombing of Pearl Harbor in 1941, images of the "Yellow Peril" presented Asian men as overly aggressive and dangerous in antiwar propaganda that was widely disseminated throughout the United States (Shek, 2006). Stereotypes of Asian American men as being effeminate emerged as well, most likely due to some of the limited work opportunities available to them being forced to take jobs considered primarily "feminine," such as launderers, cooks, and servants (Chua & Fujino, 1999).

A third and more recent image of Asian American men derives from the common racial stereotype of Asians as the "model minority." This myth suggests that "Asians are self-reliant, economically successful and politically nonresisting" (Chua & Fujino, 1999, p. 321); it became prominent in the United States after the passage of the less restrictive 1965 Immigration Act led to a second immigration wave based on family reunifications and professionals migrating from Asian countries (Takaki, 1993). Asian American men in this context are often perceived to be good family men and good providers and this image has greatly shaped and defined evolving concepts of Asian Americans.

Liu and Chang (2007) note that, in the context of predominant U.S. White male norms, negotiating masculinity is no simple or easy task for Asian American men "because they must simultaneously accept and repudiate the White masculine norm in search of alternative definitions of masculinity" (p. 199). This may lead some Asian American men to attempt to profit by adhering to these norms as well as risk being marginalized due to their racial group membership and history in the United States. Liu uses an example of a "beefcake" calendar featuring Asian men in an attempt to repudiate "geeky" or effeminate images. Unfortunately, with these efforts, "new masculinities are not formed; rather old masculine ideals are rescued and recuperated for contemporary use" (p. 199).

Regarding cultural definitions of masculinity, some research indicates that unlike White American men, Asian American men view masculinity as being complementary to femininity rather than its polar opposite (Chua & Fujino, 1999). This perspective is in line with Confucian philosophies that promote complex and flexible understandings of gender roles (Liu & Chang, 2007). For example, men may take a "yin," or submissive, role in relations with their parents and authority figures and at the same time a "yang," or masculine, response regarding a moral injustice. Nonetheless, both men and women commonly are socialized within fairly strict gender role expectations regarding values and behaviors. Moreover, the prominence of hierarchical, particularly patriarchal, relations remains a prominent feature of most Asian cultural groups (Sue & Sue, 2012).

In light of both the historical and current sociopolitical context, we explored the meanings of masculinity and gender roles among Asian/Asian American men. We interviewed 11 participants, many of whom immigrated to the United States as young boys and adolescents. Table A.9 in the appendix provides demographic information about our participants. Using the data-analytic procedures described in Chapter 1, we identified several major themes, which are described in the next section. We also integrated our key themes into a proposed theory of gender role socialization relevant for Asian and Asian American men that is incorporated in Chapter 8. In the final section of this chapter, we discuss applications of these findings for both educators and mental health professionals.

CULTURE, SOCIALIZING INFLUENCES, AND AGENCY IN GENDER ROLE CONSTRUCTIONS

In this section, we describe several key themes and processes that emerged from our analyses of participants' interviews. These include (a) cultural values, such as country of origin, centrality of family, and collectivism; (b) the *what* of gender socialization, including observation of ideal images and sources and differences between real and ideal selves; and (c) the *how* of gender socialization, including the processes of tension and agency in constructing one's own gender roles and the gender role socialization of others.

Primary Role of Cultural Values

The theme of the primary role of cultural values encompasses the broad cultural influences that contextualize the experiences of the participants interviewed. One of the big differences in participant characteristics is that several participants were international students and were not born in or did not grow up in the United States. For those participants who were U.S. citizens, there were also differences in generational status: Two participants were born in the United States and four participants moved to the United States as children.

Country of Origin

Given the cultural differences among our participants, a key theme that emerged was broad national differences between country of origin and the United States regarding cultural values. These differences were most evident with international student participants, whose migration to the United States was more recent and whose awareness of national differences was most apparent. For example, Benson made the following observation:

> The message, the message is a little bit different. I just said that like in Thailand, the family plays a bigger part in what it means to be an ideal man. And the message I get over here in the United States is, it's not quite the same. I mean, it's hard for me to say. It's not to say that families aren't important here, because I think family is important everywhere, but in terms of being the ideal man in the United States, it's a little bit different.

As Benson notes, cultural differences are central to the gender socialization process; being a man from Thailand necessarily involves his responsibilities to his family. Similarly, in his description of an ideal woman, Forrest said, "My ideal woman is someone who—I come from Asian background, and my—I guess the culture has a huge impact on me in terms of what I think women should be."

Even for participants who were largely socialized in the United States, cultural influences, especially from their parents' countries of origin, emerged as a significant source of influence in their lives. Dexter, who moved from Taiwan to the United States as a child, remembered the stories he heard there that influenced his current understanding of gender roles:

> I mean, I hear in like the story that I grew up with back in Taiwan, but I was really young. And it definitely had strong gender roles, like being respectful for young women is taking care of the mom, cleaning for them, and being a good male, an ideal male is one who protects the family, makes money. Like these old—like little tales and moral stories that we get.

For Dexter, early childhood memories growing up in Taiwan involved hearing stories that demonstrated clear gender roles for women and for men that still impacted him today.

In addition to country of origin, several participants identified bicultural influences, as was the case with Forrest:

> Well, I think, I feel like a lot of—There must be, I mean, I'm sure I'm influenced by my culture, but then I'm living in Asia for sixteen years and living in America for thirteen years, and I have, you know, I have made friends with people who come from different countries, so I feel like I don't really represent one particular culture anymore. So right now, it's hard for me to answer 'cause I feel like I have a mixture of cultural influences within myself. But I'm sure there [is] a lot of commonality across different cultures. For example, I think a lot of cultures would agree that crying is not really a good—something that men should do. Um [*pause*] but I, I believe that's changing.

Forrest, who has spent time equally in both Asia and the United States, found the cultural influences of both countries indistinguishably "mixed" in him—for example, the social unacceptability of men demonstrating some emotions, such as sadness, publicly. Furthermore, his experiences suggested that some cultural influences are generational and can change over time (e.g., attitudes toward men crying in public). Cultural differences based on national influences were often a source of tension for the participants; we discuss this later in the section on gender role socialization. For now, it is important to acknowledge that participants or their parents grew up in particular countries that were an important context in which the values and expectations surrounding gender roles were learned and played out; these contextual influences deeply affected how participants have come to understand and construct their gender roles today.

Centrality of Family

For a majority of participants, gender roles were often situated within the function of their families. For Benson, the notion of an ideal man was very much tied to the role that a father plays within a family:

> I realized that my image of an ideal man is a father who takes care of his father and does everything for the family, even though to the extent to which he also—is also subordinating his

own individual desires for the family. And being a family man, you know, going out with friends once in a while, but the family always comes first for the ideal man, at least in my mind.

Here Benson expressed a complex understanding of gender roles as embodied in the role of a father who is expected to be caretaker of his own parents and subordinate his own individual wishes to the family as a whole, while occasionally enjoying the privilege of leisure time with friends. To Alec, who grew up in China, an ideal man serves as the leader and, specifically, a leader within his family:

Yeah, for example, in China . . . it's some kind of thing in the culture that man has to be the leader in the family, an absolute leader in the family. . . . He *has* to be that. (Emphasis added.)

Thus, in addition to giving oneself to the service of one's family, Alec also expected—indeed, felt it is required—that men have absolute authority in the family, affirming cultural expectations of hierarchical and male-dominated nature of family relations (Sue & Sue, 2013).

The idea of a family and the roles different members play informs not only the roles of men but of women as well. As with men, the ideal woman was defined by her responsibility to the family for Hamish: "I'm kind of like a family man so I value someone who is really, I mean really dedicate[s] herself for the whole family." He went on to explain the relative responsibility of men and women regarding their purpose in a family:

For ideal man, he should be like, he should be more responsible . . . [a] man is like, is still the leader of a family, so he should be more responsible. On the other hand, woman, woman can be, she should be, she can be less responsible, but still need to put the, but still needs to put the family first. . . . So you can see from my dad and my mom that like my dad is like he take care of the broad view of the family, so financial status and the kinds of things like that. And my mom, she is more like go to very little detail, like discipline of children or something like that.

Thus, for Hamish and other participants, gender roles often were drawn from traditional ideas of men taking a more active, dominant, leadership role whereas a woman took a more secondary and subordinate role. Hamish also linked leadership with an increased sense of responsibility for men regarding the overall functioning and survival of the family, with women focusing more on daily details. He further described the role of the woman in the family:

> The social view upon woman is that you have that, for any woman, that she has to be a good mother, she has to like take care of their children very well. This is, this may be a little more different from man, right? So because like in most society, they don't expect men to like take your children to soccer, but for women, I think most people in this world, when they look at the ideal woman, the first that come in their minds, like okay, she has to be a good mother, she has to take care of their son, she have, she may have a career, but she also has to put the priority to the children.

Hamish regarded the family-centered role of women as an expectation that exists in most cultures ("most people in this world"). He further believed that although women may have other pursuits in life, such as a career, their children and family must still be their priority.

Some participants observed that expectations regarding men and women may be a function of expectations and values that change over time. Isidor noted:

> But you see right, like many times in the history, you see a lot of times that the woman is basically just the follower and the man just basically, the guys who lead their family to do everything. It's just, it's just in the modern time that right now, the woman turn to be more like confident about themselves, they try to be like themselves.

Even though Isidor was aware of traditional gender role beliefs, he also had observed a recent change in the social political context, as reflected by "modern times," which is linked with women's increased self-confidence. These changes also have led to differences in the public discourse, with women being more able and willing to speak openly in public, which Jules saw as a major break from the past:

> There's a big difference from the past, I can tell, yeah, I guess, yeah, when the woman wasn't able to speak out, but right now,

they can speak out and then it doesn't look so weird in public, yeah. So I guess there's a big difference from the past.

Other generational differences that participants noted concerned the relative importance or value of qualities that are important in a person. For example, Isidor, who is from Thailand, shared some of the more traditional expectations of men:

> So maybe like 20 years earlier, we tend to be taught like we're not looking for the physical body. We're looking for the value that everyone have inside like are you working hard? Do you have a good work ethic? Are you willing to protect the girls that when you marry, you're going to live a long life and have good children, that kind of stuff. We just don't talk about the physical ability that much. But, but, but we talk about it, yeah, but we did . . . not like openly or like publicly. . . . Yeah, but it's more public now.

As Isidor observed, changes in values about physical abilities, even appearance, have taken on greater importance than for previous generations, who valued more inner qualities, such as having a good work ethic. The impact of globalization, including media images promoting certain types of physical appearance (i.e., the beefcake calendar example), may be one reason for this shift in values.

Another generational theme, again perhaps linked with more modern lifestyles, was a greater expectation by some participants for women to take on the "superwoman" role in attending to matters both inside and outside of the home. Jules, for example, described an ideal woman this way:

> Actually, I can't think of any ideal woman right now, but all I can think is like my mother. Actually one, one woman that I thought of was like Hillary Clinton. Yeah, she was like pretty good. I mean, for me, I think ideal woman should be someone who's being able to work . . . and then at the same time be able to like stay home and be a good housewife. . . . [T]hey have to be able to like stand on their feet by themselves.

In addition to his mother, Jules named Hillary Clinton as an ideal woman, given her well-known roles as both political leader and faithful wife and supportive mother. These changes in beliefs reflect an increasing social acceptance of women's interests beyond the family but do not relieve women of their daily responsibilities.

In sum, the family is quite important for participants in contextualizing the roles that they see men and women play in society. Very often, images of ideal men and women were based on the roles that fathers and mothers play within a family. However, recent changes related to modern life also had begun to change some of these expectations for both men and women, with each role reflecting a little of the other: for example, emotional expressiveness for men and career pursuits for women. Even in modern times, though, the family remains central.

Collectivism

Related to the previous two themes, collectivism as a cultural value also played a prominent role in understanding gender roles across the participants. Given its salience in many Asian cultures, it is not surprising that collectivism undergirds the centrality of family in determining gender roles. For example, as we discussed earlier, Benson described his father putting his personal needs below the needs of the family. The idea that being a man sometimes involves making personal sacrifices for the needs of the family or society is influenced by collectivistic values. Jules pointed out differences between Asian and U.S. mainstream cultures in how this value is played out in the roles that members play in a family:

> Well, I mean, from my family, I mean, look at the family perspective. Like in Thailand, we usually stay together, like even though we got married, we just stay with our parents, but we have a bigger house or something like that. But here Americans, I mean, it has been like this for a long time, that when you grow up like 18 and you move out of the house, and then you leave your mother and father at home alone. So I think in Thailand, we've got lots of sense of being grateful to parents and also taking care of the elderly better, and then that's more like just how that we have lots of caring to the other people, especially to the woman's side, like your mother. But in America, I think that the caring thing is not as much as in Thailand. It's more like personal stuff, like oh, I need to get along with my life, yeah.

Jules observed that it is acceptable, even expected, for several generations of a family to live together in Thailand; this is signified by families planning to obtain a bigger house when there is a marriage, instead of making plans for moving away, as might be expected in the United States. At times, collectivistic values can take on a prescriptive role. Alec, an international student who grew up primarily in China, shared:

> Because there are lots of people in China, so you will most of the time live in your very condensed neighborhood. If you want to live like, let's say, in a very alternative life, that's against the morality of the society, people will judge you. They will talk, they will gossip, and you just cannot stay there. And also, you live in China, you should—you absolutely will have to live in a huge family. In the family, yeah. So part of it is just being around everyone else—who expect the same thing, and if you don't sort of go along with it, then people will criticize something.

Alec noted that collectivistic values are so important, particularly in promoting the family and overall society, that being different may be viewed critically, even judgmentally, such that an individual may feel compelled to move away. Grover affirmed this view by stating

> so conforming to the group by sacrificing yourself is a value. That's not a value here [in the United States].

According to Grover, a necessary component of collectivism is to sacrifice oneself for the needs of the group, a value he did not observe in the United States.

In sum, it is evident that cultural values, such as country of origin, collectivism, and familism, serve as an important backdrop in appreciating the gender role socialization of our participants. We turn now to socialization processes we saw as key themes for the construction of gender roles.

Images and Sources of Socialized Gender Roles

In this section, we discuss a second broad category of themes that emerged from our analyses that largely illuminate the process in which the participants have been exposed to gender role socialization. One key theme that emerged is the process of *observation*, that the learning of what it means to be a man or a woman originates from seeing and watching others. We first discuss what the ideal man or woman is to the participants, then we describe the sources for these ideal images and the process whereby these are realized and internalized. In the following section, we explore ways that these images are problematized and changed through conflicts that participants have encountered in the socialization process.

Ideal Images

Participants were asked to share their images of the ideal man and the ideal woman. These images were described in many ways, including: (a) physical characteristics, (b) behaviors, (c) attitudes/traits, and (d) roles and responsibilities.

Physical characteristics were one of the primary ways that the ideal man and woman were defined. On average, men have a set of different physical markers when compared to women, markers that often were highlighted by participants. Not surprisingly, men were often described as physically big and possessing powerful traits. Knute described it this way:

> I think an ideal man in society is seen as someone who is put together, and by put together, a person should be tall, I think five ten to six two is ideal. The person should be muscular, the person should look clean, and clean typically means fitting in the current trend of what looks good.

Knute conveyed very specific physical characteristics, including height dimensions, as well as being muscular and looking clean. Similarly, Isidor discussed the male physical characteristics he felt were important to attractiveness to women:

> Also, I think an ideal man should be like masculine, like sturdy, like well-built because that's, that's the way a man will look as a like, you know, when woman seeks for a man, woman will try to seek the one who thinks they can protect her or something like that. So basically if a man is well built, it will be like more attractive for her.

As both participants suggested, ideal physical features of men emphasize their muscularity and strength, with the presumption that these were important to the role of protector. Isidor further assumed these features would be attractive to women.

Our analyses also revealed a largely unspoken system of values that operates through a majority of the participants' lives, such that gender roles are prescribed within a predominantly heteronormative and sometimes heterosexist framework. Male and female gender characteristics and roles were often described in the context of men and women as romantic and sexual objects of each other. Although two of the participants identified as gay, the heteronormative framework was rarely acknowledged. Knute, a heterosexual participant, alluded to this framework when he declared that the ideal man

> should—is also heterosexual. The ideal male is and the ideal male has good guy friends and can get any girl anywhere.

In contrast to male physical characteristics, women were often described as physically weaker and diminutive. Dexter recounted a memory of his grandmother, who was always feeding him food and, at the same time, telling his sister not to eat so much. When asked to explain what the message was, he replied, "Probably men should be strong and big and women should be small and skinny people." Here, again, we see prescriptive processes as conveyed by important family members that are often a central part of the gender role socialization process.

A heteronormative framework wove through much of the narrative about women as physical beings. Knute described the ideal woman as

> supposed to be beautiful, almost effortlessly so. She's supposed to be curvy and fit. She's supposed to be sexual . . . she's supposed to be able to control herself and control her man with her sexuality, but she's still yet controlled by her man because he's the one who can say when we're going to have sex.

Dexter said:

> I guess like physical attributes of what, you know, other men and sometimes myself—we look for is—I mean, just off the top of my head, like blue eyes, blond, big breasts, slender body.

Here, heteronormative values are evident through racialized lenses, whereby the object of desire is not only viewed through straight male eyes but specifically materialized as characteristics found in women of a particular (i.e., White) race. Chet is even more direct in sharing that his image of an ideal woman is related to what he desired:

> And for looks, I personally like women with—who have partly dyed hair [*laughs*], with gold highlights, that kind of half-and-half

preference. They don't need to be that tall, maybe just medium height, say five, five four to five seven or something, I don't see myself as too tall so I'll get intimidated if the woman is too tall and what else. [*laughs.*]

Chet cited very specific physical features regarding ideal women, including height dimensions, particularly being shorter than he, in order not to feel dominated. The specificity of ideal images for women complemented those for men we described earlier. We discuss sources for these heteronormative and racialized images in a later section.

In addition to physical characteristics, ideal images of men and women were often described in terms of attributed behaviors and attitudes or traits. Isidor described an ideal woman in this way:

> [She] should be like kind of outgoing, like well, usually when you see the movie, a woman will be, will be like social, talking to their friends all the time, like doing gossiping, cooking with friends, something like that. . . . I think a woman tends to be more emotional than logical . . . so I think a woman should be like confident and humble sometimes.

In contrast, Isidor described the ideal man in this way:

> I think for a man, he should be like kind of, have the adventurer mind, like we want to travel, we want to take risks, we want to like be, not being afraid to everything, just show that we have a kind of leadership so that we can protect woman.

Thus, in addition to unique physical embodiment of ideal men and women, participants emphasized their contrasting temperaments: Women are social and emotional, whereas men are logical and risk takers. The contrasts between men and women were often most stark when participants described their understanding of the terms *masculine* and *feminine*. Alec shared that being masculine:

> is what I was told—what masculine is, there the ideal nature of the ideal man. Like the stereotype of man at the top . . . [he is] independent, and self-absorbed. . . . [I]t's kind of if you want to try to be sensitive and you're trying to be sensitive and trying to be considerate, then people will think you are feminine.

Thus Alec acknowledged that straying from idealized masculine images involves the risk of being femininized by others. Hamish, in describing men possessing power, stated that the power is demonstrated in this way:

> Like if you are . . . very smart, very intelligent, and you kind of like want to make people see that part of you, you know, like in the meeting, you always have to express your ideas and your opinions, your views on, upon other people's ideas, and it's kind of like you try to express that, you try to demonstrate that to other people that, okay, I'm intelligent, I am smarter than you.

Thus, a primary way of demonstrating power and dominance is by showing others verbal abilities that are believed to reflect well on intelligence, a major aspect of leadership and power.

Participants often defined masculinity or femininity by contrasting one against the other. In other words, masculinity is what femininity is *not*, and femininity is what masculinity is not. This finding is in contrast to Chua and Fujino's earlier findings (1999) regarding Asian men's acceptance of the complementarity of these dimensions within individuals. The notion of masculinity and femininity as incompatible with each other is an important idea that resurfaces later when we discuss the processes of gender role development. Additionally, gender roles were often regulated and enforced by invoking the strict cultural boundaries of what it means to be a woman versus what it means to be a man. For example, when asked about what *feminine* means, Grover replied that it was "someone who—well, I guess on the opposite end [of masculine]." Similarly, Alec responded that

> the message I get from what I had learned is that feminine is something to be less masculine. Like anything that is opposite to the masculine.

Defining male and female characteristics as incompatible and dichotomous thus becomes a tool of enforcement in gender role socialization.

An important characteristic associated with being a man that surfaced in many of the interviews concerned the qualities of being "successful" and "educated." Chet shared, "And you [are] brought up sort of education as something that seems to be very important." Education in turn is linked to the key to success, as Chet continued to explain:

> I think for a man, this relates back to my issue of responsibility. For a man, I think, uh, for a man, a man, you are expected to have—perhaps obtain a higher level of education so that you may be able to get into a more prestigious occupation so that you can perhaps earn more, more of a comfortable living for your family. And I think for your ideal male, you would . . . need to have a higher level of education. And be more financially comfortable. And for a woman, I think that's less important. I think it's—it's changing now obviously, but I think from my perceptions of an ideal woman is or at least has to aspire to, it's less of a significant goal. Like it's not, it's not like a woman has to become, has to be sort of earn a master's degree or be at a certain occupation, to be married, to be attractive, right? And I think that many—actually it's the opposite. Many studies have shown that the higher, the higher the education of a woman, she becomes less marriageable.

Chet affirmed that education is an important value in defining a man, particularly because it is the pathway toward success. Success here can be defined as financial security or occupational prestige. Chet shared an important link that success is framed within the context of the family as the ability of a man to provide for his wife and children. This measure of success for men is contrasted with women for whom marriage is primary and education is secondary. Many of the participants also raised the importance of "responsibility" in a man's life. Benson, for example, said, "[S]o there's a lot of responsibility for the ideal man." Chet discussed cultural messages shared by family members:

> My mom's sister is Chinese. Very, very good [*laughs*] uh, she mentioned something about, ever since I was young, what was that expression? "Ru guo ni mei you mian bao, jiu mei you ai qing" [literal translation: "If you don't have bread, you don't have love"] . . . it symbolizes, ah, I think like a sort of cultural definition of with masculinity in that it's heavily based on financial resources. So that a man has to be able . . . has to be able to financially provide for the family, and if a man is, cannot, does not have the resources or the capability at least the degree, the background, motivation to get to that particular step, he becomes that less manly. And a very good example, I think, is in Japan about—or in Korea, I think. Especially in Japan when I see these depictions

of men who are unemployed—I'm not sure if you've seen these type[s] of depictions, but some men who lose their jobs, but they continue to go to work. They pretend to go to work every morning, they still wear their suit and they go to work even though they're unemployed, but I think they're, they're embarrassed to share that information with their families. Because they're the sole breadwinner, provider in the family. Because you can go to work every day, and even though most of the time they [are] looking for jobs outside or they're standing by at homeless shelter just getting food, and they're really— . . . they absolutely don't want to disclose the fact that they are unemployed. And later on, they—in many cases, they end up committing suicide because of the fact that they don't have a job, right? And I think, and I haven't seen sort of studies, but I don't know if that's an Asian thing, or East Asian thing, or American thing or a male thing, I don't know, but just from my experience, it's—at least from Chinese culture, Chinese culture perspective, I think the financial aspect is a huge part of what people define as being manly.

As Chet poignantly shared, success and ability in leading and taking care of one's family framed within a "responsibility" narrative is considered so critical that even if a man loses his job, he continues to go through the motions of getting ready to go to work, even if it means going to a homeless shelter for a meal. Failure to live up to this responsibility also can lead to potential mental health consequences, including depression, anxiety, and, as Chet noted, suicide.

Participants often observed that a good education was not expected of women. Their role was not as provider and leader but as nurturer and caretaker of the home and children, taking a more subordinate and supportive role in the family. Isidor shared that his idea of an ideal man is someone who is "well-educated because a man mostly makes the bigger decisions than the woman does." We see how women and men are treated differently in the gender socialization process in the story of Dexter, who grew up with two sisters:

My father . . . always gave me more responsibility. He was definitely not as sweet with me. He was very stern, and you know, I took out the trash, I did these work where my sisters didn't, and it wasn't like my sisters weren't strong enough to do those things, but it was like these gender roles that we had at home. I think, I mean, some of my relatives would tell my older sisters, Well, you don't need to go to [school]. You just—all you have to do is marry someone rich or marry someone capable. Whereas for me, I was somewhat expected, like you have to go to school, you have to take care of family.

Just as with Chet, the importance of education and success were differentially applied in Dexter's family to men and women in the context of their role in the family. In both stories, we also see the influence of heteronormative values and prescriptions for gender roles; these are discussed by Chet and Dexter *only* in terms of men and women.

Although many participants described male and female characteristics and gender roles in dichotomous and clearly contrasting ways, some reported that common characteristics were expected of both men and women. Chet shared:

[T]hose two points [being planful and able to handle things when a plan does not work out], I think, are pretty important in terms of my description of the ideal woman or man. And also I think just . . . being responsible. Being responsible for yourself and for others, that's always something that I always value and that's something that is passed down from my parents . . . so I think for me, for a man or for a woman my ideal type is quite similar in terms of personality wise and in terms of outlook, and I think they would be quite similar.

Chet's emphasis on common traits highlights that, in addition to differentiated gender roles, larger cultural values and expectations are transmitted equally to both genders. In other cases, some participants discussed gendered characteristics that cross sex boundaries. Jules, for example, seemed to suggest that although men can be both masculine and feminine, he had not seen women behave in a masculine way:

Well, I mean, masculine is like, I don't—I never seen a woman be masculine before, but I mean feminine, it's kind of like masculine is more like the look outside for me, in my opinion. But feminine is more like, it can be look also, the look feminine, but I mean more likely for me, it's like the characteristic that tells you that, oh this is feminine or this is not feminine. Yeah, so if the guy who's like too sensitive and then talk too much and then like gossiping, that stuff, I would say that's like feminine side.

Even though he recognized both masculine and feminine qualities or behaviors in men, Jules noted that if men are "too sensitive" or gossip, they are acting too feminine. Here we observe subtle ways that gender role expectations are enforced. Although men may have the capacity to act feminine, it is quite evident that this behavior is socially unacceptable.

In summary, ideal images of men and women largely represent ways that characterological and behavioral expectations are different for men than for women. We reviewed physical characteristics, behaviors, attitudes/traits, and roles and responsibilities that are associated with women and men. There was some variability in the extent to which these characteristics were dichotomized by sex. Of note is the continued influence of broader cultural values of country of origin, centrality of family, and collectivism in shaping these ideal images.

Sources of Gender Roles

Participants in this study described a number of core characteristics of their ideal images of men and women. In sorting through these images, another prominent theme that emerged from the data was the sources for these images and beliefs. In other words, we explored with the participants how they came to learn about these ideas about how men and women should be. We broadly categorize these sources into three types: (a) individuals, (b) events and experiences, and (c) media.

A very influential way that the participants learn about ideal images of men and women is through important people in their lives. As expected, prominent people were often parents and other family members. Quite a number of participants responded to the question about ideal images of women and men by noting their mother and father. Hamish said, "For the ideal man, my answer would be my father." The immediacy of thinking about one's parent was another notable observation. Benson, for example, said, "Well, when I saw the word *ideal*, initially I was thinking about, you know, public figures that people know of, but then I quickly also thought about my father." Similarly, for women, Forrest reported:

> Because I have a very good mother, I feel like she should be the prototype for all daughters who are . . . sisters or mothers. That's why it's easier for me to start thinking about my mother 'cause I feel like my mother—the woman I'm describing, kind of she's like the ideal woman to me.

A major way participants acquired these images was through their observations of prominent individuals, and an important concept that emerged from the interviews was the idea of a role model. Alec said:

> Most of the time I think they learn the ideal man and woman from their parents as the role models. Or anybody else they choose to be the role model, it doesn't have to be the parents. It could be some people on the television or some people they read in the book.

Although not all participants identified parents or these important sources of gender roles as role models per se, their function as such was evident. Through observation of behaviors and attitudes/traits attributed to these role models, participants came to admire and acquire an image of how a woman or man should be. In most cases, through direct observations, participants saw in their fathers and mothers characteristics that they presumed matched with the appropriate gender. That is to say, in fathers they saw and thus learned what it meant to be a man, and in mothers they saw what it meant to be a woman.

Gender matching of observed characteristics is the only socialization process participants described. For example, there were times when participants learned what it means to be a man from observing a woman. Here, again, the ideas of admiration and role models are relevant. In admiring someone and seeing him or her as a role model, certain characteristics were integrated into the participant's sense of what it means to be a man, even if the role model was not a man. A good example is with Edward, who lost his father in his grade school years. Here he described what he learned about being a man and a father from his mother:

> When my father passed away when I was nine, it was really hard for my mother and she didn't have much education. She finished junior high, junior high school in Taiwan, which means nothing here 'cause she doesn't know English, and she, uh, she worked minimum wage for a while and tried to learn English, and she eventually got a job at the post office, which was like a government job, very steady, had good benefits, and, and from the story that she's told me, like her attitude, um, has kind of been, been my, been my ideal maybe, 'cause she would say some people wait for the best job, but she said if there's work to be

done, then she'll take it. She worked, everywhere she goes, like she works as hard as she can, and she told me the story about how she worked, worked at a restaurant where she wasn't guaranteed a position, and she just kept working, and then the next day she went and they said they didn't really have any room for her to work and they gave her four dollars for the, for the subway fare . . . and she took those four dollars and went and got a newspaper and started looking for another job right away that same day. Um, she didn't want to go back home without, you know, without another job. And so there's like a persistence, . . . she, no matter . . . what she's paid, she would work her, her hardest, and so just not, not giving up. And she actually got the job at the post office by studying really hard for the civil service exam, and she kind of had to take it until she made it [*laughs*]. She still doesn't know much English but she's good with people and they help her and she finds, finds her way through, learns what she needs to do at her job, and then she, she's been able to do it for a long time now. And so her approach to providing and work, I kind of see that as something that I want, want to emulate and pick up for myself, and that's why I would imagine, I would want from, from like a father or for men.

Edward's experience highlights the power of observation and the function that admiration and role models play in participants' lives. Although his mother was not the same sex as he is, he learned through her what it means to be a man by watching her work hard and sacrifice on behalf of her family. It is possible that his mother served as such a strong role model in Edward's life because she possessed many of the traits (i.e., sacrifice, perseverance, and hardworking) and served the role (i.e., provider to the family) that would have been expected for a man. However, as we will see in the next theme, without admiration, participants do not internalize these observations.

In some cases, some individuals served what we call anti–role models in participants' lives. In contrast to role models, anti–role models are individuals to whom participants have developed negative views. Instead of admiration, these are individuals whom clients learned to not look up to or emulate. Edward talked about an uncle in the family that served this role:

My uncle, he—I see him as very dependent on his mother still, and . . . he's a grown man and he can't do, do certain things for himself, or won't because it's been done for him. And . . . would say that's not an ideal man because, uh, 'cause if somebody does something for you, like you, you thank them or you show appreciation for that . . . or like if they weren't there in your life, like would things just, would you not be able to survive [*laughs*], like I guess survival is, it's another part of it, though. . . . I guess my idea of the ideal man is more of a reaction to an example of seeing the opposite of, of what I've seen maybe.

In contrast to his mother's example, Edward observed the behaviors of a man who is overly dependent on other family members and is not grateful for what others do for him. If having leadership and a sense of responsibility are important characteristics of a man, Edward concluded that his uncle is someone who possesses neither. Through him, Edward learned what an ideal man is *not*.

The impact of role models also can change during one's life; that is, once a role model, not always a role model. For Alec, an individual he once admired and aspired to be became someone whom he no longer viewed this way. Alec, who identifies as gay, shared a story about his first intimate relationship with a man:

So he is a military man, he's a military guy, so most of the time he, he doesn't talk much. He's a man of few words. Not few words. Little words. Really, really, really, he doesn't talk most of the time and when we're together, lots of time—most of the time, he doesn't talk at all. He'll just sit there. I was, I was, and I felt like that's the man I wanted to be. Tight-lipped, poker-faced, indifferent to everything, self-absorbed. . . . Then this relationship ended up in a disaster, and this whole ideal just suddenly broke down.

Alec went on to explain that he realized that whereas he initially admired and saw his boyfriend as "successful" in the beginning, in the end he recognized that these traits were too extreme. With the breakup of the relationship and his realization that he was not happy when they were together, he decided to change his idea of success and what he saw as admirable traits that he wanted to integrate into his gender role.

As many scholars have noted, parents are central to the gender socialization of children (Eccles, Jacobs, & Harold, 1990; Lytton & Romney, 1991), so it is understandable that they were often quite prominent in serving as models for many participants. However, other participants mentioned other influential individuals as well. For some participants, public figures served as both positive models (e.g., Michael Jordan [Benson], Hillary Clinton and Condoleezza Rice [Chet]) as well as negative models (e.g., Bill Clinton and Eliott Spitzer [Benson]). For others, such as Dexter, Grover, and Benson, siblings or other family members like uncles were important figures in shaping their experiences in the socialization process. Still another important source for gender socialization involved friends and teachers. Chet, for example, shared:

> The individuals that they select to surround themselves with that have enormous impact on—on their personality, on their value[s], on their identity in general, so I think perhaps friends, your friends, the friends that you spend time with probably will have more of an impact over time than your, than your parents or your family because maybe it's even more—or you value their opinion more when they're your closest family members.

Although parents and other families may exert tremendous influence over one's own gender role socialization, Chet's view suggests that other people can become influential as individuals gain greater autonomy over the formation of their social circle. Moreover, family influences may diminish over time while peer influences increase.

Events and experiences constitute another important source in the gender socialization of participants. Dexter told a story of when he was about 8 or 9 and met a gardener who was working for his family. The gardener was going through some difficulties in life that included some financial problems and shared them with Dexter. Dexter, being a "sensitive" child, subsequently became very emotional and cried when he was with his father. The rest of the story shows the power of events and critical incidences shaping gender roles:

> And I just started crying and I just started tearing up, and then when I went home, my father was—I mean, went in the house, my dad was like, Why are you crying? I gave the man [the gardener] the month advance. Why were you crying? And I was telling him, Well, you know, it's sad, why does his arm have to be hurt? Why does—and he's like, No, no, this is it, I gave him the money, stop crying. Don't cry. Like what is wrong with you? Why are you crying? Like he's not our family and, you know, that just—and I was bawling and he's just—he was really angry at me. He didn't want me to cry, and I mean I knew that I shouldn't,

you know, cry, and I was trying my best to not, you know, so. I think, I mean he had a hard life himself, and the messages that were sent to him—his father passed away when he was very young—was you have to be a man. You have a lot of other stuff to take care of. There's other things in life that are way worse than whatever that you're going through, and so like you have to toughen up and be there for the rest of your family. So I think his message is, I understand that it's sad, but every man has to do what they have to do. So the gardener has to do what he has to do to get his, and we have to do what we have to do, and you can't worry about other people and cry and feel for other people, or you're going to get stepped on, or you need to stay strong like for the rest of our family. I think that was his message.

Dexter's moving story emphasized the importance of needing to be there, be tough, for one's own family. Dexter likely saw his father as a role model in this instance as he made a difficult decision not to expend limited emotional resources on grieving for another's painful experience or family. The socialization of gender roles occurred here not through direct observation of a role model but through a role model's interpretation of an event. Furthermore, we again see the transmission of the ideal image of a man through qualities of toughness and responsibility in protecting one's family.

Another example of influential events also involves Dexter, who, as mentioned, grew up with two sisters:

> I just remember some conversations that I would have as a kid, like I would tell them, You know, it's not my fault I'm a boy. Like that's not my fault Mom treats me like this, or you know—and you know, they would tell me, Well, it's—we never asked you not to be a boy, you know, but we ask you to have the understanding and recognizing the certain rights that you have that we don't have, and you know, like we need you to be aware. And like for me at the time, I was just like, What can I do? What can I do? And they were like, We don't want you to do anything. And that leaves me totally confused! [*laughs*] Like what do you do? But you know, I think, like I guess as I grow older, I think I translate that more into like recognizing your privilege, and even at the times when you don't recognize your privilege, to be aware of like the things that you may possibly not recognize.

Again, through certain life experiences, gender role and identity issues were made salient for Dexter through important people in his life. Dexter's experiences also raise the topic of male privilege for the first time. Participants varied in the extent to which they explicitly discussed their self-awareness about male privilege, and those who did were in the minority. Knute is another participant who was aware of and struggled through issues of male privilege. He said, for example:

> There are times, though, where I wonder if I'm, I'm complicit in affirming the structures that exist and wondering what I can do to fight them. According to certain theories and theorists of privilege, you never give up on privilege, it always exists, so what can I do every day to fight that?

Both Dexter and Knute were aware of the impact of differential power statuses accorded to men. Dexter found it difficult to reject the differential treatment, particularly as it came from an important family member, whereas Knute struggled with the daily dilemma of fighting privilege. For both men, it seemed socially risky to challenge these patriarchal expectations. In the next section, we discuss in more detail the issue of self-awareness in the gender role socialization process.

Finally, many participants cite media as an important source for learning what it means to be a man or a woman. Isidor observed that media plays a big role in shaping ideal images of men and women.

> So I think the commercial media have a great role that shows us kind of how the man, how the ideal man look like, how the ideal girls look like, women. . . . So what the commercial advertisement[s] are trying to do right now are basically produce the ideal image. So that the customer will believe that if they purchase on the, like use their products or they go to the hotels or that place that they advertisement—that they advertise, they will have that kind of ideal experience, too.

Isidor noted the power of the media to produce ideal images that make those exposed to them desire what is represented and believe that the images are achievable; these media images likely influenced the specific physical characterizations participants described for both men and women. Hamish drew a distinction between the images presented in the United States and in Asia:

> I mean, like in each, I mean each region of the world they see ideal man or ideal woman in different ways. Like, for example, . . .

the male actor in the U.S. . . . , they possess an image of like a badass, like you know you see Johnny Depp, he's like wearing jeans and like trying to propose a bad boy image. But if you see like movie stars in Hong Kong or Korea, it's kind of like more elegant people and they dress clean and very, very gentle.

Hamish observed that images of men and women are qualitatively different between Asian countries and the United States. However, other participants, such as Isidor, suggested that because of the globalization of media, Asian media have been influenced by Western standards by becoming more focused on sexualized images of bodies. Consequently, these globalization forces are causing a homogenization of ideal images of men and women.

Some participants who grew up mostly in the United States expressed a heightened sensitivity to the representation of men and women through racialized lenses. They observed that the media does not merely represent images of ideal men and women; often these are positive or glorified images of *White* men and women as well as negatively stereotyped images of Asian men and women. For Asian Americans exposed to these racialized images of ideal men and women, their gender role socialization was marked by conflict. Knute, for example, shared:

Asian men, you know, in this society are very much emasculated in part, you know, because there's a stereotype of Asian man having small penises, right? And so there's this emasculation of Asian men, they're not strong, they're too nerdy.

He goes on to talk about an experience whereby a White friend said "me love you long time" to him:

It's like a term U.S. movies depicting what Vietnamese prostitutes said to U.S. soldiers during the Vietnam War: "Me love you long time." So for a White American friend to say that to an Asian American male friend both implies it's [a] colonialist imperialist kind of mentality, and simultaneously it emasculates and effeminizes me.

In both of these experiences, Knute wrestled with negative stereotypes of Asian men and women in the media that are highly racialized and oppressive, although he was able to see these images as external to his own definition of manhood. This is an important dynamic to keep in mind as we discuss how these experiences come to influence the gender role constructions of the participants we interviewed.

Tension and Agency in Gender Role Socialization

In this section, we introduce concepts that help pull together previous themes that emerged from our data analysis. Whereas earlier we focused largely on the *what* of the gender role socialization process (images and sources), here we focus more on *how* the emergent thematic categories relate to each other. Figure 6.1 depicts a model that represents how our participants were socialized about their gender roles. We suggest that cultural values (upper circle) operate in the background of the socialization process (middle circle) that, in turn, involves the observation of ideal images from a number of sources. Through this process, a participant arrives at a temporally situated gender role or identity. We believe it is temporally situated because the gender role socialization process changes over time. Furthermore, it is iterative in the sense that one's own gender role in turn socializes the gender roles of others.

One broad idea we would like to introduce is *tension*, based on our interpretation of the experiences of the men we interviewed. It is related to the concept of *gender role conflict* (O'Neil, 2008) in the existing literature; we have chosen to rename it to allow our data analyses to stay close to participant narratives. Although the gender socialization process may seem smooth and natural, there are times when certain events or experiences cause some tension in participants' socialization processes. During these moments of tension and conflict, a participant has the opportunity to reject or integrate particular gender roles and identities. One way that tension is created is when cultural values clash. Earlier we highlighted ways that cultural values may differ between the country of origin and the United States. When cultural values are incongruent with each other, participants must process conflicting goals and priorities. To the extent that the United States is more individualistic and Asian cultural values are more collectivistic and family focused, an Asian American male growing up in the United States must somehow resolve what it means to be a man from these competing perspectives. Our data analyses are consistent with existing research that has found that acculturation and enculturation factors influence the gender identities and experiences

Culture, Socializing Influences, and Agency in Gender Role Constructions 195

Cultural Values
- Country of Origin
- Centrality of Family
- Collectivism

Socialization Process

Observation
- Ideal Images:
  - Physical
  - Behavior
  - Attitude/Traits
  - Roles/Responsibilities
- Sources:
  - Individuals
  - Events/Experiences
  - Media

Tension
- Stereotypes of Asians and Asian Americans
- Cultural Values Between Asia and U.S.
- Generational Differences
- Self and Ideal

Agency

Gender Role

Gender Socialization of Others

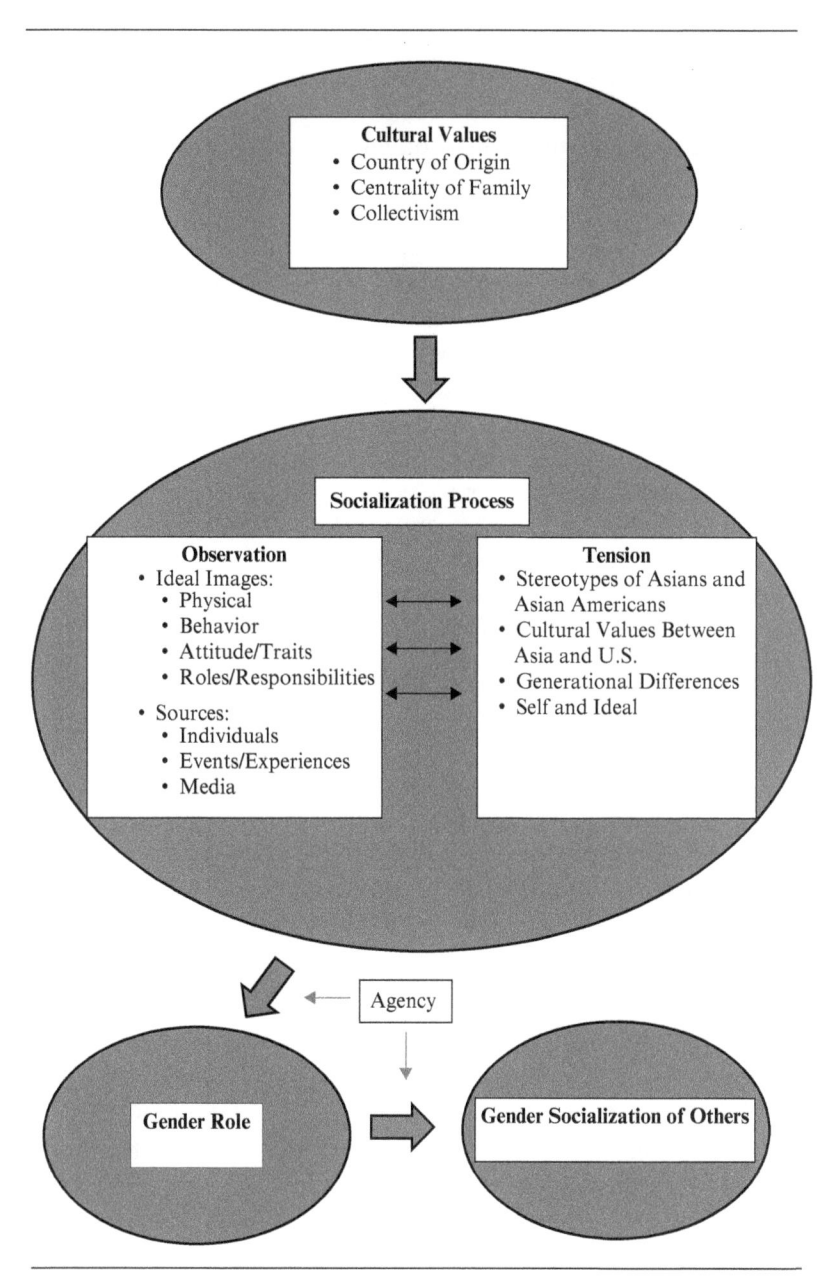

Figure 6.1 Proposed Model of Gender Role Socialization of Asian/Asian American Men

of Asian American men (Kim, O'Neil, & Owen, 1996; Liu & Iwamoto, 2006). Adherence to both traditionally Asian values and American values has been found to result in gender role conflicts.

For the participants we interviewed, sources of tension may originate from a number of sources described earlier. For example, tension may be created because of generational differences in ideal images of men and women. A number of participants observed that expectations for gender roles have evolved over time. When expectations are incongruent over time, the potential for tension is present. Negative stereotypes of Asian men and women in U.S. society were another source of tension. Participants discussed several familiar racial stereotypes of Asian men and women. Grover, for example, talked about representations of Asian men having small penises, and Hamish talked about images of Asian men being smaller in stature and size when compared to men of other races. These stereotypes can create strong tension in our participants because the stereotypes problematize their presumed gender roles via the public representation and discourse of their masculinity. Wrestling with public "ideal" images of manhood and their own personal ideal images is often a source of tension. Knute, for example, shared this:

> I think that the term *ideal* [. . .] the term *ideal male* is the representation of what society wants and I think society wants what the media tells it to want, which is the media being controlled by a select group of the ideal men that I just described. [*Sighs.*] I think for myself, the ideal male is the one who self-recognizes his own privilege, recognizes his own status, is self-aware, recognizes that simply because we are male, we get certain things given to us, but that's when it's automatically given to us.

A second broad concept we would like to introduce here is the idea of *agency*. In the interviews, participants varied in the degree to which the gender socialization process was impacted by their own internal processes (i.e., agency). In some cases, participants actively engaged in the process of integrating gender role expectations into their own gender role constructions. We saw this most often when participants were strongly influenced by role models and anti–role models and individuals' strong reactions to others who came to symbolize "best of" versus "worst of" examples of being a man. In other experiences, participants experienced pressure to conform to certain gender role expectations from external sources. These external sources seemed to emerge most often or most strongly when participants were perceived to be crossing the boundaries of their ascribed gender. Isidor described the common existence of transgender women in his home country of Thailand. He shared this experience when he was younger:

> Because I have my own sister, and basically we hang out a lot, so when my sister ask me if I want to do like cooking, pretending, you know, I just go along with her and somehow, I don't really know, somehow I just come to like it, too. So basically my parents . . . [tease] "Hey, are you going to be like a transgender or something, a gay or something?" . . . I think that's kind of affect[ed] my value[s] too because like am I supposed to choose something like that? You know, I just never thought about that before, but when my parents point out that just doing like cooking–pretending–makes you more like a girl rather than like a guy, it's just like makes me feel strange, because that's not the issue at all.

With Isidor's experience, we see the intergenerational transmission of gender norms. Furthermore, behaviors and attitudes originally experienced as neutral become gendered (i.e., typical or expected of one sex but not the other) and, over time, become a gender role norm that is enforced. In contrast to what were previously unconscious ways of behaving as a young boy, Isidor is taught by his parents to become more conscious of how his behaviors come to represent his gender.

The idea of conscious and unconscious processes of gender role socialization is helpful when understanding the experiences of these participants. Knute shared this experience:

> You know, I think this idea of being a man. . . . I think I'll use the term *good job* too because that's something I feel, you know, for—with the exception of me getting a PhD, I haven't been seen by my family as being a man, you know, as a teacher, and I worked with youth, but I wasn't a doctor, lawyer, businessman, you know, something successful. Those are the jobs that a man needs to have. In college, I tried dating Asian women and I think I was naturally attracted more to Asian women, but my ambitions weren't there, and since college, my ambitions weren't there. I've never had a problem dating non-Asian women, and this is a gross generalization, but in terms of Asian women, I feel like I'm not the man. What's interesting is for me, I'm not without fault here because it's true, and there actually have been times when there were Asian women who were attracted to me, but they don't fit my box of what an Asian woman should be. So it's—I'm being judged and in turn I judge other people, and so it kind of becomes this ridiculous scenario.

Here we see Knute wrestle consciously with cultural expectations of his gender with regard to his attractiveness as a sexual partner. At the same time, Knute is affected by the partly unconscious ways in which he transmits the cultural expectations that he finds problematic. These gender role norms, as we discussed earlier, can come from a number of sources, including friends, teachers, and the media.

One other important observation that we made is that although we have focused on the gender socialization of participants, we found that participants often discussed their impact on the gender socialization of *others*. For example, Chet aptly described the idea that gender socialization occurs iteratively:

> The individuals that [a person] selects to surround themselves with that have enormous impact on their personality, on their value[s], on their identity in general, so I think perhaps friends, your friends, the friends that you spend time with, probably will have more of an impact over time than your . . . than your parents or your family because maybe it's even more—or you value their opinion more when they're your closest family members. I think, I think some of the messages we receive are from our friends, and then of course, our friends receive those messages from their friends or from the media . . .

In sum, we first introduced the concept of tension that arises from wrestling with disparate images of gender roles. Second, we introduced the idea of agency, reflecting the extent to which participants actively or consciously take part in their gender role construction versus when gender role socialization arises from external pressures or subconscious/covert influences. Finally, we suggested that participants are not only the recipients of gender role socialization but in turn play a role in the gender role socialization of others. These three concepts, taken together, help to link the thematic categories we believe are important to the gender role constructions of Asian men.

APPLICATIONS FOR MENTAL HEALTH PROFESSIONALS AND EDUCATORS

In this section, we describe applications for mental health professionals and educators. These applications center on (a) the multifaceted nature of gender role socialization, (b) the varying sources of gender role socialization, and (c) the ongoing process of gender role constructions.

Multifaceted Gender Role Socialization

One of our most prominent conclusions is that gender role socialization is a multifaceted process. Through the experiences of the men we interviewed in this study, we encountered the complexity and cultural context of this process. A key theme of this book and chapter is the concept of *intersectionality*, which helps anchor our findings and suggested applications. As our participants noted, gender role socialization occurs within multiple cultural contexts that are defined by nationality, ethnicity, and immigration experiences. These experiences provide the background that helps contextualize and influence the other more specific themes that emerged in our analyses. Intersectionality is helpful in understanding these themes because we see how broad cultural and racial/ethnic factors moderate the various ways our participants come to see the roles of men and women in their lives.

With our participants, a configuration of cultural factors likely unique to Asian populations was prominent in their gender role narratives. Most prominent among these factors were the values surrounding family and collectivistic ideals. Numerous participants emphasized that male and female gender roles are often organized around cultural prescriptions for the family. Other researchers have highlighted the importance of cultural values in Asian communities (e.g., Kim, Atkinson, & Umemoto, 2001; Kim, Atkinson, & Yang, 1999) and provide some suggestions regarding how to intervene effectively with Asian male clients who may experience difficulties with values clashes. For example, Chu and Akutsu (2010) note that cultural conflict between generations can be quite common in Asian American families, particularly in younger men's attempts to uphold their responsibilities to the family, including caring for older parents, marrying someone of a similar background, producing children, and achieving success in an acceptable field, such as medicine or business. Failing to be the family's primary breadwinner, as sometimes happens with immigrant families, also can lead to psychological distress and, sometimes, domestic violence (Sue, 2001). Chu and Akutsu describe a type of male gender role strain of particular concern for Asian men, *discrepancy strain*, which they define as "the emotional or psychological distress that one may experience when one does not live up to internalized ideals and expectations" (p. 89) associated with culturally prescribed gender roles. One source of discrepancy strain is the precarious position of patriarchal power due to immigration status and acculturation to Western values that promote egalitarian attitudes, particularly in younger men. Chu and Akutsu further note that family conflict can be a risk for depression and suicide, and urge assessment of potential sources of discrepancy strain between generations within the family.

A number of mental health scholars (Chu & Akutsu, 2010; Sue, 2001) suggest the need to work within cultural values, especially those that are gender prescribed. Although some scholars have emphasized problem-focused coping strategies as culturally consonant with cultural expectations of emotional restraint and forebearance, Chu and Akutsu suggest a careful assessment of both client and context variables before moving forward with such strategies, since the level of family conflict (low versus high) may be linked with the ultimate outcome of these interventions. They further describe three culturally sensitive approaches for Asian American men in the midst of generational masculinity strains: (a) *unilateral acculturation*, involving the one-way conformity of the client to traditional Asian values and norms or separation from the family; (b) *integrative acculturation and bicultural frame switching*, involving learning about both Asian and Western values and norms and changing one's behavior based on the context; and (c) *internal and external negotiation*, in which the entire family is involved to identify areas of compromise and resolution. Chu and Akutsu identify this last option as the optimal, albeit the most sophisticated, approach. As we found with our participants, both immigrant (recent and distant) and U.S.-born individuals were influenced by native cultural values to varying degrees, so assessing these values will be critical for effective therapy to move forward. Moreover, clashes in values may be present for some participants, whereas others may have found ways to uniquely incorporate these values into their gender role constructions.

It is important to acknowledge that the cultural influences of the gender role socialization process are multifaceted and that important cross-cultural differences may further affect the definitions of masculinity among Asian men. For example, Sue (2001) identified several key cultural differences between Asian American and White/Euro-American men, including collectivism versus individualism; hierarchical versus egalitarian relationships; restraint of emotions versus expression of emotion as a sign of maturity; respect versus challenge of authority; and modesty versus self-promotion. At the same time, acculturation and enculturation statuses may vary across individuals, and these would have an influential effect on the strength of these cultural messages. Miller and Lim (2010) recently described the multiple complex processes of acculturation that may be at play for Asian and Asian American men as they sift through these many values. In particular, they highlight both the domain- and the context-specific components that may affect acculturation of these values, such that an Asian man might prefer to focus on hierarchical relationships and roles within his family of origin but practice egalitarian ways of interacting with either his spouse or coworkers. However, learning to navigate effectively across different contexts for different domains (e.g., language use, values, etc.) can be a major source of stress. For example, they suggest that young Asian men, particularly those who were born or have lived primarily in the United States, may experience *enculturative* stress, arising from pressure to conform to more traditional gender role behaviors.

Regarding educational concerns of Asian men, adhering to cultural values can be highly motivating but also very anxiety provoking in pursuing educational goals and aspirations. As Kwong-Liem and Mutow (2010) note, Asian American men may be socialized to aspire to those careers as befits their gender role expectations, particularly as provider and enhancer of family prestige. For the career development of Asian American men, Kwan and Mutow distinguish between unique personal factors reflecting who they really are and what they want to do from received messages about what is expected of them via cultural and contextual factors. In addition to cultural and family expectations, Kwan and Mutow also caution that the impact of the "model minority" myth may cause some Asian men to exclude certain educational and career goals because there is a presumption by others and perhaps by the individual himself that only certain careers (i.e., science, technology, and management) are acceptable and attainable. Teachers and advisors also may buy into these stereotypes and erroneously guide Asian

American male students to pursue vocational paths that do not truly reflect their interests or aptitudes. Kwan and Mutow urge educational and career professionals to become aware of biases that affect the kinds of opportunities or learning activities they provide to these students.

We encourage mental health practitioners and educators to employ these suggestions in gaining greater understanding of the individuals that they work with. Understanding gender role and gender role socialization of Asian and Asian American men can have important applications for both mental health and education (Liu & Iwamoto, 2006, 2007).

Many Sources of Gender Role Socialization

A second application of our analyses is based on varying sources of gender role socialization. For our participants—and this point is related to previous applications about the influence of broad cultural Asian values—the impact of family and cultural prescriptions surrounding the roles of men and women in the context of familial goals appear to be most prominent. However, prescriptive expectations do not always mean that the gender roles of Asian and Asian American men are completely congruent with these prescriptions. We saw that, at times, participants integrated these prescriptions and expectations into their identity quite willingly and sometimes unconsciously. However, there are also instances when participants react quite consciously against these social expectations of their gender role. Moreover, as participants informed us, other sources of gender role socialization may originate from family members, friends, and the media.

In working with Asian and Asian American men, exploring and adequately assessing the sources of gender role socialization is an important task because each individual may have a very unique constellation of influences. For mental health practitioners and educators, a good place to start in exploring these sources is with family, because family members appear to be early and strong influences on individuals, particularly in establishing the centrality of familial and collectivistic values in shaping the gender roles of Asian and Asian American men. Continuing with our previous suggestion of openly exploring learned cultural assumptions about gender roles, we encourage mental health practitioners and educators to openly explore where and how the individuals they work with learn messages about gender roles.

In addition to cultural values from multiple sources, it also is important to understand the potential impact of negative racial stereotypes on the gender role socialization of Asian and Asian American men. Liang, Rivera, Nathwani, Dang, and Douroux (2010) described the potential influences of gendered racism, particularly in the form of these stereotypes, on Asian and Asian American men. As our participants noted, stereotypes played a role in how they constructed their gender roles, particularly in their strong reactions to the public discourse on Asian masculinity. Liang et al. poignantly observe the multiple impacts these stereotypes can have on the psychological functioning of Asian males—for example, a less-than-ideal body image based on internalization of negative images (e.g., obsession with muscularity or lean physique). They suggest that mental health practitioners explore the kinds of images that Asian boys and men have been exposed to and possibly internalized, because these may lead to apathy or substance abuse.

Educators also might directly address these issues in classroom settings by providing positive images of Asian and Asian American leaders or conducting activities in which students identify positive role models. Internet educational and psychoeducational activities also might be excellent resources for both mental health professionals and educators to help clients and students explore the multiple sources affecting their gender role socialization and as a way of fighting the negative impact of racial stereotypes. Chang and Yeh (2003, in Chang & Wong, 2010) provide a number of helpful guidelines for organizing groups for Asian and Asian American men online.

Ongoing Gender Role Construction

Last, our analyses underscore the importance of understanding the *process* of gender role construction. Gender role socialization occurs over time and is not stagnant. Our participants, like those in other chapters, were in constant process of listening to and evaluating the images and sources of the roles. Our participants' constructions of their gender roles changed over time and are likely to continue to do so in the future. An important finding of the study is that in the course of constructing their gender roles, participants may encounter both conscious and unconscious messages. At times, these messages may create psychological tension, and negotiations and resolutions of these points of conflict are important events to understand. Moreover, in becoming gender socialized, participants become players in the socialization of others in their lives. The idea that gender role socialization can occur both consciously and unconsciously points to its ubiquitous nature of the gender socialization process. Furthermore, these findings suggest that gender roles and identities are to a great extent fluid and malleable. This finding has important implications for mental health practitioners and educators who facilitate understanding and change within individuals.

By approaching the socialization process as an evolving and dynamic one, mental health practitioners and educators can help the individuals they work with understand the possibility of developing greater self-awareness and agency in constructing their gender roles. Although some roles are influential and evolve unconsciously, as our participants have shown, when greater awareness and agency are present, individuals can have more influence on the particular gender role that they would like to nurture. This is a powerful message for mental health practitioners, educators, and positive change agents to help individuals understand. By acknowledging and working with the dynamic messages of gender role expectations, practitioners and educators can help individuals develop greater ownership in the gender roles and gender identities they are comfortable constructing and also help them become more conscientious and psychologically healthy change agents in the gender role socialization of others.

REFERENCES

Chang, T., & Wong, R. P. (2010). Using the Internet to provide support, psychoeducation, and self-help to Asian American men. In W. M. Liu, D. K. Iwamoto, & M. H. Chae (Eds.), *Culturally responsive counseling with Asian American men* (pp. 259–278). New York, NY: Routledge.

Chu, J. P., & Akutsu, P. D. (2010). Intergenerational masculinity strain among Asian American men: Emotion, coping and therapy approaches. In W. M. Lui, D. K. Iwamoto, & M. H. Chae (Eds.), *Culturally responsive counseling with Asian American men* (pp. 83–107). New York, NY: Routledge.

Chua, P., & Fujino, D.C. (1999). Negotiating new Asian-American masculinities: Attitudes and gender expectations. *Journal of Men's Studies, 7*(3), 391–413.

Eccles, J. S., Jacobs, J. E., & Harold, R. D. (1990). Gender role stereotypes, expectancy effects, and parents' socialization of gender differences. *Journal of Social Issues, 46*, 186–201.

Kim, B. S. K., Atkinson, D. R., & Umemoto, D. (2001). Asian cultural values and the counseling process: Current knowledge and directions for future research. The *Counseling Psychologist, 29*, 570–603.

Kim, B. S. K., Atkinson, D. R., & Yang, P. H. (1999). The Asian Values Scale: Development, factor analysis, validation, and reliability. *Journal of Counseling Psychology, 46*, 342–352.

Kim, E. J., O'Neil, J. M., & Owen, S. V. (1996). Asian-American men's acculturation and gender-role conflict. *Psychological Reports, 79*, 95–104.

Kwong-Liem, K. K., & Mutow, J. E. (2010). Career development of Asian American men: Stereotyping influences of being Asian American, a man, and "me." In W. M. Lui, D. K. Iwamoto, & M. H. Chae (Eds.), *Culturally responsive counseling with Asian American men* (pp. 171–190). New York, NY: Routledge.

Liang, C. T. H., Rivera, A. L. Y., Nathwani, A., Dang, P., & Douroux, A. N. (2010). Dealing with gendered racism and racial identity among Asian American men. In W. M. Lui, D. K. Iwamoto, & M. H. Chae (Eds.), *Culturally responsive counseling with Asian American men* (pp. 63–81). New York, NY: Routledge.

Liu, W. M., & Chang, T. (2007). Asian American masculinities. In F.T.L. Leong, A. G. Inman, A. Ebreo, L. H. Yang, L. Kinoshita, & M. Fu (Eds.), *Handbook of Asian American psychology* (pp. 197–211). Thousand Oaks, CA: Sage.

Liu, W. M., & Iwamoto, D. K. (2006). Asian American men's gender role conflict: The role of Asian values, self-esteem, and psychological distress. *Psychology of Men & Masculinity, 7*(3), 153–164.

Liu, W. M., & Iwamoto, D. K. (2007). Conformity to masculine norms, Asian values, coping strategies, peer group influences and substance use among Asian American men. *Psychology of Men & Masculinity, 8*, 25–39.

Liu, C. H., Murakami, J., Eap, S., & Hall, G.N.C. (2009). Who are Asian Americans? An overview of history, immigration, and communities. In N. Tewari & A. N. Alvarez (Eds.), *Asian American psychology: Current perspectives* (pp. 1–29). New York, NY: Psychology Press.

Lytton, H., & Romney, D. M. (1991). Parents' differential socialization of boys and girls: A meta-analysis. *Psychological Bulletin, 109*, 267–296.

Miller, M. J., & Lim, R. H. (2010). A domain- and context-specific view of acculturation: Implications for counseling Asian American men. In W. M. Lui, D. K. Iwamoto, & M. H. Chae (Eds.), *Culturally responsive counseling with Asian American men* (pp. 39–62). New York, NY: Routledge.

O'Neil, J. M. (2008). Summarizing 25 years of research on men's gender role conflict using gender role conflict scale: New research paradigms and clinical implications. The *Counseling Psychologist, 38,* 358–445.

Shek, Y. L. (2006). Asian American masculinity: A review of literature. *Journal of Men's Studies, 14,* 379–391.

Sue, D. (2001). Asian American masculinity and therapy: The concept of masculinity in Asian American males. In G. R. Brooks & G. E. Good (Eds.), *The new handbook of psychotherapy and counseling with men: A comprehensive guide to setting, problems, and treatment approaches* (Vol. 2, pp. 780–795). San Francisco, CA: Jossey-Bass.

Sue, D. W., & Sue, D. (2013). Counseling the culturally diverse: Theory and practice (6th ed). New York: Wiley.

Takaki, R. (1993). *A different mirror: A history of multicultural America.* New York, NY: Little, Brown.

U.S. Census Bureau (2010). Profile of general population and housing characteristics: 2010 demographic profile data. Retrieved from http://www.nyc.gov/html/dcp/pdf/census/census2010/t_sf1_dp_nyc.pdf.

U.S. Census Bureau (2011). Facts for features: Asian/Pacific American Heritage Month: May 2011. Retrieved from http://www.census.gov/newsroom/releases/pdf/cb11ff-asian.pdf

Chapter Seven

ASIAN AMERICAN FEMALE GENDER ROLES
Melissa J. Corpus and Marie L. Miville

Asian Americans consist of approximately 30 subgroups, which include a large scope of cultural traditions, religious/spiritual beliefs, and languages (U.S. Commission on Civil Rights, 1992, as cited in Sue, Mak, & Sue, 1998). In addition to experiencing similar historical influences of the migration patterns and discriminatory U.S. policies briefly described in Chapter 6, Asian and Asian American women also are socialized through cultural expectations about their presumed gender roles. For example, Wang (2001) notes the influence of Confucian philosophies on many Asian ethnic groups by prescribing virtues relevant to women, including behavior (i.e., must agree with "feudal ethics"), speech (i.e., talk less and only at appropriate times and settings), appearance (i.e., graceful and pleasant), and tasks (i.e., dutifully completing household chores). Confucian philosophies also include three "obediences" in reference to which women should obey throughout their lives: first father, then husband, and, finally, son. Moreover, Wang contends that the cultural value of filial piety reinforces hierarchical and patriarchal family structures in most Asian communities, "leaving the status of women institutionally underclassed" (p. 73). As a result of these expectations, Wang further suggests that many Asian and Asian American women may experience "gendered differential role strain" (p. 76), an example of which refers to the expectation of women to bear (and favor) sons, relegating their own, as well as their daughters', educational and career interests to a secondary status. Even today, pursuing educational and career interests as primary goals may lead to psychological conflict and distress for some Asian and Asian American women (Kawahara & Fu, 2007).

Asian American women also have been impacted by some of the same negative stereotypes in the United States described in Chapter 6, including the "model minority myth," the "Yellow

Peril," and the "perpetual foreigner." This last image refers to the presumed iconic image of Americans in general as being phenotypically and culturally White (i.e., blond hair, blue eyes, barbecues, and baseball), casting Asian Americans as perpetually foreign, regardless of the number of generations one's family has lived in the country (Suzuki, Ahluwalia, & Alimchandani, 2013). Moreover, as with other women of color, Asian American woman have been impacted by gendered racist images reflecting (a) the "'good' Asian female as being subservient, passive, and docile"; (b) the erotic or sensual woman, a stereotype that arose in the context of anti-immigration policies toward Asians in the late 1800s (i.e., lacking morality) and still in use to promote images of Asian and Asian American women as dehumanized sex workers; (c) the untrustworthy, manipulative "Dragon Lady"; and (d) the "extremely conscientious, hardworking, sexless employee or 'busy worker bee'" (Kawahara & Fu, 2007, pp. 182–183). Although these images starkly contrast each other, they each serve to mask oppressive U.S. policies and practices, with the overarching impact of marginalizing the experiences of Asian American women and potentially silencing their unique voices.

In the mid- to late 20th century, a number of mental health and educational scholars began to call for the exploration and development of theories and interventions that incorporate the multiple and varied cultural and immigration experiences of Asian Americans (Kawahara & Fu, 2007; Suzuki et al., 2012). These calls were part of the larger civil rights and social justice movements for people of color, women, and sexual minority individuals in the United States. For Asian American communities, these movements became the impetus for "bilingual education, ethnic studies programs, the removal of stereotypic images in the media, and an emphasis on resisting oppression" (Suzuki et al., p. 193). Through informal networks available through "chain immigration" (immigration patterns of joining family and friends in the United States), ethnic enclaves (e.g., Chinatowns, Koreatowns), and community churches, Asian American women were able to gather together to discuss the impact of racism and sexism, and other oppressive forces in their lives (Suzuki et al., 2012). A collective Asian American women's movement was formed to combat social injustice but has struggled at times for leadership and progress, due to multiple competing pressures on women, such as family responsibilities, cultural expectations, and economic difficulties (Kawahara & Fu). Today, however, many Asian and Asian American women are engaged in redefining their roles in their families and their communities, as well as the larger society.

Although some existing psychological and educational literature has shed light on gender-related issues (e.g., outcomes related to sexism), most research on gender and gender roles has not incorporated racial-ethnic contexts, including those for Asian and Asian American women. Further, a majority of studies have not investigated the various cultural pathways that influence one's understandings of gender and gender roles. Finally, much of the research in this area has been quantitative, which arguably may not be suitable for underrepresented or marginalized groups since many measures and theories are culturally bound. As a result, we explored racial-ethnic and other influences on the gender role constructions among Asian and Asian American women. We interviewed 13 Asian and Asian American women living in the United States, a majority of whom were born in the United States. Demographic information about our participants is presented in Table A.10 in the appendix. Data were analyzed using the procedures outlined in Chapter 1.

MODEL MINORITY, MODEL WOMAN

Our analyses of participants' interviews revealed the confluence of cultural factors that inform their gender role socialization and their lived experiences as gendered beings. *Model minority, model woman* emerged as the core narrative shared by participants. This narrative reflects the myth or presumption that Asian American women are expected to meet idealized prescriptive standards in the United States. In other words, Asian American women are expected to fulfill both the model minority stereotype—that is, not rock the boat—while being academically ambitious, achievement oriented, and financially successful. They also felt expected to fulfill stringent culturally informed gender roles common for most Asian American women, including being subservient to men in the family, supportive of their husbands, and sacrificial of personal educational or professional attainment for the sake of their families. In short, our participants felt they were at the intersection of both stereotypes and cultural scripts regarding their gender roles. This intersection was often difficult for participants to reconcile, given some of the inherent contradictions and similarities among these expectations.

The core narrative, model minority, model woman, is composed of three key themes: (a) gender role socialization, (b) negotiating intersections, and (c) pathways to passivity (see also Table A.11). *Gender role socialization* consists of the gamut of cultural pathways that influence perceptions of gender. Participants indicated that movies, television, religion, school, and familial cultural values impart overt and covert messages regarding gender roles. Data revealed that television shows and parents' behavior in particular conveyed implicit behavioral expectations about gender roles and heterosexuality. Most respondents also described the pervasive influence of familial messages concerning gender roles. However, with the exception of Filipina participants, few participants described how the specific ethnic background of their parents informed their understanding of gender roles.

Participants clearly indicated that there is considerable pressure on women to conform to their gender roles, as doing so often is perceived as a primary way of preserving culture (Gil & Vazquez, 1996). The common cultural understanding of many participants was that they are expected to follow the cultural norms of their family and/or society—for example, devoting their lives to the men in their family. Several Asian American women disclosed that their mothers explicitly and implicitly conveyed that their lives should be viewed as a supportive role for their fathers and husbands. Others indicated that their mothers conveyed messages regarding the expectation to adopt specific physical appearances (e.g., wearing makeup and feminine clothing) and to take up wifely duties (e.g., women serving as sexual objects for their husbands). In fact, a few participants shared that their mothers often rigidly modeled this behavior to their daughters.

The second major theme is *pathways of passivity,* which represents the various messages emphasizing passivity in relationship to race and gender. When participants were asked about messages specific to their Asian background, they shared various messages relating to passivity, submissiveness, and lack of assertiveness. Similarly, when participants were asked what it means to be a woman, messages regarding submissiveness and deference also emerged. Taken together, passive behavior (e.g., not rocking the boat) was a common message reflecting what it means both to be a woman and to be Asian. Although these messages appeared to be very consistent with race-ethnicity and gender, most participants, with the exception of Filipina participants, did not openly discuss their intersecting identities in an integrated fashion. That is, respondents often spoke from a unitary perspective, sharing perspectives about being a woman or Asian but not as an Asian American woman.

Although participants described examples of rigid expectations and beliefs regarding gender and gender roles as conveyed by family members, participants maintained their own unique beliefs despite these cultural scripts. That is, most of the participants created their own meanings about gender and gender roles. Our participants' narratives also revealed that many held an idealized image of being an Asian American woman. Moreover, they were faced with high expectations steeped in stringently held cultural values. In short, our participants indicated that they must contend with the stereotype of the model minority as well as the ideal way of being a woman and enacting their gender roles. Interestingly, many participants grappled with two sets of scripts, reflecting a "superwoman" ethos. That is, an overwhelming majority of respondents were pursuing educational and career goals and taking care of their families at the same time. In sum, participants attempted to preserve the traditional caretaking and nurturing role despite juggling full-time careers.

Negotiating intersections is the third theoretical category that emerged from our data. Deference to men is a consistent general belief in many Asian communities that participants observed their mothers upholding. However, most Asian American participants appeared to hold disparate, even contrary, perspectives from that of their parents. Irrespective of age and country of origin, all participants endorsed bicultural values, though bicultural gendered mores were demonstrated differently among participants. Most respondents ascribed to U.S. values of independence and were pursuing their educational goals and professional careers to satisfy their own personal needs and desires. However, although several participants valued their careers and education, they simultaneously upheld the traditional maternal supportive role, in which caretaking and nurturing were important qualities. Further, several participants also maintained certain traditional cultural values of femininity. For example, participants agreed that the word *feminine* connotes a "ladylike" appearance (e.g., skirts, makeup, etc.) and specific behaviors (e.g., nurturing, caretaking, and emoting). Overall, most Asian American women in our study ascribed to their own unique beliefs, a blend of their cultural heritage as well as their personally constructed gendered beliefs. Among openly identified lesbian participants, constant negotiation of their understanding of gender, sexual orientation, and gender roles was also discussed. Some participants revealed that religious scripts emphasized by their parents (e.g., marriage between a man and a woman) inherently conveyed heteronormative assumptions. Messages regarding specific feminine physical appearances (e.g., attention to makeup and long hair) indirectly conveyed these assumptions as well, given that these appearances are meant to physically attract men. There also was an absence of fluidity of gender roles or for inclusion of nonheterosexuality within these deeply held religious beliefs. In fact, many respondents directly referenced their parents' religious beliefs and/or the Bible to relay how they had learned gendered scripts.

Gender Role Socialization

Several important themes were represented as part of gender role socialization, including (a) the cultural value of filial piety, (b) the impact of religion and religious beliefs, and (c) emotional and physical components of gender and gender roles.

Filial Piety

Asian American women participants appeared to be strongly influenced by filial piety, a sense of obligation to one's parents and/or elder family members. In many Asian cultures, filial piety includes being good to one's parents inside and outside of the home to maintain a good reputation for parents and ancestors, complying with parents' desires (rebellion is frowned on), carrying out personal sacrifices, and performing one's job well to help obtain material things for parents. Given the indices of filial piety, these broad messages informed participants' understanding of gender and gender roles. More specifically, filial piety indirectly conveyed the importance of heterosexual marriage and procreation. In line with Asian American cultural values, many participants viewed fulfilling gender roles of heterosexuality through being a wife and mother as demonstrating respect and honor for one's parents. For example,

Cynthia, a 31-year-old Filipina American lesbian-identified woman who works for a magazine publication, noted how she struggled with the pressures of fulfilling presumed heterosexual roles. She noted that she had to negotiate and think critically as an adult, shifting her perspective of her initial familial influences and her own beliefs. Denise, a 51-year-old Japanese American bisexual woman who works in the insurance field, shared similar sentiments. She felt conflicted that her lesbian relationship with her partner (who is not Japanese) was not congruent with the deeply ingrained heterosexual, procreative cultural norms of her family. As a young girl, filial piety in her family also involved accepting lower educational and career aspirations as compared with her brothers. Denise grew up hearing that girls are not expected to pursue a career because they are expected to serve as supports to their husbands. She learned during her formative years that, in contrast, boys in her family had higher expectations to fulfill, as they were encouraged to pursue a college education and career for the sake of filial piety, while the girls in her family were discouraged from pursuing these goals. Essentially, boys were groomed to be breadwinners and financially support their wives and children as well as, eventually, their parents. Thus, college education was more important for the boys than the girls in the family. Denise shared:

> Expectations were more—Like a perfect example or one example would be like one of my—I have three sisters and one brother. So one of my sisters wanted to go to graduate school in the mainland, but my dad didn't want to pay for it. And, and basically all three of us, we went to school locally, college locally. But my brother didn't have a choice. My father forced him to go away to school. And ironically, he didn't want to go away! [*laughs*] . . . He had to go away to get the better education, make the better living. Whereas it wasn't like—worth it to pay for us to, you know, whatever.

As Denise observed, cultural expectations regarding gendered differences were so strong in her family that although her sister wanted to go away to college, her father refused to send her, while at the same time he paid for an education for his son that the son did not even want. Denise further acknowledged that fulfilling cultural obligations did not seem to benefit her. In her personal life, she and other female relatives distanced themselves from the constraints of Japanese cultural expectations:

> I mean, it's just ironic in that way that I think the women in my family I know went out, instead of falling into that typical norm, we all, we all went outside [these norms]. So, not to say that there still wasn't that male-female, but I think it's just ironic, I think, that we went searching outside . . .

Jessica, a 30-year-old Filipina woman, observed that cultural expectations were vastly different for boys and girls in her family. Boys were expected to fulfill higher expectations, which afforded them certain privileges at an earlier age. However, higher expectations prepared boys (regardless of their birth order in the family) for greater responsibilities, especially since they were expected to fulfill obligations of taking care of one's family and parents as they get older:

> I also have a little brother who was born six years after me, and even though I was the firstborn, my little brother got to do everything I couldn't do at the different ages, right? Got to drive the car first, got to go on dates first. Age-wise, even though I didn't get to do those things until at a much later age, so I mean they reinforced that with siblings as well, like treating them different . . . it just reinforced—it wasn't a surprise. I mean, it reinforced the belief that, you know, guys—boys are different, they have different responsibilities. They can carry—actually they can carry more responsibility earlier, right.

Thus, the privileges of being male regarding career and educational opportunities as well as being afforded certain privileges and status in the family also came with higher expectations to be a provider to one's own family as well as care for one's parents as they aged.

Impact of Religion

Throughout the interviews, many respondents revealed that they learned about gender expression and gender roles through religion, including how they even understood idealized ways of physical appearance as well as expected behaviors with their husbands. For example, Corazon, a 70-year-old, married, heterosexual Filipina woman, directly quoted religious scriptures as a notable influence on gender role socialization. When asked "What is the ideal woman?" she integrated God and Christianity within her understanding:

> The ideal woman is someone who can, decides to get married, have a family, and responsible, should get responsibility, should be to raise children who will not be a burden to society. And what I mean by burden to society, they should be raised like citizens and _____ having the faith, have the faith and the belief in God and believing in God is something that I think should be obedient to what the laws of God is, you know, which we call the Ten Commandments.

Thus, for many participants, religious beliefs were critical in specifying that gender roles of women are sacred and ensure that children are cared for and that both families and the larger society are maintained.

However, several participants felt that religious beliefs about gender were heteronormative and did not seem to allow for nonheterosexual, non–gender-conforming ways of being. Sherry, a 30-year-old lesbian-identified Filipina American woman, candidly talked about her mother's emphasis on religion and appropriate physical appearance for women:

> I think it was just preserving classic femininity in everything I did, from the way that you looked to the way that you acted. I think my mom was pretty extreme. I mean, she would quote Bible verses about a woman's hair is her honor, right? So if I wanted short hair, it was like No! If you cut your hair, it's like a defilement.

As Sherry noted, her mother instilled religious beliefs in her about multiple aspects of her gender role expression regarding her physical appearance, using strong language (e.g., "defilement") if Sherry did not conform. Maria, a 30-year-old heterosexual Filipina American woman, was informed by religious beliefs that nonheterosexuality was unacceptable. The following excerpt explicitly reveals the lack of tolerance:

> So I went to the Bible reading, and it was [*pause*], he was invited to go because his parents wanted him to go because that was their week to speak out loud to the group. And—did I tell you about this? And it was their turn that week, so we sat there and I was so uncomfortable because the topic of their little talk was the way a man should be and the way a woman should be. And

it was so uncomfortable because obviously my gay friend who had already come out to his parents, you know, was probably pretty uncomfortable listening to his parents talk about that in front of the whole, the whole group of people. And they pretty much said, you know, there's a man and there's a woman and then there's this third sex, and it's like a forbidden sex, or you know, there's these people that think that they're, you know, a different type or whatever. I don't know, but it put gay people, you know, in a different— I guess it assumed that a man and a woman should get married, you know, because we were talking about there's a man of the household and a woman of the household.

Maria's story highlights how religious beliefs can become part of the social world, as people come together to openly discuss heteronormative expectations that only men and women can establish a household. These beliefs might be held so strongly that parents may shame or embarrass their adult children who are living an alternative lifestyle in front of the congregation, as happened to Maria's gay friend.

Emotional and Physical Components of Gender

Respondents consistently stated that the word *feminine* is related to specific characteristics of verbal and physical expression that were learned through nuanced familial interactions and explicit messages from parents. For example, participants shared that *feminine* meant maintaining a physical appearance with a specific goal in mind, attracting men, and this typically involved wearing revealing clothing, makeup, and long hair. Andrea, a 31-year-old heterosexual Filipina woman, characterized the word *feminine* as reflecting both physical and emotional aspects:

I guess the first words that come to my mind: dresses and nice hair, makeup, being "proper." Like, you know, sitting with your legs together and not being too loud and feminine [*pause*]. Being delicate, that's what I think of, feminine. Like, well, okay, by delicate, I don't mean vulnerable, but I mean like [*pause*] not harsh. Sweet, to be sweet, and not like overly loud, rough.

And later she explained:

Nothing is coming to mind. I guess it would be like hair, makeup, long frilly hair, you have to look very girly, you have to be refined, wear certain clothing that shows your feminine side. . . . Masculine would be, I guess, well, I don't know. When I see the word *masculine*, I'm thinking of a female in dark colors and having her hair pulled back, so everything is done like a man, and acting very strong in their mannerisms and their work, the choice of work is very strong as well, other than the female is a little bit more soft and a little bit more, their actions have a—it's different.

Andrea adhered to traditional notions of femininity as involving being soft, pleasant, and delicate and saw this in opposition to what masculinity embodies: strength. Interestingly, Andrea was able to imagine a female as expressing masculine traits and described this as being "like a man."

Participants also noted that women were expected to demonstrate less physical strength and skill compared to men. While men were expected to have strong, imposing figures, women were expected to be less physically skilled in athletics. Women were expected to be less physically aggressive and maintain a softer appearance. One participant captures this sentiment:

Girls aren't supposed to do so well in playing [sports] [*laughs*], you're not supposed to be [*laughs*], you're not supposed to like . . . Like in gym class, they would separate us out and then like the boys would go shoot baskets on the one side and play Thunder and Lightning, and the girls would play on the other side, and then the gym teacher like pulled me over to play like with the boys' side because I think that [girls are] supposed to be less skillful.

Cynthia had similar observations about women and their physical strength:

I guess I was like in my first or second grade or something, and because I grew up with all my boy cousins, I could play baseball. And not a blood uncle but kind of—he was coaching his nephew, one of my—one of the guys that I grew up with, and he wanted me to play literally. But I guess at that time, it was a big thing, and then eventually I couldn't play because I was a girl. But I could play, but because I was a girl, I couldn't play.

While physical attributes were consistently mentioned, emotional characteristics were also related to the word *feminine*. Descriptors related to the word *feminine* included: supportive, soft, caring, sweet, and nurturing. Denise related the word *feminine* to being more considerate of others. She stated that feminine is associated with being "emotional, but maybe more soft, more empathetic, more considerate, or almost thinking of other people."

Pathways of Passivity

The pathways of passivity theme had two subcomponents regarding how women are expected to play subordinate roles in the family as well as society: division of labor and the use of double messages.

Division of Labor

Most participants revealed that they learned about gender roles from their immediate family, particularly their parents. Prescribed gender roles included ways of communication as well as responsibilities within the house. Our participants revealed that women in their families often held more passive roles within the household (e.g., men made the decisions). Women also were generally socialized to communicate in a nonassertive manner (e.g., nonconfrontational, compliant). Further, participants commented that there were certain household responsibilities unique to women, whereas men were viewed as the breadwinners. Notably, participants did not describe specific household chores that men are responsible for, such as work typically associated with men (e.g., yardwork, taking out the garbage, or other forms of physical labor around the house). Rather, participants generally stated that men are responsible for finances. Additionally, power and/or authority within the household were clearly divided between men and women. The majority of respondents were socialized to understand that men had the power because their opinion is rendered the most important, whereas the woman's role is to be deferent, as Andrea described:

> It's typical, the man is the breadwinner, the man is the head of the household, the man is supposed to be the leader, he's supposed to be able to be the one that supports the family. And the woman is to be the nurturer, the person that takes care of the house for the children, it's the weaker of the two and always relies on, uh, a man to support her financially.

However, some Filipina respondents described different roles in the household. These participants described a division of labor that reflected a more matriarchal household; thus, women determined children's schooling and discipline as well as controlled finances. Cynthia observed that her parents demonstrated a more equitable relationship while other families followed culturally prescribed gender roles (e.g., man served as breadwinner, woman was in charge of household):

> Well, I think that it's kind of different 'cause at our house, I mean, my parents have switched like the cooking, the caretaking, whatever . . . , I would say that they both had equal parts. I would observe like from our family friends and famil[ies] in the community, . . . it seemed like the male is someone that maybe earned—well, yeah, I mean, who brought in the income and the woman like stayed home and, um, took care of the children and cooked the food.

Cynthia's story reveals some individual differences in her family, where the family roles and responsibilities were marked by egalitarian attitudes, in contrast to other families in her community. Her story also indicates the potential differences that exist in terms of cultural prescriptions among Asian ethnic groups. That is, although Confucian philosophies about virtues and obedience may be a predominant influence even to this day in cultural prescriptions of female gender roles, important differences exist among ethnic groups that must be explored, rather than be presumed, by mental health professionals and educators (Suzuki et al., 2012; Wang, 2001).

Double Messages

Throughout the interviews, it was abundantly clear that participants had to contend with messages communicating passivity and inferiority via gendered cultural expectations and racial stereotypes about Asians. Behavioral expectations of women appeared to be related to passivity and compliance in relationships with men. Details regarding intonation and volume of speech were notable, as these expectations appeared to be associated with communicating in a more demure, less assertive way. For example, Karen, a 27-year-old Korean American, described women's style of modest communication as "demure or quiet. Soft-spoken, maybe sometimes too nice." Another participant, Denise, shared how she feels unequal to a man:

> I was for a long time thinking that I have limits to what I can . . . cannot do or can say or cannot say or, um, the rights that I have are not as, the same as a man. That I'm not equal to

a man. I think that's what I really want to say, that in itself there is just—you know, that I'm equal to a man.

As Denise noted, she internalized, at least for a time, the belief of her inferiority to men, although eventually she began to counter this with her own belief that in fact she was an equal. She further described expectations regarding limited communication by women, particularly if a woman disagrees with a man: "Pretty much the woman can't really say what they, what they really feel. They have to check their emotions every time."

Another Filipina American woman named Ashley commented that women are expected to be obedient. She noted that an ideal woman is "obedient and quiet, calm, educated, you know, smart, respectful." Ashley further elaborated on these expectations, underscoring the extent of a woman's need to be obedient:

> The man in the family has the last say and has the right to tell the woman what he thinks she should wear or what they think they should do for social type of—in social situations or what they should be doing on the weekends or the appropriate way to act.

Karen further elaborated and described women as the "weaker" part of the relationship, given their lack of authority within the family:

> Well, she's the one that is perceived to be the weaker part of the unit because she's the one that doesn't have any say-so in, um, the major decisions of how the family should be run or which way the family should go.

Thus, as Karen, Denise, and Ashley all note, cultural expectations regarding the subordinate role of women were mirrored in the ways they were expected to silence or suppress their voices, at least in relation to men in their families. Wang (2001) writes that these expectations reflect long-held beliefs that promote patriarchal structures of many Asian families. However, as Denise found, she began to develop her own more egalitarian views as she grew older, coming to believe she had equal rights as men. Homma-True (1997) cautions that although many Asian American women may come to wish to be autonomous and not subordinate their wishes to their husbands, they may not be able to change their family's belief systems. Instead, she suggests helping these women face their own negative internalizations, as Denise did, if these beliefs are interrupting their sense of self-esteem and causing psychological distress.

In addition to messages that participants received about the inferiority of women, all participants consistently indicated that they received similar negative messages about Asians as a racial group in the United States. Respondents shared that they believe other racial groups perceive Asians as compliant and nonassertive. In fact, these characteristics were often discussed in a positive manner rather than as negative stereotypes, given that Asians are seen as people who do not rock the boat in work settings. Although intelligence was a characteristic that was associated with being an ideal woman and Asian, participants believed intellectual prowess to be tempered by the qualities and expectations of submissiveness, passivity, and nonassertive behavior. Candace commented:

Whites view Asian women as very subservient. [. . .] I think they view them as being very, you know, always being so intelligent, and I think they view the Asian men as being very dominant.

Karen also described the model minority myth in the context of other racial-ethnic groups:

I still feel they think of them as very passive, like almost equal to Jewish people [laughs], very much equated with Jewish people, like they're the model minority. I mean, I experience that at work, you know. That they, you know—it works to, I think, Asian people's advantage at times, you know. They see a resume, they automatically think A, B, and C when that's not necessarily true.

And further:

Someone who is educated and successful and blends in and doesn't cause any problems, doesn't cause any riots—not riots, but just doesn't cause any problem, but just kind of blends in with the majority.

As both Candace and Karen indicated, the model minority myth continues to exert its influence in today's society. On one hand, this myth specifies seemingly positive qualities regarding intelligence and a good work ethic that still serves to dehumanize Asians and Asian Americans. This is particularly true for women, who must contend with a dual stereotype of being perceived as subservient due to their gender and race.

Negotiating Intersections

Negotiating intersections is the last theoretical category that emerged from our data. As mentioned previously, most participants were socialized to internalize beliefs about women that were related to being compliant, submissive, weaker, heterosexual, feminine, and inferior. These beliefs were transmitted by multiple sources, including parents, extended relatives, media, and school settings that imparted these messages indirectly and directly. Although most women were aware of messages that communicated the cultural values of their inferiority and passivity, the majority of participants constructed their own beliefs about gender and gender roles.

Making It on My Own

Given the differences in generation status, religious background, educational attainment, and sexual orientation, participants constructed their lives as gendered beings in a variety of ways. Blending traditional U.S./American values of independence, individuality, and autonomy with traditional Asian values of conformity, compliancy, and emotional reserve was a common theme. In this sample, participants clearly valued their careers and education but simultaneously preserved some traditional ways of expressing their femininity (e.g., long hair, makeup, soft-spoken) and beliefs of what it means to be a woman. Overall, caretaking, nurturing, wearing makeup, long hair, and skirts, and communicating in a soft, nonassertive manner were behaviors that some consciously enacted as feminine traits, although others did not. The inconsistency in beliefs within this sample demonstrates the uniqueness of personal constructs that each woman held as well as the importance of the participants' unique ethnicities and other diverse dimensions. In particular, openly identified lesbians negotiated their sexual orientation and beliefs about gender expression and presentation with some of the religious values that they were socialized with. Candace described her ability to critically think about some of the messages that she grew up with:

> I think it's tough for people to kind of get a grasp of where their gender role ideals come from, you know. I mean, they think it's

from their parents, but it's really evolving as they . . . become adults and learn to critically think, and it's a constant battle. I mean, I battle with it all the time.

Candace shared that constructing her gender role is a constantly evolving process that can be fraught with conflict. Denise revealed that she sought out people from different cultures, given that she did not want to be subservient in a relationship, as she was groomed to be in her own culture.

Japanese culture, you know, men got everything. You know, and women were more subservient in gender, in general. And so I knew I didn't want that. So probably a lot of that led to me looking outside of my culture or race or whatever, although—yeah, so probably because of that, you know, I was looking for something different. So probably something more equal.

As a result of her not adhering to the belief of women's inferiority, Denise was led to seek people beyond her cultural background, in hopes of finding others who might share her own evolving views. Rather than seeking out another culture, Cynthia acknowledged that she simply had come to believe that masculinity and femininity have a scope of different meanings, depending on their cultural context. According to Cynthia, masculinity among lesbians and heterosexual men is expressed differently yet similarly. She described her beliefs about masculinity in various contexts:

I guess, you know, acting like a guy, you know, kind of being—well, I think of it as more *machismo*, like being a total guy style, you know. I don't know how to express it. I guess when I think about it with lesbians, it's different. [*laughs*] It just complicates things! More like they dress more androgynous and they're definitely more the caretaker or the breadwinner and they take control of things. I think that's how I see it.

Despite, or because of, cultural prescriptions regarding gender roles, Cynthia was able to construct her own unique views of masculinity and femininity. In addition to gender and race-ethnicity, sexual orientation also influenced how these meanings were derived for Cynthia, Candace, and Denise. Being able to think critically about gender role messages and to observe the impact of these messages on oneself and others was key to being able to construct more personally relevant gender roles for participants.

APPLICATIONS FOR MENTAL HEALTH PROFESSIONALS AND EDUCATORS

Our participants' poignant narratives provide a number of insights and implications for mental health professionals and educators working with Asian American women as well as with other populations that have multiple, marginalized identities. Given the key themes of gender role socialization, pathways to passivity, and negotiation of multiple identities, it is important for clinicians to be mindful of creating a welcoming environment to allow Asian American women to feel accepted. In this section, we provide suggestions for attending to and affirming the breadth of gender role values and expressions, developing a collaborative stance with clients and students, and affirming their multiple pathways and multiple selves.

Breadth of Gender Role Values and Expressions

As emerged through our analyses, Asian American female participants endorsed a breadth of unique gendered values that were informed by their racial-ethnic and gender role socialization. On the whole, most participants acknowledged that they had been socialized in more traditional cultural expectations regarding women's roles in the family and society. Many had heard messages from parents and others reflecting gendered beliefs described in the literature, such as subordination to men and feminine self-expressions (i.e., graceful and delicate) (Wang, 2001). On one hand, affirming the value of women's supportive roles in the family may be important for some women who have accepted these cultural prescriptions, perhaps due to deeply held religious and spiritual beliefs. Connecting these clients with others sharing similar beliefs and problems in living, perhaps through a community church, may promote their well-being by helping them to build a supportive community. For example, Serafica, Weng, and Kim (2000) described that multiple relationships built through social networks have been extremely important to the psychological adjustment of Asian and Asian American women, including helping them adjust to problems and situations relevant to immigration concerns. From their extensive literature review, Serafica et al. found that becoming immersed in social networks, as might be found in church or religious communities, facilitated women's engagement in a larger social network.

Other participants expressed conflicts and emotions about accepting these culturally prescribed beliefs, including their struggles when internalizing attitudes about their presumed inferior status and abilities. As a consequence, some Asian and Asian American women may experience the gendered differential role strain described earlier (Wang, 2001), which has shaped the expectations and sense of self-efficacy about assuming roles beyond the family of many generations of Asian and Asian American women. Thus, as Homma-True (1997) suggested, it may be more effective to help some women focus on changing their internalizations of culturally prescribed gender roles rather than attempting to change the family's views.

Still other participants said that they personally held more flexible gender role values and even expectations that were unique and, at times, contrary to cultural expectations. For these women, it will be important to provide a safe and supportive space within the therapeutic dyad as well as through other relationships and social networks to explore these flexible definitions and expressions. Serafica et al. (2000) note that social networks were a primary source of the women's movement in Asian American communities and that these networks continue to empower women to "reconstruct their personal identities and redefine their roles" in many ways, including engaging in traditionally masculine behaviors and activities, challenging sexism in one's ethnic community, and even escaping domestic violence or sex work (p. 169). Similarly, in her research with a group of Asian American women engaged in social advocacy work, Louie (2000a) found these women had engaged in a number of community efforts, such as providing social services to recent immigrants or counseling services to abused women. Louie noted that these women also demonstrated a strong internal locus of control that helped identify and organize against instances of social injustice as well as an increased sense of self-worth and affiliation with others. However, she observed the need for more leadership and mentoring opportunities for women engaged in such work.

In sum, rather than assuming that all Asian American women share the same core values and beliefs about gender and gender roles, it is important for mental health professionals and educators to be mindful of both common cultural expectations as well as personally constructed gender role beliefs and expressions that incorporate or redefine these prescriptions. Suzuki et al. (2012) urge professionals to consider and be inclusive of the multiple group identities that often are at play for Asian American women, including ethnicity, national origin, ability status, and socioeconomic status. Chen (2009, in Suzuki et al.) highlighted three ways Asian American women can negotiate among these identities: "(a) focusing on one of the identities, such as race *or* ethnicity *or* gender; (b) compartmentalizing one's identities into separate categories; and (c) integrating one's identities into one holistic identity" (p. 192). Each strategy may be effective, depending on time and context, and it is possible that given the unique setting, individuals may use one or more strategies.

Adopting a Collaborative Stance

Given our findings that indicate that socialization of multiple pathways of passivity is potentially relevant for Asian American women, we suggest mental health professionals and educators to create a collaborative stance with their clients and students. For example, in light of the potential socialized tendency of Asian American female clients toward passivity and compliance within sessions, clinicians need to be aware of the uneven power dynamic within the therapeutic dyad. For example, feminist therapists who emphasize assertiveness as an adaptive quality will need to attend to the unique nuances of their clients' contexts, such as their relations with spouses. Homma-True (1997) acknowledged that "assertiveness training can be effective for those who are being exploited at work if it focused on the specific situation and careful attention is given to separate and maintain an acceptable pattern of behavior within the context of the Asian American community" (p. 424). Homma-True also suggested that mental health professionals of similar racial-ethnic backgrounds can serve as positive role models for clients in terms of negotiating among the varying demands of one's family and community.

Mental health practitioners also are encouraged to help their clients identify and negotiate their personal values. Similarly, we suggest mental health professionals to be cognizant of their own personal values and biases regarding gender and gender roles when working with Asian American women. For example, participants' narratives illustrate that some Asian American women continue to uphold traditional values in the home environment (e.g., passive communication; caretaking role). Given that many therapists typically hold a more egalitarian viewpoint of relationships and household responsibilities, we suggest that mental health professionals be mindful that their clients may hold different, even conflicting, values. Although clinicians may perceive their client to be "too passive," clients instead may view their role as collectivistic and an appropriate, valued role within their family. A lack of awareness regarding heterogeneous mores/values within this demographic group may be harmful, as Asian American women may subscribe to gendered beliefs not consistent with prevailing Western norms. Louie (2000b) suggests that one way of conceptualizing interpersonal relationships for Asian and Asian American women is to understand the value of *interdependence* rather than independence, in which "others are partially included within the boundaries of the self because relations with others are the defining features of the self" (p. 213).

In addition to mental health professionals, educators are encouraged to take a similar culturally aware collaborative stance. Recent statistics show that, despite cultural prescriptions regarding women not pursuing their educational aspirations, more Asian American women are obtaining college-level degrees than their male counterparts (*Catalyst*, 2012). However, they continue to earn less ($751 versus $970) than men but more than women of any other racial-ethnic group, and remain severely underrepresented in major leadership roles in most educational and business settings. Thus, educators have the potential to be effective in facilitating the educational and career aspirations of Asian American female students. Educators can attend to the key theoretical categories, such as gender socialization (e.g., influence of school and family), given that the developmental trajectory of girls and young women in higher education contains highly influential messages concerning gender. School environments in the United States are settings that typically encourage academic exploration, attainment of higher education, and pursuit of professional interests. Our analyses reveal that Asian American female participants receive contrary messages from their families regarding the need and importance of pursuing advanced degrees. Thus, educators must beware of their own Western biases and presumptions about academic and professional independence and autonomy, underscoring the importance of education and careers within this framework. Moreover, parents may socialize the qualities of passivity, caretaking, as well as deference to and support of one's husband in their young daughters, setting up further potential conflicts between the home and school/career environments for young Asian American girls. Thus, we urge educators to adapt educational strategies that incorporate their students' cultural values, perhaps framing an education with improving a young woman's culturally sanctioned role to support her family. Moreover, to enable better educational and professional outcomes, educators might provide opportunities for their students, particularly Asian American females, to explore in school settings their own gender role beliefs, perhaps through the use of possible selves activities mentioned in previous chapters.

Affirming Multiple Pathways, Multiple Selves

As we heard through our participants' narratives, many were engaged in constant constructions of their gender roles, both in their families and in the larger society. They also interwove other diverse dimensions of their identity, based on their ethnicity (e.g., Filipino, Chinese, Japanese) and sexual orientation, as part of these gender role definitions. Mental health professionals and educators can provide critical support for these explorations along many paths and settings as Asian and Asian American women negotiate their roles. Chin (2000) affirms the normative struggles of Asian and Asian American women as they encounter the multiple complex challenges of immigration, language acquisition, racism, and sexism, using the term *interactive dualism* "to describe the evolutionary and historical perspectives, the oppression of socioeconomic and sociopolitical contexts, and the diversity of experiences and cultural groups that come together, interact, and influence one another" (p. 227). Chin further notes the tendency of these forces to "both interact yet remain separate," leading to "inherent tension and [reflecting] the inability to eliminate and amalgamate differences" (p. 227). Thus, constant struggle and continuous constructions do not necessarily reflect confusion, dysfunction, or even doubt over one's self-definitions. Instead, using bicultural or even multicultural lenses (i.e., incorporating multiple dimensions of diversity, as based on race, ethnicity, abilities, social class, etc.), we encourage mental health professionals and educators to approach and help frame these struggles and changing definitions as "rational, appropriate, adaptive, and healthy. In other words, [multiple] selves are OK" (Chin, p. 227).

REFERENCES

Asian-American women in the United States. *Catalyst* (2012, April 26). Retrieved from http://www.catalyst.org/publication/224/asian-american-women

Chin, J. L. (2000). Paradigms for Asian American women: Power and connections. *Relationships among Asian American women* (pp. 223–230). Washington, DC: American Psychological Association.

Gil, R. M., & Vazquez, C. I. (1996). *The Maria paradox: How Latinas can merge Old World traditions with New World self-esteem.* New York, NY: Perigee.

Homma-True, R. (1997). Asian American women. In E. Lee (Ed.), *Working with Asian Americans: A guide for clinicians* (pp. 420–427). New York, NY: Guilford Press.

Kawahara, D. M., & Fu, M. (2007). The psychology and mental health of Asian American women. In F.T.L. Leong, A. G. Inman, A. Ebreo, L. H. Yang, L. Kinoshita, & M. Fu (Eds.), *Handbook of Asian American psychology* (pp. 181–196). Thousand Oaks, CA: Sage.

Louie, K. B. (2000a). Asian American women and social advocacy. In J. L. Chin (Ed.), *Relationships among Asian American women* (pp. 13–23). Washington, DC: American Psychological Association.

Louie, S. C. (2000b). Interpersonal relationships: Independence versus interdependence. In J. L. Chin (Ed.), *Relationships among Asian American women* (pp. 211–222). Washington, DC: American Psychological Association.

Serafica, F. C., Weng, A., & Kim, H. K. (2000). Friendships and social networks among Asian American women. In J. L. Chin (Ed.), *Relationships among Asian American women* (pp. 151–175). Washington, DC: American Psychological Association.

Sue, D., Mak, W. S., & Sue, D. W. (1998). Ethnic identity. In L. Lee & N. W. S. Zane (Eds.), *Handbook of Asian American psychology* (pp. 289–323). Thousand Oaks, CA: Sage.

Suzuki, L. A., Ahluwalia, M. K., & Alimchandani, A. (2012). Asian American women's feminism: Sociopolitical history and clinical considerations. In C. Z. Enns & E. N. Williams (Eds.), *The*

Oxford handbook of feminist multicultural counseling psychology (pp. 183–198). Oxford, England: Oxford University Press.

Wang, V. O. (2001). Hold up the sky: Reproductive decision making by Asian women in America. In D. E. Pope-Davis & H. L. K. Coleman (Eds.), *The intersection of race, class, and gender in multicultural counseling* (pp. 71–88). Thousand Oaks, CA: Sage.

Chapter Eight

NEGOTIATING MULTICULTURAL GENDER ROLES
A Proposed Model

Marie L. Miville, Lucinda Bratini, Melissa J. Corpus, Michael Y. Lau, and Jorja A. K. Redway

For much of the 20th century, psychologists conceptualized gender in terms of differences between men and women, typically framed as stable personality traits, masculinity and femininity, that invariantly distinguished the two sexes (Spence, 2011). Interestingly, Shields and Dicicco (2011) note that the originating research conducted in the 1930s was driven by an interest in identifying "sexual inversion," or homosexuality (i.e., identifying gay and lesbian individuals by their endorsement of feminine and masculine traits, respectively). However, by the mid- to late-20th century, with the rise of feminist psychology in the 1960s and 1970s, the study of gender became more complex, as mental health professionals began advancing the idea that perhaps masculinity and femininity, still presumed to be personality traits, were orthogonal rather than bipolar dimensions. During this time, psychological health was conceptualized as "balanced" individuals having both sets of attributes (Spence, 2011). However, even this approach proved flawed, not only because of the lack of evidence for this contention but, more seriously, because the study of gender was still framed as an unacknowledged endorsement of sex-based stereotypes (Shields & Dicicco, 2011).

From the late 1980s onward, gender began to be studied "in context" rather than as inherent traits (Deaux & Major, 1987, in Shields & Dicicco, 2011). Part of this reconceputalization involved reframing gender roles (i.e., behaviors that enact presumed qualities of masculinity and femininity) as embedded within the larger sociopolitical context reflective of hierarchical power relations. A social constructionist approach, such as the approach we took in this book, conceives of gender as a "*process*—often characterized as 'doing gender'—which simultaneously creates and reinforces cultural meanings of gender and the systems of power and oppression on which it rests" (emphasis in original; Shields & Dicicco, 2011, p. 495). In other words, gender, and its relevant constructs, "emerges through social interactions as a negotiated statement of identity . . . [it] is not something that one achieves . . . rather it is continually practiced in social interactions large and small" (p. 495).

As we noted in Chapter 1, research on the psychology of gender has been critiqued as representing only part of the story and that cultural and oppressive experiences based on other social group memberships, such as race-ethnicity, social class, and sexual orientation, also must be incorporated into theory and research in this area (Cole, 2009; Hurtado, 2010). Our current series of interview studies focused on describing how men and women of diverse racial-ethnic groups constructed their gender roles. As was apparent from our participants' narratives, several important parallel themes and processes emerged, suggesting commonalities of experiences among men and women of color regarding their constructions of gender and gender roles. In this chapter, we suggest a theoretical model, based on our analyses and interpretations of these narratives, for conceptualizing gender roles, incorporating both race-ethnicity and gender as important contextual variables in describing these roles. Throughout, we also provide suggestions for applications of this model for mental health professionals and educators.

SUMMARY OF OUR ANALYSES

As our participants informed us, racial-ethnic group membership greatly affected how they constructed or "did" gender. For example, many of our participants described sex-typed norms and attitudes that they learned in their youth from parents, extended family members, peers, and religious and educational institutions that communicated cultural expectations regarding masculinity and femininity (Spence, 2011)—that is, norms linked with either being male or being female. Examples of cultural values imbuing participants' understandings of gender roles involved *respeto* among Latinas/os, filial piety among Asians/Asian Americans, and knowing one's history among African Americans. Many cultural expectations centered on the complementary roles that men and women play in the family structure and their respective racial-ethnic communities that help ensure their survival and success. Participants from all racial-ethnic groups we interviewed indicated that men typically were viewed in a leadership role with responsibilities as protectors and providers, whereas women were expected to be caregivers, nurturing, and subordinate to men in the family. Strong expectations regarding the embodiment of gender (i.e., men as muscular and tough, women as soft and curvy) as well as its expression or presentation (e.g., women wear makeup, men do not cross their legs) also were communicated during childhood and youth in a variety of ways through a number of people, most significantly parents and extended family. Social consequences often resulted if these expectations were violated, such as embarrassment or shame to oneself and one's family as well as social isolation. The heteronormative presumptions of culturally based gender roles were clearly evident in participant narratives, yet only a few participants, mostly those who identified themselves as gay, lesbian, or bisexual, were conscious of these presumptions.

The larger society, particularly through the media, had a tremendous impact on most of our participants as well, not only in communicating traditional gender roles and their expressions or presentations as linked with masculinity and femininity but also in negative stereotypes that existed for both men and women of color. The term *gendered racism* (Essed, 1991, in Thomas, Witherspoon, & Speight, 2008) has been coined to describe the multiple ways that racist and sexist attitudes, beliefs, and discriminatory behaviors can become intertwined into a single phenomenon. Both female and male participants from all racial-ethnic groups shared such experiences, particularly as negative stereotypes passed on through television shows, movies, journal reporting, and popular music. Stereotyped images, both positive and negative, were perceived as communicating the social locations of participants as persons of color in the larger society (e.g., "bottom of the barrel"). Media exposure was often associated with strong emotional reactions among participants that included anger, frustration, disgust, grief, and anxiety. Moreover, several people highlighted the internalization of these images, both through their own individual attitudes and behaviors as well as by significant others within their own racial-ethnic communities.

At the same time, many participants emphasized that they were in a constant process of constructing their gender roles. That is, although most participants were aware of the continuous bombardment of conflicting expectations and norms arising from a variety of socializing agents and institutions, they also perceived themselves to be their own negotiator of the roles they wished to take on and the ways they wished to express or present their gender. Some of their insights arose from exposure to important people in their lives who might have shown them how to behave as either men or women, even though this might not have been the presumed role of these individuals (e.g., mothers serving as teachers or even liberators for their sons regarding emotional expressiveness). A number of participants also viewed the larger society as relaxing many of the previous prescriptions surrounding gender roles, particularly for men (i.e., men now can wear pink).

A more conscious negotiation of gender identities and gender roles seemed to begin most commonly in young adulthood as participants transitioned from childhood and dependency to taking on life responsibilities, including seeking an education or employment or raising a family of their own. It is important to note that many participants did not necessarily reject the original gender role expectations or norms taught them by their parents, extended families, and spiritual/religious communities. Indeed, many men and women continued to find these embodied roles to be a useful means—for some even sacred paths—by which to structure their families and lives. Thus, most participants continued to center their definitions of gender roles within a web of cultural and spiritual values and significant relationships, most typically within their families as well as their racial-ethnic communities.

However, the uneven power relations among men and women within these families and communities were sometimes linked with distress, depression, and anxiety, particularly for women. Although many men of color were supportive of egalitarian attitudes and norms, they were ambivalent about ceding their more dominant leadership roles both in their families and in society at large. At the same time, many men found alternative ways to define their masculine roles that emphasized respect and role modeling rather than overt domination and subjugation of others. Although women were often interested in maintaining their more nurturing roles, at least within the family, they often felt silenced and restricted in their more passive roles. Many pursued autonomous lives beyond the family, often engaging in educational or professional pursuits while still maintaining caretaking roles within the family, although they felt conflicted about doing so. However, a number of women of color struggled with the demands brought on by taking on multiple roles, in the family and at work, often feeling challenged to take on a "superwoman" mentality. This type of mentality was a common source of psychological distress.

MULTICULTURAL GENDER ROLE MODEL

Figure 8.1 presents our emergent model of multicultural gender roles, as grounded by our analyses of participants' narratives. We based our model on a review of the core narratives or theoretical codes that emerged from each set of participants (the analyses we presented in Chapters 2 through 7). At the core of our model is the primary narrative of *negotiating gender roles*. As described, individuals are raised and socialized about what it means to be male or female as well as the gender roles that are linked with either of these genders. Sources of information and socialization include (a) unique cultural values, expectations, and norms; (b) traditional notions of masculinity and femininity shared across cultural groups; (c) socializing agents and institutions; and (d) racial-ethnic and gender stereotypes. These sources often interact with each other in terms of congruent and conflicting messages about the ways an individual can and should behave as a gendered being and the roles in which an individual may or should engage. Each individual thus perceives and negotiates what his or her gender roles might be as a result of these ongoing complex socialization processes. We suggest that gender role negotiation is made up of a number of important processes for many women and men of color, such as letting go of imposed restrictions of traditional notions of masculinity and femininity, even focusing on non–gender-based constructs to define their gender roles. For example, a key gender role theme for most interviewees was participating in, contributing to, and taking responsibility for the survival and success of their families (i.e., being an adult). We further suggest that the process of role negotiation is constant and fluid, and it is possible for individuals to express themselves in one way (soft and feminine) in one setting or context, in another way (tough and autonomous) in another setting, and even in ways that may not reflect traditional bifurcated roles of masculinity and femininity.

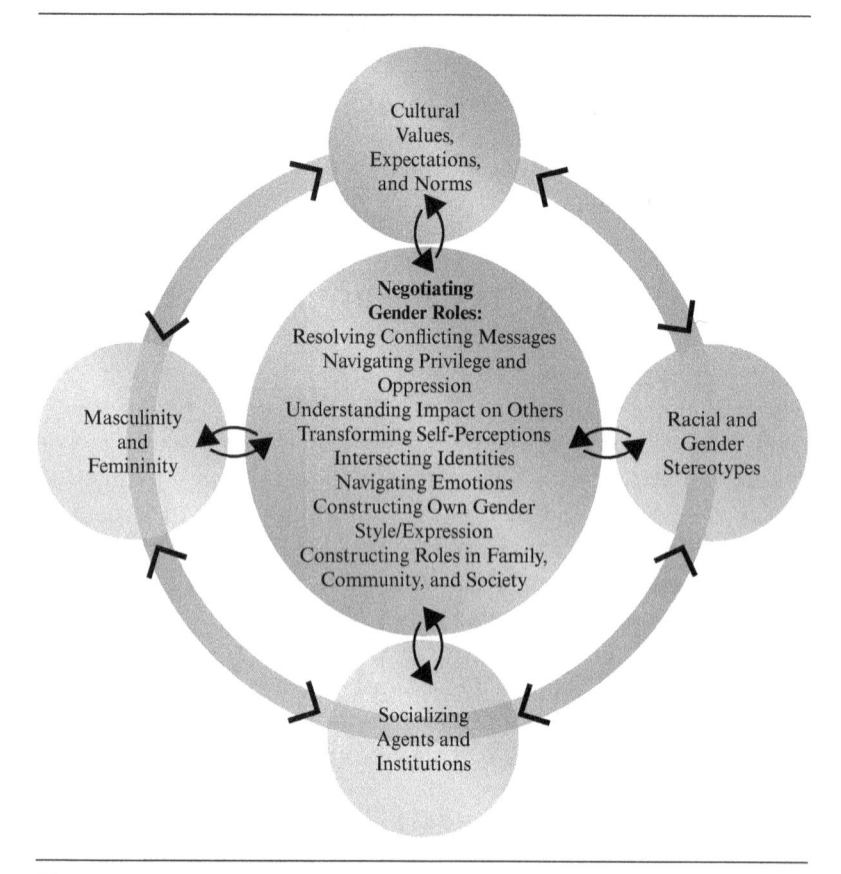

Figure 8.1 Emergent Multicultural Gender Role Model

In negotiating gender roles, we highlight a number of components that may be important for people of color; these include:

1. Resolving conflicts
2. Navigating privilege and oppression
3. Understanding one's impact on others
4. Transforming self-perceptions
5. Intersecting identities
6. Navigating emotions
7. Constructing own gender styles/expressions
8. Constructing roles in family, community, and society

Each person of color may be affected by any, some, or all of these role negotiation processes throughout the lifetime; moreover, future research may define other processes. We describe each of these processes in brief detail next.

Resolving Conflicts

As a result of gender role socialization via many different people, institutions, and events, individuals are exposed to a complex array of messages about how to construct their gender roles. For example, many cultural values regarding the gender roles of women focus on their supportive and nurturing roles in the family, which can contrast with more Western notions promoting egalitarian roles and autonomous/individualistic values, particularly in the United States.

Becoming aware of these areas of conflict often is a major aspect of negotiating gender roles, particularly as individuals construct their own meanings in light of these multiple messages, values, and norms. Resolutions of these conflicts may involve finding congruence, perhaps by discovering a community supportive of one's negotiated roles, such as the social networks described for Asian American women in Chapter 7. Moreover, simply accepting the reality of multiple perspectives, expectations, and norms, however mixed these may be, is also a critical aspect of satisfaction and self-acceptance as a gendered being. Particular settings, events, or people may at times make gender role conflicts salient throughout the lifetime and lead to further role negotiations within and among individuals. As previously noted, negotiating among the multitude of messages, communities, and oppressive experiences is normative for people of color (Chin, 2000), so it is critical for mental health professionals and educators to provide affirmation and support, including the use of self-disclosure, to resolve these conflicts for clients and students.

Navigating Privilege and Oppression

Because both race-ethnicity and gender exist within a larger sociopolitical context marked by dominative power relations, women and men of color are affected throughout their lives by these dominant/subordinate relations. As noted previously, men may experience marginalization in the larger society resulting from overt racist beliefs as both an individual of color and as a man of color (e.g., being viewed as a threat by Whites). However, within their racial-ethnic communities, men often were viewed in a leadership role that many participants still adhered to. Many male participants were positive about taking on this more dominant role, most likely as a result of enculturation within their ethnic community about their presumed roles in the family. Some participants also expressed ambivalence in terms of letting go of this role, perhaps because of a well-placed concern about their marginalization in the larger society. At the same time, many men expressed support for women's rights to self-expression and, in some cases, autonomy. Several scholars (e.g., Abalos, 2002; Franklin, 2004) have suggested ways in which men of color can continue to be leaders in their families and communities without necessarily suppressing the rights and voices of women of color. For example, Franklin (2004) outlined 12 steps of empowerment for African American men that involved taking risks, seeking supports, and finding a spiritual anchor. He incorporates a spiritual quote that may be relevant for men from diverse racial-ethnic backgrounds—"Now faith is the substance of things hoped for, the evidence of things not seen" (p. 195)—as inspiration for men to seek destiny and optimism rather than fear and suppression of others. Abalos (2002) similarly calls for a transformation of gender roles in which men and women together co-create families that promote love and nurturance for all. Both Abalos and Franklin emphasize mutuality and respect as important characteristics of culturally diverse families.

For women, their experiences of multiple oppressions were perceived as "double jeopardy" across all racial-ethnic groups. Many felt targeted in the larger society as "less than" because of their race and their gender, describing the bombardment of objectified and exoticized images to which they are exposed. These oppressive experiences were then compounded with cultural expectations of subordinate roles within their own racial-ethnic communities and families, leading many participants to feel as if they are truly at the bottom of the ladder. As a consequence, a number of women of color felt pressured to enact a superwoman role as someone who can do it "all" in light of multiple family and work demands for which they expect to receive little support or recognition. Thus, strategies that facilitate self-reflexivity and critical consciousness, particularly within a "context of hope" (Dillard, 2000, in Hurtado, 2010), may help women of color to be able to stand back and stand up to these multiple layers of oppressive ideologies. The words of bell hooks are poignantly relevant: "[E]ndurance is not to be confused with transformation" (1981, in Speight, Isom, & Thomas, 2012, p. 128); negotiating gender roles occurs as part of the larger process of "self-making and self-inventing . . .

propelled by a self-loving and self-trusting made possible by overcoming a colonized mind, body, and soul" (West & Gates, 1992, in Speight et al., p. 128).

Understanding One's Impact on Others

A number of participants observed that engaging in traditional gender roles, particularly in ways that are not mindful, and acting out from internalizations of gendered racism, can lead to potentially harmful impacts on self and others. For example, Latino men described some of the negative consequences that resulted from engaging in stereotyped *machista*, or hypermasculine, behaviors they observed in male relatives and consciously chose another, more respectful path toward expressing their masculinities. Taking responsibility for the impact of one's actions was a theme that reverberated as well among many African American male participants in their efforts to define themselves as men rather than boys. Moreover, family and responsibilities toward family members were central to many of the narratives of the participants we interviewed, and understanding one's impact on others has implications for these important relationships. Participants also discussed the significant influence that parents and other family members played in their gender role socialization. Therefore, understanding one's own impact on others has the potential of positively impacting these relationships.

We suggest that this process is likely different for men and women of color. For men, as our participants acknowledged, internalizing gendered racist stereotypes may involve enacting roles that are oppressive, even harmful, to others, such as engaging in sexually promiscuous, alcoholic, or violent behaviors. For many women, enabling these behaviors on the part of their male partners as well as taking on the majority of responsibilities for maintaining their families may lead to physical and mental distress. Earlier chapters discussed a number of strategies for interrupting and calling to attention these internalized negative beliefs about one's race-ethnicity and gender. Helping clients and students to critically examine these beliefs as well as to observe and accept the consequences of their behaviors, particularly their impact on others, might begin to help individuals to transform their beliefs and self-images about what is possible to do and achieve in life as a woman or man of color.

Transforming Self-Perceptions

As noted earlier, some of the sources of gender role socializations include racial-ethnic cultural values as well as negative stereotypes about these values and norms. As a result, a number of participants discussed their struggles in differentiating between cultural prescriptions and stereotypes in constructing gender roles, especially as these roles apply to an individual's personal life. Some individuals may adopt gender roles that are very much in line with what is culturally expected although they find a unique enactment of doing so; others may revise these prescriptions.

Re-creating prescribed gender roles may prove liberating for some people as they begin to view themselves in flexible, diverse ways. For example, one major theme that was apparent for many women of color was to retain their roles as mothers and caregivers yet still feel free, even supported, to pursue an education or a profession. This may be particularly salient for women living in poverty or as single parents, since pursuing an education may facilitate increased opportunities toward social and economic advancement. Mental health professionals and educators might focus on helping individuals clarify their understandings regarding cultural expectations of their gender roles and how these expectations currently are being enacted or not in their lives. Such dialogues will help clients and students articulate sources of current conflicts and also illuminate opportunities to re-create themselves within these racial-cultural contexts.

Eurocentric standards of beauty and notions of the ideal body image were also closely linked to traditional definitions of what is masculine or feminine. Recognition and celebration of physical diversity while resisting mainstream or conventional ideals can therefore facilitate increased positive self-perceptions and forms another path toward transforming self-perceptions among men and women of color. As Belgrave (2009) suggested, helping clients and students become media critics may help them not only debunk negative or colonized images of beauty but offer up a chance to make visible, and enhance, positive images that are based on their own heritage.

Intersecting Identities

In addition to race-ethnicity and gender, participants also highlighted the impact of other social group experiences, including sexual orientation, religion, and social class. The social meaning attached to these identities immediately impacts how one is perceived as well as subsequent interpersonal interactions, behaviors, and attitudes. Although we did not specifically focus on these experiences, participants spontaneously described them because of their impact on their gender role construction. Thus, it is important to be aware that negotiating gender roles will likely involve a number of social group experiences for each individual. Moreover, when exploring gender roles, it may become apparent that these other intersecting identities may be "hidden" from self and others. Some individuals may be unaware of or uncomfortable with these identities for several reasons (e.g., potential conflicts with cultural prescriptions or religious values). Most of our participants were in their early adult years. Therefore, it is understandable, even expected, that their knowledge of more complex and layered identities was only starting to emerge. For other individuals, the invisibility may be related to oppressive reasons (e.g., internalized homophobia or classism as well as heteronormative norms in either one's racial-ethnic community and/or the larger society), such that it is taboo or even unsafe to acknowledge, let alone explore, these sides of their identity. Thus, it is important to be mindful that negotiating gender roles not only involves race-ethnicity and gender but other significant social group memberships that are at play. Helping to make these other aspects of self more apparent will facilitate their more conscious integration into people's gender roles.

Navigating Emotions

Negotiating gender roles, particularly in light of cultural norms, traditional notions of masculinity and femininity, and exposure to overt racist and sexist stereotypes, leads to many emotions that can be distressing as well as harmful behaviors, if they are not managed well. Becoming aware of the breadth and depth of these emotions may help individuals more clearly and consciously understand the decisions they make regarding their gender role expressions. For example, a young African American student may embrace a negative stereotype about himself as a means of resisting it or for fear of being labeled a "sellout" by his peers. Similarly, an African American woman may feel pressured to both put up a "strong front" while, at the same time, be forgiving of a male partner's transgressions in their relationship. Cultural expectations and norms also are important to incorporate in developing interventions and activities. For example, emotional restraint and forbearance are key cultural norms for many Asian and Asian American individuals. Chu and Akutsu (2010) offered strategies for incorporating individuals' acculturation levels in developing interventions that incorporate these norms.

Learning to navigate one's emotions, particularly if these can help drive or motivate change in self, one's communities, and even the larger society, may be an important positive outcome of negotiating gender roles. For example, some male participants integrated feminist and social justice–oriented attitudes after wrestling with feelings of guilt and anger over their own privilege and power. In addition, some female participants learned how to embody and assert their womanhood without sacrificing their own racial-ethnic ideals. Thus, learning to articulate the breadth and depth of emotions that accompany gender role construction may lead to ever more transformative definitions and decisions.

Constructing Own Gender Styles/Expressions

As noted, gender is a process, and expressing or presenting one's gender can be constructed in many ways. These expressions may reflect very traditional notions of masculinity or femininity, particularly as these might be expressed within one's racial-ethnic community. For example, participants highlighted how gender role styles might be embodied, such as pants that are worn low on the hip, driving trucks instead of cars, dressing in makeup and high heels, and the like. However, a number of participants also identified ways that individuals might construct their gender style that may be counter to tradition (e.g., women wearing presumably masculine clothes) as well as differ across settings (e.g., bar versus a job interview).

Moreover, norms defining masculinity and femininity vary across cultures, and some participants reported that what is considered within the bounds of masculinity in one culture may not be considered so in the broader U.S. society. For example, humility and deference are considered desirable qualities in many Asian cultures but do not typify what is considered masculine (or even feminine) in U.S. culture. As such, constructions of gender styles and expressions can be fraught with conflict and uncertainty, particularly in negotiating these styles within multiple cultural frameworks. Being affirming and supportive of individuals' gender style and expression is critical to facilitating their gender role constructions. Exploring one's own expectations and biases about gender expressions (e.g., thoughts and feelings about individuals who might violate cultural prescriptions regarding speech and dress) is important to do as part of becoming a supportive therapist or teacher.

Constructing Roles in Family, Community, and Society

One of the most poignant themes expressed by our participants was the notion that giving to one's family and community, and even the larger society, is critical for any adult; indeed, many felt this is what differentiates the roles of adults in the family from those of children. Thus, constructing gender roles is crucially linked with being a contributing member of one's family and community. The word *responsibility* was one of the most commonly used terms by all participants, often conveying the notion that whatever clothes an individual wears, or how one walks or talks, is not really what is important in negotiating gender roles. What is important is the positive impact one has on others, particularly in being a good role model for younger generations. Communicating and holding up the expectations of responsibility as family and community standards will be key to helping individuals negotiate their gender roles. In the words of Malcolm X, "A man who stands for nothing will fall for anything" (in Boyd-Franklin & Franklin, 2000, p. 156). Developing a game plan that involves goals and activities with young people of color may help them pursue a more constructive gender role path.

For most of our participants, the notion of family was often, if not exclusively, expressed through heteronormative frameworks. Although families can be a source of strength and meaning for individuals, it also is evident that heteronormative conceptions of families may be alienating for gay, lesbian, questioning, and transgender individuals. For these individuals, meeting the responsibilities of their families may be more problematic and potentially distressing. On a more positive note, these individuals can play an important role in challenging these heteronormative assumptions regarding gender roles and gendered responsibilities in families and in opening them up for transformation.

FUTURE DIRECTIONS FOR RESEARCH AND PRACTICE

The major impetus of our research journey has been to explore ways that people of color today understand themselves, their communities, and the world at large through the lenses of race-ethnicity and gender. We interviewed more than 60 individuals who shared their perspectives, stories, thoughts, and feelings with us. We approached our research from a qualitative perspective in the belief that this strategy might be an ideal approach to allow unique voices and narratives to be brought forth into the open.

We have presented a model that we believe is based on the many varied experiences of our interviewees. Despite the diversity of our participants, we were struck by the multiple parallel themes and processes that emerged from our data. To be sure, some of these themes may be a product of our interview approach; that is, all interviews were conducted using a similar set of interview questions, albeit by different individuals. Thus, different models of gender role construction might emerge from different conversations based on other types of questions, responses, and individuals. Moreover, many of our participants were fairly young (mostly in their 20s or early 30s). It would be interesting to see how individuals who are older or from other generations might view this process as well as what were important sources of socialization. We also recruited individuals who self-identified as either male *or* female; and experiences of people who do not identify as such were not included here. Finally, we explored the experiences of three primary diverse racial-ethnic groups in the United States. Future research might explore racial-ethnic groups not included (e.g., Indigenous/Native American, Middle Eastern/Arab), those who are identified as of mixed racial-ethnic heritage as well as having diverse experiences within each of these groups.

Our data analysis chapters included extensive considerations of applications for both mental health professionals and educators. Suffice to say that our model incorporates many of the applications previously described. Moreover, our model provides a constellation representation of the dynamics of gender role socialization and negotiation through which mental health professionals and educators can better understand the clients and students with whom they interact. Our research methodology involving qualitative analyses of interviews was a useful template for revealing participants' gender role constructions. Mental health professionals and educators might adopt such interviewing strategies to help individuals discuss and understand these issues. Another implication is that discussing one's gender role does not only increase one's own self-understanding; by being mindful to the socializing agents of the gender roles of others, such an understanding can have broader effects on larger sociocultural issues (e.g., perpetuation of oppression or discrimination) and the gender role constructions of others. Therefore, an implication of our model as a whole is that individuals can become active and more self-aware negotiators of gender roles, and mental health professionals and educators can play a facilitative role in helping individuals in their negotiations. Finally, it is important for both mental health professionals and educators to understand that there is no single "healthy" path toward gender role development. Instead, it is more accurate to explore how each individual constructs and negotiates these roles across settings over her or his lifetime.

CONCLUDING REMARKS

We believe our model captures some of the complexities involved in negotiating gender roles that will be helpful for mental health professionals and educators in their work with clients and students across an array of settings. We do not intend our model to be viewed as an essentialized portrait that represents the experiences of all people of color. Instead, our model describes many of the sources and processes potentially involved in gender role construction within the current context of existing power relations. We hope the model and the stories of our participants have helped illuminate some of the complexities and nuances involved in becoming a man or woman of color in today's world.

REFERENCES

Abalos, D. T. (2002). *The Latino male: A radical redefinition.* Boulder, CO: Lynne Rienner.

Belgrave, F. Z. (2009). *African American girls: Reframing perceptions and changing experiences.* New York, NY: Springer.

Boyd-Franklin, N., & Franklin, A. J. (2000). *Boys into men: Raising our African American teenage sons.* New York, NY: Dutton.

Chin, J. L. (2000). Paradigms for Asian American women: Power and connections. *Relationships among Asian American women* (pp. 223–230). Washington, DC: American Psychological Association.

Chu, J. P., & Akutsu, P. D. (2010). Intergenerational masculinity strain among Asian American men: Emotion, coping and therapy approaches. In W. M. Lui, D. K. Iwamoto, & M. H. Chae (Eds.), *Culturally responsive counseling with Asian American men* (pp. 83–107). New York, NY: Routledge.

Cole, E. R. (2009). Intersectionality and research in psychology. *American Psychologist, 64,* 170–180.

Franklin, A. J. (2004). *From brotherhood to manhood: How Black men rescue their relationships and dreams from the invisibility syndrome.* Hoboken, NJ: Wiley.

Hurtado, A. (2010). Multiple lenses: Multicultural feminist theory. In H. Landrine & N. F. Russo (Eds.), *Handbook of diversity in feminist psychology* (pp. 29–54). New York, NY: Springer.

Shields, S. A., & Dicicco, E. C. (2011). The social psychology of sex and gender: From gender differences to doing gender. *Psychology of Women Quarterly, 35,* 491–499.

Speight, S. L., Isom, D. A., & Thomas, A. J. (2012). From Hottentot to Superwoman: Issues of identity and mental health for African American women. In C. Z. Enns & E. N. Williams (Eds.), *The Oxford handbook of feminist multicultural counseling psychology* (pp. 115–130). Oxford, England: Oxford University Press.

Spence, J. T. (2011). Off with the old, on with the new. *Psychology of Women Quarterly, 35,* 504–509.

Thomas, A. J., Witherspoon, K. M., & Speight, S. L. (2008). Gendered racism, psychological distress, and coping styles of African American women. *Cultural Diversity and Ethnic Minority Psychology, 14,* 307–314.

Appendix

SUPPORTING RESEARCH MATERIALS

GENDER ROLE INTERVIEW GUIDE

1. Can you share what you wrote for the question "What/who is/are the ideal man and woman" (follow-up from written question on demographic form)?
2. What does being a man/woman mean to you—how do you define this?
3. How do people learn these kinds of images?
4. What kinds of messages are taught about how men and women are supposed to be? (Probe racial/cultural traditions about gender roles.) How do people learn these messages?
5. What does it mean to be "feminine"? What does it mean to be "masculine"? (Reverse order for male groups.) Probe cultural terms (e.g., *machismo/marianismo*, "cool pose" or acting tough).
6. Do you recall a specific experience where you learned how men and women are supposed to be or how you are supposed to act as a man or woman? (Probe sources of messages: family, media, peers and teachers, partners and spouses, culture, religion/spiritual traditions.)
7. Are you familiar with the term *feminism* or *womanism*? What do these mean to you?
8. How do others (Whites) view "race/gender persons" (e.g., Black men, Black women, Latinos, Latinas, Asian/Asian American men, Asian/Asian American women).
9. What have we missed? What have we not asked that you would want us to ask about gender (being a male or female and _____ name race/ethnicity)?

CHAPTER TABLES: PARTICIPANT DEMOGRAPHIC INFORMATION AND CORE NARRATIVES/THEMES

Table A.1 Demographic Information of African American Male Participants

Gender	Sexual Orientation	Age	Race-Ethnicity	Parental Education	Social Class	Employment	Place of Birth	Racial Composition of Neighborhood	Primary Language
M	Gay	45	Biracial: African American and Native American	Father: grade school Mother: high school	Working class	Graduate student	New York	Childhood: nearly 100% minority Currently: nearly 100% White	English
M	Heterosexual	27	African American	Father: professional degree Mother: bachelor's degree	Middle class	Employee in educational system	Louisiana	Childhood: 25% minority, 75% White Currently: nearly 100% minority	English
M	Heterosexual	26	African American	Father: high school Mother: grade school	Working class	Graduate student	New York	Childhood: nearly 100% minority Currently: nearly 100% minority	English

M	Heterosexual	28	African American	Father: bachelor's degree Mother: high school	Middle class	High school teacher	New York	Childhood: nearly 100% minority Currently: 25% minority, 75% White	English
M	Heterosexual	26	African American	Father: high school Mother: trade school	Middle class	Graduate student	Louisiana	Childhood: nearly 100% minority Currently: 25% minority, 75% White	Bilingual

Note: Demographic information on three participants was not available.

Table A.2 Core Narrative and Key Themes of African American Male Gender Roles

Core Narrative: Negotiating Gender Roles					
Key Themes					
Responsibility and Leadership	Evaluating Multiple Messages from Multiple Sources	Negotiating Stereotypes	Navigating Privilege and Oppression	Constructing Flexible Gender Roles and Styles
Awareness of consequences of actions/Impact on others	Parents	Communication of social location	Support of civil rights for women in larger society	Awareness of traditional definitions of masculinity and femininity
Taking a stand	Extended family	Internalization	Ambivalence about women's "place," especially in family context	Embodiment of traits in either men or women
"No excuses"	Religion/church community	Resistance strategies		
	School settings, including teachers and peers			
	Racial-cultural values			
	Media			

Table A.3 Demographic Information of African American Female Participants

Gender	Race	Ethnicity	Age	Sexual Orientation	Social Class	Occupation	Primary Language(s) Spoken	Place of Birth	Approximate racial composition of neighborhood
Female	Black	African American	23	Heterosexual	Upper class	Student	English	California	75% minority, 25% White
Female	Black	African	39	Heterosexual	Middle class	Student	English, Kiswahili, Ateso, Luganda	Uganda	Nearly 100% minority
Female	Black	African American	23	Bisexual	Middle class	Student	English, Spanish	New York	Nearly 100% minority
Female	Black	African American	22	Heterosexual	Middle class	Student	English	Connecticut	Nearly 100% White
Female	Black	African American	23	Heterosexual	Middle class	Student	English	California	25% minority, 75% White
Female	Black	African American	28	Bisexual	Middle class	Student	English, Spanish	New York	50% minority, 50% White
Female	Black	African American	26	Heterosexual	Working class	Student	English, Spanish	California	25% minority, 75% White
Female	Black	African American	30	Not reported	Working class	Elementary school teacher	English	New York	75% minority, 25% White

Table A.4 Core Narrative and Key Themes of African American Female Gender Roles

Core Narrative: Conflict and Evolution of Gender Roles
Key Themes
1. Gender socialization: The influence of past experiences on present attitudes
2. Silent strength: Notions of the "strong" versus "weak" woman
3. "Binary" conceptualizations of masculinity and femininity: Either/or parameters regarding what defines masculine and feminine
4. Less than ideal: The misunderstood and misrepresented Black/African American female
5. "Bottom of the barrel": The dilemma of being Black/African American and female

Table A.5 Demographic Information of Latino Participants

Gender	Sexual Orientation	Age	Race-Ethnicity	Parental Education	Social Class	Employment	Place of Birth	Racial composition of neighborhood	Primary language
M	Gay	34	Latino	Father: grade school Mother: grade school	Middle class	Employee	California	Nearly 100% minority	Bilingual – English/Spanish
M	Gay	36	Mexican	Father: high school Mother: high school	Middle class	Employee/student	California	75% minority, 25% White	English
M	Heterosexual	36	Hispanic	Father: grade school Mother: bachelor's degree	Working class	Employee	El Salvador	75% minority, 25% White	Bilingual – English/Spanish
M	Heterosexual	31–35*	Hispanic	Father: trade school Mother: did not attend school	Working class	Employee/Army	California	75% minority, 25% White	English

(*Continued*)

Table A.5 (Continued)

Gender	Sexual Orientation	Age	Race-Ethnicity	Parental Education	Social Class	Employment	Place of Birth	Racial composition of neighborhood	Primary language
M	Gay	18–25	Latino	Father: high school Mother: high school	Working class	Employee	California	Nearly 100% minority	English
M	Gay	18–25	Latino	Father: grade school Mother: declined	Working class	Employee	California	75% minority, 25% White	Bilingual – English/Spanish
M	Heterosexual	26–30	Hispanic	Father: master's degree Mother: bachelor's degree	Middle class	Employee	Peru	25% minority, 75% White	English
M	Heterosexual	18–25	Mexican	Father: bachelor's degree Mother: bachelor's degree	Middle class	Employee	California	25% minority, 75% White	English
M	Bisexual	18–25	Latino	Father: did not attend school Mother: grade school	Working class	Student	California	Nearly 100% minority	Bilingual – English/Spanish

M	Gay	26–30	Latino	Father: high school Mother: trade school	Working class	Student	California	75% minority, 25% White	English
M	Heterosexual	18–25	Hispanic	Father: bachelor's degree Mother: associate's degree	Working class	Employee	California	75% minority, 25% White	English
M	Heterosexual	26–30	Latino	Father: high school Mother: high school	Middle class	Student	USA	25% minority, 75% White	Bilingual – English/ Spanish

*Remaining participants responded to age range item.

Table A.6 Core Narrative and Key Themes of Latino Gender Roles

Core Narrative: Defining Male Gender Roles within a Latino Cultural/Family Context

Key Themes			
Masculinity Influences	Parental Influences	Social/Cultural Influences	Developing One's Own Definition of Being a Latino Man
Physical definitions and characteristics of Latino men	Egalitarian relations between men and women	Role of the family	Reflection of messages
Traditional gender roles	Instilling sense of ethnic pride	Role of religion	Life experiences
Machismo and *caballerismo*	Emotional expression versus emotional restriction		Impact on others
Stereotypes	Strengthening and building Latino masculinity		

Table A.7 Demographic Information of Latina Participants

Gender	Sexual Orientation	Age	Race	Ethnicity	Social Class	Employment	Place of Birth	Racial Composition of Neighborhood	Primary Language
F	Heterosexual	30	Latina	Mexican American	Middle class	Court investigator	San Jose, CA	50% White, 50% minority	English
F	Heterosexual	30	Latina	Mexican American	Middle class/ working class	Administrative assistant	San Jose, CA	50% White, 50% minority	English
F	Lesbian	21	Biracial	Puerto Rican/ African American	Middle class	College student	New York, NY	Nearly 100% White	English
F	Heterosexual	30	Hispanic	Dominican American	Working class	After-school program coordinator	New York, NY	Nearly 100% minority	English/ Bilingual
F	Heterosexual	46	Hispanic	Peruvian	Middle class	Clinical psychologist	Peru	Nearly 100% minority	Bilingual
F	Heterosexual	43	Hispanic	Dominican	Working class	Cleaning industry	Dominican Republic	Nearly 100% minority	Spanish
F	Bisexual	19	Latina	Mexican	Working class	College student	Bronx, NY	Nearly 100% minority	Bilingual

(*Continued*)

Table A.7 (*Continued*)

Gender	Sexual Orientation	Age	Race	Ethnicity	Social Class	Employment	Place of Birth	Racial Composition of Neighborhood	Primary Language
F	Heterosexual	30	Latina	Ecuadorian	Middle class	Marketing	Queens, NY	50% White, 50% minority	English/Bilingual
F	Heterosexual	31	Latina	Puerto Rican	Working class	Domestic violence hot-line specialist	Brooklyn, NY	Nearly 100% Minority	English
F	Heterosexual	29	Latina	Puerto Rican and Dominican	Working class	Community service coordinator	New York, NY	50% White, 50% minority	English/Bilingual

Table A.8 Core Narrative and Key Themes of Latina Gender Roles

Core Story: Latinas in the Process of Negotiating Roles

Key Themes

Racial-Cultural Expectations	Identity Constructs	From Internalized Ideals to My Own Values
Agents of gendered lessons	Gender identity	Renegotiating values
Messages about gender	Racial-cultural identity	Questioning expectations
Cultural expectations:		Transforming definitions
Respeto (Respect)		
Subject to men		
Ladylike/girly girl		
Superwoman		
Expectations or stereotypes?		

Table A.9 Demographic Information of Asian/Asian American Men

Participant	Age	Race/Ethnicity	Birth Country	Age of immigration to U.S.	Sexual Orientation
1	24	Asian American Taiwanese American	Taiwan	6	Straight
2	27	Asian	Thailand	26 (international student)	Straight
3	28	Asian American/Chinese American	United States	N/A	Straight
4	29	Asian	Taiwan	16.5 (international student)	Gay
5	—	—	China	— (international student)	Gay
6	25	Asian Taiwanese	Taiwan	3	Heterosexual
7	19	Asian	Thailand	18 (international student)	Straight
8	—	—	Thailand	—	—
9	23	Asian	Thailand	22 (international student)	Straight
10	26	Taiwanese	Taiwan	3	Heterosexual
11	30	Asian, Taiwanese American	United States	N/A	Heterosexual

Note: We retained the exact race/ethnicity and sexual orientation terms used by the participants. Demographic information for two of the participants was incomplete (Participants 5 and 8).

Table A.10 Demographic Information of Asian/Asian American Women

Gender	Age	Race	Ethnicity	Education	Neighborhood Grew Up	Racial Composition of Neighborhood	Primary Language
F	31	Asian	Filipina	Bachelor's degree	Suburban	100% minority	English
F	32	Asian	Filipina	Bachelor's degree	Suburban	25% minority; 75% White	English
F	32	Asian	Filipina	Master's degree	Suburban	75% minority 25% White	English
F	30	Asian	Filipina	Some college	Suburban	50% minority 50% White	English
F	70	Asian	Filipina	Some college	Urban	Nearly 100% minority	Bilingual
F	32	Asian	Filipina	Doctorate	Suburban	50% minority 50% White	English
F	67	Asian	Filipina	Some college	Urban	Nearly 100% minority	Bilingual
F	53	Asian	Filipina	Some college	Urban	100% minority	English
F	27	Asian	Korean	College	Suburban	75% minority; 25% White	English
F	30	Asian	Filipina	JD	Suburban	25% minority; 75% White	English
F	51	Asian	Japanese	Bachelor's degree	Suburban	75% minority; 25% White	English
F	32	Asian	Chinese/Filipina	Bachelor's degree	Suburban	50% minority; 50% White	English
F	28	Asian	Filipina	Bachelor's degree	Suburban	75% minority; 25% White	English

Table A.11 Core Narrative and Key Themes for Asian/Asian American Women's Gender Roles

Core Narrative: Model Minority, Model Woman		
Key Themes		
Aspects	Pathways of Passivity	Negotiating Intersections
Filial piety	Division of labor	Making it on my own
Impact of religion	Double messages	
Emotional and physical aspect of gender		

Acknowledgments

We wish to first thank all our participants who willingly volunteered to be interviewed and shared so deeply of their lives. We also thank the many students who began our research journey with us several years ago, including Christine Sainvil, LeLaina Romero, Lisa Rosenzweig, Gregory Payton, Naoko Hashimoto, Shikha Gulati, and Mie Uzuno. We thank Gabriella Oldham for the provision of her excellent transcription services, and Kristine Gamarel, Mei Kuang, and Sylwia Misiewicz for their assistance with Chapter 6. We thank Teachers College, Columbia University, and the University of Miami, each of which provided the priceless gifts of time and space to develop this book project. We are also grateful to the following colleagues who reviewed the material and provided valuable feedback: Joseph G. Ponterotto, PhD, Professor, Fordham University and Lisa Spanierman, PhD, Associate Professor, McGill University Finally, we would like to thank the staff at John Wiley & Sons, particularly Rachel Livsey, for her incisive editorial feedback and suggestions; Amanda Orenstein, for her administrative support; and Thomas Caruso, for his production editing.

About the Editor

Marie L. Miville, PhD, is an associate professor of psychology and education and chair of the Department of Counseling and Clinical Psychology, Teachers College, Columbia University. Dr. Miville is the author of more than 50 publications dealing with multicultural issues in counseling and psychology. She is the editor of the Around the Winter Roundtable Forum in *The Counseling Psychologist* and is currently serving or has served on several editorial boards, including *Journal of Counseling Psychology*, *Journal of Latina/o Psychology*, *Cultural Diversity and Ethnic Minority Psychology*, and *Training and Education in Professional Psychology*. Dr. Miville is a past chair of the Council of Counseling Psychology Training Programs (CCPTP) and was co-chair of the joint Division 17/CCPTP Special Task Group that developed the Integrative Training Model, a competency-based model integrating multiple aspects of diversity. Dr. Miville also helped to develop the Counseling Psychology Model Training Values Statement Addressing Diversity (http://www.ccptp.org/trainingdirectorpage6.html) and was among a group of authors who won the "2009 Major Contribution Award" for a series of articles about the statement published in *The Counseling Psychologist*. Dr. Miville is a Fellow of the American Psychological Association (Division 17 and 45).

Contributors

Marilyn C. Ampuero, EdM
Mental Research Institute
Palo Alto, CA

Lucinda Bratini, PhD
*John Jay College of Criminal Justice,
City University of New York*
New York, NY

Yu-Kang Chen, MA
Teachers College, Columbia University
New York, NY

Melissa J. Corpus, PhD
Center of Cognitive Assessment
New York, NY

Manuel A. Diaz, MA
Teachers College, Columbia University
New York, NY

Natalia Gil, BA
Teachers College, Columbia University
New York, NY

Jill Huang, EdM
Fordham University
New York, NY

Michael Y. Lau, PhD
Teachers College, Columbia University
New York, NY

Jorja A. K. Redway, MA
Teachers College, Columbia University
New York, NY

Joel Sahadath, MA
Housing Works
New York, NY

Author Index

Abalos, D. T., 122, 125, 129, 238
Adams, V. L. L., 65, 91
Ahluwalia, M. K., 208
Akutsu, P. D., 199, 200, 242
Alexander, M., 23
Alimchandani, A., 208
Almquist, 65
Alston, R. J., 23
Anderson, T. C., 12, 99
Anzaldua, G., 157, 161, 166
Arciniega, G. M., 12, 13, 99, 104, 108
Arredondo, P., 9, 97, 133, 166, 167
Arrizon, 134
Atkinson, D. R., 199

Babbitt, L. G., 66
Baca Zinn, M., 8
Bacigalupe, G., 12, 98
Banchero, R., 98
Barret, B., 10
Beattie, P. M., 98
Beauboeuf-Lafontant, T., 67
Beecher, H. W., 8
Belgrave, F. Z., 70, 73, 78, 81, 85, 90, 92, 240

Bem, S. L., 66
Bethea-Whitfield, P., 65, 71, 91
Boyd-Franklin, N., 36, 39, 52, 57, 58, 69, 70, 243
Burke, P. J., 2, 3, 4, 15

Caldwell, L. D., 13
Cameron, E., 66
Carlstrom, A. H., 98
Casas, J. M., 12, 13, 98, 99
Castellanos, J., 134, 152, 162, 164, 167
Catalyst, 227
Cavazos, A., 13, 99
Chafetz, 3
Chang, 203
Chang, T., 170, 203
Charmaz, K., 15, 16
Cherry, M., xiv, 2
Chin, J. L., 228, 229, 237
Chinn, P., 10, 11
Chu, J. P., 199, 200, 242
Chua, P., 169, 170, 182
Cole, E. R., 66, 232
Cole, J. B., 67, 71, 73, 87
Collier, 3
Comas-Diaz, L., 7, 66

269

Cones, J. H., 14, 49, 57, 59, 62
Connell, 14
Corbin, J., 16
Corpus, M., 10
Cournoyer, R. L., xiv, 2
Damas Jr., A., 7
Dang, P., 203
Davidson, M. M., 5
Davis, A. Y., 8
de Beauvoir, Simone, 4
de Esparaza, C. A. R., 12
DeFranc, W., xiv, 2
Dicicco, E. C., xiv, 231, 232
Dillard, 238
Douroux, A. N., 203

Eap, S., 169
Eccles, J. S., 182
Enns, C. Z., 4, 154
Espin, O. M., 8, 153–154, 156, 164
Essed, 24, 233

Falicov, C. J., 13, 99, 100, 122
Fann, M. D., 24
Fassinger, R. E., 15–16
Ferguson, A. D., 4, 6, 7, 9, 10, 14
Franklin, A. J., 24, 36, 39, 43, 48, 52, 57, 58, 60, 62, 69, 70, 238, 243
Fry, R., 97
Fu, M., 207, 208, 209
Fujino, D. C., 169, 170, 182

Gallardo-Cooper, M., 9, 97, 133
Garrett, M. T., 10
Gates, 239
Gayles, T. A., 23
Gil, R. M., 9, 133, 134, 146, 149, 151, 153, 156, 164, 210
Gilmore, D., 5
Ginoria, A., 166
Glenn, K., 128
Gloria, A. M., 134, 152, 162, 164, 167
Gonzalez, J., 97
Greene, B., 9
Guy-Sheftall, B., 67, 71, 73, 87

Hall, G.N.C., 169
Hambrick, A., 76
Harley, D. A., 73
Harold, R. D., 182
Harper, S. R., 24
Helmreich, R., 66
Heppner, M. J., 5
Hernton, 87
Homma-True, R., 220, 225, 226
Hondagneu-Sotelo, P., 8
hooks, b., 7, 153, 238
Hurtado, A., xiii, 9, 12, 13, 99, 154, 232, 238
Huston, M., 166

Institute for Women's Policy Research, 3
Isom, D. A., 238
Iwamoto, D. K., 195, 202

Jacobs, J. E., 182
Jones, J., 6
Jones, L. S., 3, 4

Kawahara, D. M., 207, 208, 209
Kim, B. S. K., 199
Kim, E. J., 195
Kim, H. K., 224
King, K. R., 66
Kwong-Liem, K. K., 201

LaFromboise, T. D., 65, 91
Lalonde, R. N., 66
Liang, C. T. H., 203
Lim, R. H., 201
Liu, C. H., 169
Liu, W. M., 170, 195, 202
Lobel, M., 66
Lopez, M. H., 97
Lorde, A., 9
Louie, S. C., 225, 227
Lucal, B., 2
Lytton, H., 189

Mahalik, J. R., xiv, 2
Mak, W. S., 207
Mead, M., 3
Mendoza-Romero, J., 98
Messner, M. A., 8
Miller, M. J., 201
Mincy, 23
Mirande, A., 98, 99, 110, 118
Miville, M. L., 4, 6, 7, 9, 10, 14, 17, 97

Mora, R., 126, 127
Morales, 12, 89
Morales, E., 12
Munoz-Laboy, M., 126
Murakami, J., 169
Mutow, J. E., 201

Nadal, K., 10
Napolitano, J. M., xiv, 2
Nathwani, A., 203
Nguyen, A. B., 66

Obama, B., 28
O'Neil, J. M., 5, 12, 194, 195
Ontai, L. L., 7
Owen, S. V., 195
Oyserman, D., 92

Parham, T. A., 13, 14
Patterson, L. A., 66
Petersen, 65
Pido, A., 10
Pleck, J., 99
Raffaelli, M., 7
Reid, P. T., 7, 66
Rice, D. W., 24
Rivera, A. L. Y., 203
Romney, D. M., 189

Santiago-Rivera, A., 97, 98, 118, 123, 133
Santiago-Rivera, A. L., 9, 12
Savitt, D. J., 166
Schwing, A. E., 24, 59
Sellers, R. M., 7

Serafica, F. C., 224, 225
Serrano, R., 128, 129
Settles, I. H., 7, 66
Shek, Y. L., 169, 170
Shields, S. A., xiv, 231, 232
Sinha, M., 12, 13, 99
Solberg, V. S. H., 98
Speight, S. L., 24, 59, 233, 238, 239
Spelman, E. V., 66
Spence, J. T., 66, 231, 232
Staten, D., 23
Stets, J. E., 2, 3, 4, 15
Strapp, J., 66
Strauss, A. L., 16
Sue, D., 6, 7, 12, 171, 174, 199, 200, 201, 207
Sue, D. W., 6, 7, 171, 174, 207
Suzuki, L. A., 208, 219, 226

Tafoya, T., 10
Takaki, R., 169, 170
Thomas, A. J., 24, 59, 233, 238
Tinsely-Jones, H. A., 6
Torres, J. B., 98
Tovar-Blank, Z. G., 12, 99
Tracey, T. J. G., 12, 99
Tryon, G. S., 4
Turner, J. A., 12
Umemoto, D., 199

U.S. Census Bureau, 97, 169
U.S. Commission on Civil Rights, 207

Vasquez, C. I., 9
Vazquez, C. I., 133, 134, 146, 149, 151, 153, 156, 164, 210
Villereal, G. L., 13, 99
Virella, K., 23, 24

Wagenheim, B. R., 98
Wang, V. O., 207, 219, 220, 224, 225
Weng, A., 224
West, 239
Wester, S. R., 13, 99
White, J. L., 13, 14, 49, 57, 59, 62
Williams, E. N., 154
Winograd, G., 4
Witherspoon, K. M., 24, 233
Wong, R. P., 203
Wong, Y. J., 24
Woods-Giscombé, C. L., 66
Wyatt, G., 9
Wyatt, G. E., 65, 81, 84, 90, 112

Yang, P. H., 199
Yeh, 203

Subject Index

Adolescence, 4
Affirmation of pathways/
　selves, 228–229
African American men:
　core themes/
　　subthemes, 24–25
　education and, 23–24
　empowerment for, 238
　extended family, 36–38
　fathers and, 30–33
　flexible roles/styles,
　　52–54
　impact on others, 239
　media and, 43–45
　mothers/female relatives
　　and, 33–36
　negotiating gender roles,
　　54–56
　parents and, 29–30
　peer influences, 40–42
　privilege, oppression and,
　　49–52
　racial-cultural background,
　　42–43
　religion/church members
　　and, 38–39
　responsibility and
　　leadership, 25–29
　school settings and, 39–40
　stereotypes and, 13–14,
　　45–49
African Americans. *See*
　African American men;
　African American women
African American women:
　conflict and evolution of gen-
　　der roles (*see* Conflict and
　　evolution of gender roles)
　educators/mental health
　　professionals and, 88–94
　generally, 65–67
Anti-Asian sentiments,
　169, 170
Asia, 173
Asian American women:
　Asian communities and, 10
　child-rearing and, 11
　education and, 211,
　　227–228
　educators/mental health
　　professionals and,
　　224–229

273

Asian American women (*continued*)
- gender roles (*see* Gender role socialization)
- generally, 207–209
- making it on my own, 222–224
- model minority/model woman, 209–212
- passivity and (*see* Passivity)
- stereotypes and, 207–208
- three "obediences," 207

Asian cultures, 242

Asians/Asian American cultural values. *See also* Confucian philosophies
- centrality of family, 173–177
- collectivism, 177–178
- country of origin, 172–173
- generally, 171–172

Asians/Asian American men:
- child-rearing and, 11
- cultural values (*see* Asians/Asian American cultural values)
- generally, 169–171
- socialized gender roles (*see* Socialized gender roles)
- stereotypes, 170
- stereotypes and, 12

Asians/Asian Americans:
- men (*see* Asians/Asian American men)
- women (*see* Asian American women)

Binary conceptualizations of masculinity/femininity

Black Girls Rock! Inc., 93

"Black Is Beautiful," 82

Black Liberation movement, 8

Blacks. *See* African American men; African American women

Body images, positive, 126–127

"Bottom of the barrel" dilemma, 84–88, 233

Caballerismo, 13, 99, 100, 104–111

"Chain immigration," 208

Children's toys, 147

China, 11, 169, 178

Church membership. *See* Religion/church membership

Civil rights movements, 208

Collaborative Couple Communication, 129

Collectivism, 177–178

Community, roles in, 243

Conflict and evolution of gender roles:
- binary conceptualizations, masculinity/femininity, 76–81
- "bottom of the barrel" dilemma, 84–88
- educators/mental health professionals and, 89–91
- gender socialization, 68–74

generally, 67–68
less than ideal image,
    81–84
silent strength, 74–76,
    91–92
Conflict resolution, 237
Confucian philosophies, 11,
    170–171, 207
Constructivist grounded
    theory (CGT). *See also*
    Grounded theory (GT)
    overview, 14–16
    researchers' worldviews
    and, 16–17
Country of origin, 178
Cultural deprivation, 13
Cultural values, 232, 234, 242

Deference to men, 211
Division of labor, 218–219
Dominant/subordinate
    relations, 237
Double messages, 219–222

Education, 207
Educational settings. *See*
    School settings
Educators:
    affirmation, pathways/
        selves, 228–229
    body images, positive,
        126–127
    collaborative stance,
        226–228
    dialogue/exploration and,
        165–166

family expectations/respon-
    sibilities, 163–165
femininity/female gender
    roles, 89–91
flexible roles/identities,
    60–63
gender roles, positive bal-
    anced, 127–128
gender role transforma-
    tions, 166–167
gender role values/expres-
    sions, 224–226
healthy relationships,
    129–130
Latina gender roles,
    162–167
leadership development,
    56–58
negative stereotypes and,
    58–60
redefining gender roles,
    92–94
as role models, 40
self-silencing and strength,
    91–92
Egalitarian relations, 114–117
Egalitarian views, 220
ELC. *See* Executive
    Leadership Council
    (ELC)
Emergent gender role
    model. *See* Multicultural
    gender role model:
Emotions, 241–242
Enculturation, 237–238
Ethgendered prejudice, 66

Ethnic enclaves, 208
Ethnic pride:
  Black, 82
  Latina/o, 117–118
Ethnocentric monoculturalism, 7
Evolution of gender roles. *See* Conflict and evolution of gender roles
Executive Leadership Council (ELC), 93–94
Extended family, 36–38

Familism, 178
Family. *See also* Extended family; Fathers; Mothers
  centrality of, 173–177
  extended, 36–38
  gender roles in, 238
  heteronormative conceptions and, 243
  role of, 121–122
  roles in, 37, 243
Fathers:
  of African American men, 30–33
  Asian American women and, 207, 210, 213
  as role models, 30
Female gender roles. *See also* African American women; Asian American women; Latina socialization
  conflicting definitions of, 89–91
Female relatives, 33–36. *See also* Mothers
Femininity. *See also* "Ladylike" appearance/behavior
  Asians/Asian Americans and, 181–182, 216–217, 222
  binary conceptualizations of, 76–81
  conflicting definitions of, 89–91
  as stable personality trait, 231
  traditional notions of, 242
Feminism, 4, 154
Filial piety, 212–214
Filipina American, 211, 215–216, 218–219
Filipino culture, 10
Films, 155
Flexible roles/styles, 52–54
Future directions, 244–245

Gay individuals, 180, 189, 216, 243
Gender:
  defined, 2
  as a process, 231–232, 242
  studied "in context," 231
Gender-based disparities, 3, 5
Gendered racism, 24, 233
Gender identity. *See* Identity constructs

Gender role conflict
  (GRC), 5
Gender roles. *See also* Role
  model(s)
  conflict and evolution (*see*
    Conflict and evolution of
    gender roles)
  defined, 2
  Latina/o, traditional,
    103–104
  negotiating (*see* Negotiating
    gender roles)
  positive balanced,
    127–128
  redefining, 92–94
  reframing of, 231
  socialization (*see* Gender
    role socialization)
  sources of, Asian/Asian
    American, 186–194
  transformations, 166–167
  values/expressions,
    224–226
Gender role socialization.
  See also Socialized
  gender roles
  cultural pathways to, 210
  emotional/physical
    components, 216–217
  filial piety, 212–214
  religion, impact of,
    214–216
Gender socialization, 68–74,
  189
Gender stereotypes. *See*
  Stereotypes

Gender styles/expressions,
  242–243
Gender wage gap, 3
GRC. *See* Gender role conflict
  (GRC)
Grounded theory (GT), 2.
  See also Constructivist
  grounded theory (CGT)
GT. *See* Grounded theory
  (GT)

HBCU. *See* Historically
  Black college/university
  (HBCU)
Head Start, 92
Healthy relationships,
  129–130
Heteronormative framework/
  assumptions, 179–180,
  212, 233, 243
Heterosexuality, 210, 212
Historically Black college/
  university (HBCU):
  peer influences and, 41–42
  styles of maleness and,
    28, 62
Homosexuality, 231. *See also*
  Gay individuals; Lesbians

Identity constructs:
  gender identity, 4,
    151–155, 232
  generally, 135, 136, 150
  racial-cultural identity,
    155–157
Immigration Act (1965), 170

India, 169
Interactive dualism, 228
Internalized ideals/own values:
  generally, 135, 157–158
  questioning gendered expectations, 160–161
  renegotiating gendered values, 159–160
  transforming definitions, 161–162
Internalized racism, 38
Internet, 139
Invisible dignity, 76

Japan, 169
Japanese culture, 223

Korea, 169
Korean American, 219–220

Labor. *See* Division of labor
"Ladylike" appearance/behavior, 146–148, 211–212. *See also* Femininity
La fuerza potente, 146
Latina gender roles. *See also* Marianismo
  educators/mental health professionals and, 162–167
  generally, 133–136
  identity (*see* Identity constructs)
  internalized ideals/own values (*see* Internalized ideals/own values)
  sexuality, 135
  socialization (*see* Latina socialization)
Latina/o communities:
  caballerismo, 13
  female gender roles (*see* Latina gender roles)
  machismo, 12–13, 98–99, 100
  male gender roles (*see* Latino gender roles)
  marianismo, 9
  men and, 12
  relational resilience, 122
Latina socialization:
  educational/work settings, 140–141
  gender expectations/Latina stereotypes, 149–150
  ladylike/girly girl, 146–148
  messages about gender, 141–143
  racial-cultural expectations, 144–145
  socializing agents, 136–141
  subject to men, 145
  superwoman, 148–149
Latino gender roles:
  caballerismo, 99
  generally, 97–100
  machismo, 98–99, 100

machistas, 239
masculinity influences
  (*see* Latino masculinity
  influences)
one's own definition of,
  124–125
parental influences
  (*see* Parental influences,
  Latina/o)
social/cultural influences,
  121–123
Latino masculinity
  influences:
gender roles, traditional,
  103–104
generally, 100–101
machismo and
  caballerismo, 104–111
perceiving stereotypes,
  111–113
physical definitions/
  characteristics, 101–103
Leadership development:
educators and, 56–58
negative stereotypes and,
  58–60
responsibility and,
  25–29
Lesbians:
Asian American, 212,
  215, 222
families and, 243
Latina, 134, 136–137
machismo and, 223
Less than ideal image, 81–84
Literature, 155

Machismo:
caballerismo and, 13,
  99–100, 104–111
lesbians and, 223
marianismo and, 133
psychological risk and,
  12–13
stereotypes and,
  98–99, 149
Machistas, 106, 107, 239
Malcolm X, 58, 243
Male. *See* Caballerismo;
  Machismo; Masculinity;
  Men of color
"Manifest Destiny" policy,
  97–100
Marginalization, 237
Marianismo:
as cultural norm, 9
defined, 133
educators/mental health
  professionals and,
  166, 167
gender identity and, 151
"Maria Paradox," 9, 149
The Maria Paradox
  (Gil and Vazquez), 134
Masculinity. *See also*
  Machismo; Machistas
Asians/Asian Americans
  and, 181–182
binary conceptualizations
  of, 78, 80
machismo and, 127
parental influences, Latino,
  119–121

Masculinity (*continued*)
  as stable personality trait, 231
  traditional notions of, 242
  traits associated with, 3
Mead, Margaret, 3
Media. *See also* TV shows
  African American men and, 43–45
  American socialization and, 138
Men of color. *See also* Asians/Asian American men; Latino gender roles
  Black, 13–14, 17–18 (*see also* African American men)
  generally, 14
  Latino, 12–13
Mental health professionals. *See* Educators
Mentoring programs, 62
Modeling behavior. *See* Role models
"Model minority myth," 170, 207, 209–212
Mothers. *See also* Parental influences
  of African American men, 33–36
  of Asian American women, 210, 211
Multicultural gender role model, 235–236

National Coalition of 100 Black Women, Inc. (NCBW 100), 93
Native Americans, 10
NCAAM, 58
NCBW. *See* National Coalition of 100 Black Women, Inc. (NCBW 100)
Negotiating gender roles:
  African American men and, 54–56
  at core of model, xv, 235
Nonheterosexuality, 212

"Obediences," 207
Observation, 178
Oppression:
  African American men and, 49–52
  institutionalized beliefs and, 7, 9
  internalization of, 9
  navigating, 237–239
  social group memberships and, 232
  women and, 238–238

Parental influences. *See also* Fathers; Filial piety; Role model(s)
  of African American men, 29–30
  gender roles and, 189, 210

Latina/o (*see* Parental influences, Latina/o)
maternal, 33–36, 210, 211. *See also* Mothers
Parental influences, Latina/o:
  egalitarian relations, 114–117
  emotional expression/restriction, 118–119
  ethnic pride instilled, 117–118
  Latino masculinity, strengthening/building, 119–121
Passivity:
  division of labor, 218–219
  double messages, 219–222
  for woman/Asian, 210–211
Patriarchy. *See also* Fathers; Parental influences
  negative impact of, 4–5
  women of color and, 8
Peer influences, 40–42. *See also* School settings
People of color. *See also specific racial group*
  racism and, 6
  role negotiation processes and, 236
"Perpetual foreigner," 208
The Philippines, 169
Popular culture, 137. *See also* Media; TV shows
Power-based constructions of gender, 4

Power position:
  men and, 11
  sociopolitical context and, 237
Privilege:
  African American men and, 49–52
  navigating, 237–239
Project Naja, 92

Racial-cultural background, 42–43
"Racialized masculinities," 14
Racism:
  defined, 6–7
  gendered, 24, 233
  health and, 11
  internalization of, 38
  marginalization and, 237
  social injustice and, 208
Relational resilience, 122
Relationships, healthy, 129–130
Religion/church membership:
  African American men and, 38–39, 58
  gendered expectations and, 140, 212
  impact of, 214–216
  role of, 122–123
Responsibility and leadership:
  African American men, 25–29
  role construction and, 243

Rites-of-passage mentoring programs, 57, 62
Role model(s). *See also* Gender roles; Parental influences
  becoming a, 37
  changing during life, 189
  close to home, 28
  family members as, 30, 60, 110, 114, 140, 141, 143, 160, 187, 188
  gender socialization and, 141–142
  lack of positive, 14
  leadership and, 25, 27 (*see also* Leadership development)
  mentoring and, 93
  mothers as, 33–34
  negative, 18, 41, 61
  positive, 27–28, 37, 41, 57, 90
  responsibility and, 25–26
  social institutions and, 39
  teachers as, 40

School settings:
  African American men and, 39–40
  Latinas and, 140–141
Self-awareness, 245
Self-disclosure, 237
Self-perceptions, 240
Self-reflexivity, 238
Self-silencing/strength, 74–76, 91–92

Seneca Falls Declaration, 7–8
Sex-based stereotypes, 231
Sexism:
  defined, 5
  health and, 11
  social injustice and, 208
  women of color and, 8
Sex-typed norms/attitudes, 232
"Sexual inversion," 231
Sexuality. *See also* Heterosexuality; Homosexuality
  Latina/o, 135
Sexual objectification, 210
Sexual orientation, 212, 223. *See also* Gay individuals; Lesbians
Social constructionist approach, 231–232
Social/cultural influences:
  family, role of, 121–123
  religion, role of, 122–123
Social group memberships, 232
Social institutions, 39
Socialized gender roles. *See also* Gender role socialization; Latina socialization
  generally, 178–179
  ideal images, 179–186
  sources of gender roles, 186–194
Socializing agents/institutions, 234

Social justice movements, 208
Social status, 3
Society, roles in, 243
Sociopolitical context, 237
Spiritual values, 234. *See also* Religion/church membership
Stereotypes:
 African American men and, 45–49
 Asian/Asian American, 170, 207–208
 gender, 4, 231
 Latina/o, 12–13, 111–113, 145–146
 negative, 58–60
 social locations and, 233
 "Superwoman" mentality, 148–149, 235, 238

Taiwan, 172–173
Teachers, 40. *See also* Educators
Thailand, 177
Three "obediences," 207
Transgender individuals, 243
TV shows, 44, 83, 137–139, 210

U.S. culture, 242

Western biases, 228
Women of color. *See also* Asian American women; Female gender roles
 Black, 8, 9 (*see also* African American women)
 Filipina American, 10
 generally, 11
 Latina, 9–10 (*see also* Latina gender roles)
 Native American, 10
 oppression and, 238–238
Women's rights:
 movement, 7–8
 self-expression and, 238

"Yellow Peril," 170, 207–208
"Yin" and "yang," 170–171
Young adulthood, 234